Advanced Praise for *Intrapreneurs*

"Never has the mission of Intrapreneurs been more critical. The bigger the company the slower they move in a world that moves faster every day. Intrapreneurs are the way for traditional organizations to intentionally and profitably move at today's speed of business. Susan provides valuable insight into Intrapreneurs".

Rick McPartlin,
CEO of The Revenue Game®

"Your newest book, *Intrapreneurs: - Who, What, How and Why*, brings together the relationship between process and the human component within an organization. You emphasize the challenges and constraints of an organization's structure and process that are obstacles to creating an effective intrapreneurial culture. Your book contains material I can implement in creating the entrepreneurial mindset in the classroom."

Don Reimer,
Professor, Lawrence Technological University

"Backed by a wealth of research, over a decade of working with and coaching intrapreneurs and her own personal intrapreneurial journey, Susan Foley provides a very readable and actionable series of checkpoints and checklists to ensure you address the PEOPLE part of the innovation and business growth equation. You'll learn to understand how to spot, support and motivate your intrapreneurs and identify the natural tension and potential sources of conflict between your new ventures and the core business. Want-to-be intrapreneurs or ones seeking to perfect their skills, business leaders struggling to drive and sustain innovations and heads of HR, people, talent and leadership charged with developing job competencies for a rapidly changing world will greatly benefit from reading *Intrapreneurs - Who, What, How and Why*. The book is very well written and filled with real-world examples and actionable recommendations to help you understand the talent and competencies required to drive innovations into successful businesses."

Guillaume Hervé,
President G3point0 Consulting
Author, *Winning at Intrapreneurship*

""I am always inspired by your writings. The points you make are exactly how I define my work, but you crystallize the process and make it very clear on what and how we are motivated along with what drives us Intrapreneurs. I recommend this book to anyone interested in change, transformation and the rebuild or better build process that move organizations to the next level. It takes dedication, persistence, and the inner drive. Of course, you also have fun with the process since this is why we do what we do. Bring it on!"

Lina Gallotto EVP,
Barton Associates

A thoughtful book about intrapreneurs. Easy to read and an abundance of good advice on how to become an intrapreneur"

Kevin DeSouza,
Professor at QUT Business School
Author of *Intrapreneurship: Managing Ideas within Your Organization*

"In this book Susan Foley, a renowned expert in the field, provides a very detailed and complementary *tour d'horizon* about the topic. As it is composed of a compilation of posts, she regularly published the past 10 years, this book provides a global and comprehensive picture of the phenomenon since it addresses the topic from very different angles. In addition, it is very pleasant to read, both acute and specific. As it alternates very concrete and actionable propositions engaging to act and valuable and smart thoughts having taken a step back, this book will undoubtedly be of interest to anyone who discovers the topic and is willing to implement it from scratch (then used as a handbook) but also to seasoned practitioners of intrapreneurship providing them with in-depth reflections.

"A must-read book for anyone who considers intrapreneurship more than just a fad."

Olivier Leclerc
Head of intrapreneurship at Safran

"I had the opportunity to work as an Intrapreneur in a very large international organization (Unilever) and to teach the subject at the International MBA program at HEC Montreal. I have used many of Susan Foley's insights while teaching my classes. She has a deep understanding of the world of Intrapreneurs. While the need for Intrapreneurs is clearly identified, the challenges to make it a success remain high. Why? Because of the "*Corporate Immune System*" that most organizations have that tends to fight the Intrapreneurs. Susan's latest book will help organizations better understand the Intrapreneurs and protect them from the "*Corporate Immune System.*" This book is full of valuable insights on Intrapreneurs."

Serban Teodoresco
VP EMEA Region, NSF International

Intrapreneurs

Who, What, How, and Why

Susan Foley

Explore the World of Intrapreneurs

Intrapreneurs – Who, What, How and Why

Intrapreneurs – Who, What, How and Why
www.intrapreneurs-wwhw.com

First Edition 2020

ISBN: 978-1-7349569-0-0

Visit website at: www.corporate-entrepreneurs.com

Cover Design; Clark Kenyon
Cover photograph: Joanna Skoczen from iStock / Getty Images

This book was printed in the United States of America by KDP Publishing

Table of Contents

Introduction

Intrapreneurs – Who, What, How and Why explores the world of Intrapreneurs. They are individuals inside organizations that are building new businesses, new products, services and processes that create value and generate new revenue growth. Often referred to as corporate entrepreneurs, mavericks, change agents and internal entrepreneurs.

The book was inspired by a network of Intrapreneurs from around the world that are changing business as usual. They are changing the way we work, the way we look at opportunities, solve problems and leverage technology to address social and business issues. They are rewriting the rules and leading organizations into the future.

They are the catalyst for change and growth in a world that has become more complex and uncertain.

Yet, despite the hype and growing interest in Intrapreneurs there has been a lack of understanding about who these individuals are, what they do, how they do it, and why it is important.

We've spent the last decades working with intrapreneurs and researching who they are, what they do, how they are different and the value they bring to organizations. We've found that they possess a unique combination of competencies that distinguish them from their peers. It wasn't just one or two competencies but the breadth and depth of those competencies that separated them from others.

We've also found that they look at the world through a different lens. They have a different mindset, thinking process, decision making and propensity to act. These factors influence what they do and how they do it. These success factors often determine their effectiveness and success as an intrapreneur.

More importantly we've learned that being an Intrapreneur is not an intellectual exercise it is developed and refined through experience. Not by doing business as usual but by taking the initiative to try something new, different, and unconventional. It's all about the challenge. The bigger, more difficult the challenge the better. Intrapreneurs are not afraid to fail, only concerned if they don't try.

We've worked with Intrapreneurs around the globe to understand who they are inside and out.

The book *Intrapreneurs – Who, What, How and Why* is a collection of articles that explore these issues and provide insight into what it means and what it takes to be an Intrapreneur.

We also look at Intrapreneurship, nuances, intrapreneur profile, success factors, aspirations, challenges, future, value, leadership and talent. We've organized the book into these general categories so you can wander through each chapter as you see fit.

Our goal is to provide you with a foundation for understanding Intrapreneurs – the Who, What, How and Why behind them and how they are creating the future as they learn and grow.

We also invite you to explore your own Intrapreneurial orientation as you gain a deeper insight into the world of Intrapreneurs.

Terminology, Themes, Insights and Lessons Learned

Terminology

In the book *Intrapreneurs – Who, What, How and Why* we use different words to describe the same things. For example:

- Corporate Entrepreneurship = Intrapreneurship
- Entrepreneurial = Intrapreneurial
- Entrepreneurial Leaders = Intrapreneurial Leaders
- Intrapreneurs = Corporate Entrepreneurs, Internal Entrepreneurs, Change Agents

Part of the challenge is that there is no common definition for many of these terms and they are often used interchangeably. We have done that as well throughout the book.

Themes

You will notice some reoccurring themes as you read through the book *Intrapreneurs – Who, What, How and Why.* These themes serve to emphasize and reinforce key aspects of what it takes to be an intrapreneur inside an established organization.

Our hope is that once you finish reading the book you will be able to reference some of the key themes for yourself, your team and the organization.

Insights

The essence of the book is based on the insights we have gained while working with Intrapreneurs from around the world. As well, as the research that we have conducted to better understand the nuances and differences that distinguish intrapreneurs from others.

Our goal has been to bridge the gap between theory and reality.

Lessons Learned

The biggest contribution to this book has come from the intrapreneurs and entrepreneurial leaders that have shared their journey with us. Their successes and failures and the lessons that they have learned being an intrapreneur inside organizations.

We are grateful to all of them and acknowledge the contribution they are making to creating a better future.

We have assembled a collection of articles that have been published over time and are more relevant and timelier today than when they were written. Enjoy!

Foreword

Intrapreneurship: Simple yet Complex

A friend of mine gave me a lapel pin in the shape of a corkscrew. The card with it read, 'Simple yet complex.' Years earlier we had started a business selling wine albums for individuals that wanted to keep track of their favorite wines. I was working at HP at the time and made frequent trips to California for work so always spent a few extra vacation days selling the albums to the vineyards in Napa Valley and Sonoma. It was a kick to see the wine albums in the gift shops.

Of course, while visiting the various wineries I was asked to try their newest wines. So, you can imagine that by midafternoon I was ready for a nap by the pool. This little entrepreneurial venture taught me a lot about being an entrepreneur. All while having a full-time job selling business computers in Boston.

The combination of working in a large organization and running my own business on the side laid the foundation for the rest of my career. It was the excitement of building a new business while having the stability of being employed that inspired and motivated me. It was not a conscious decision; it was something that seemed to evolve and develop over time.

It led me to other entrepreneurial pursuits inside large organizations. Identifying and developing new products and services and building new businesses. Each opportunity brought with it new challenges, lessons to be learned, problems to solve, obstacles to overcome and resistance to deal with. These became the parameters of work that kept me energized and engaged.

These are the same things that are driving workers today. They want an opportunity to be entrepreneurial at work. They want to take on the biggest challenges, solve the toughest problems, drive change, make a difference and have an impact. They want an environment that allows them to express themselves through their work. At the same time organizations want to become more entrepreneurial, generate new business growth; improve productivity and employee engagement, innovation and financial performance. They see intrapreneurship as a way forward.

So why is it we do not hear more stories about entrepreneurial success inside existing organizations? These are the very things that organizations want and need but struggle to achieve. What seems to be holding them back? What's getting in the way? Why are workers so disengaged, disillusioned at work, electing to go out on their own? These are questions being asked in the C-suite and in the board room.

The problem is that intrapreneurship is not an intellectual exercise it is grounded and formed from experience. If there aren't opportunities for workers to be entrepreneurial then you can't expect them to be entrepreneurial. If there isn't an infrastructure to support intrapreneurship, then it won't succeed. It is why so many organizations are turning to intrapreneurship. They see it as an answer to these issues. That's why we see incubators, accelerators and new venture businesses gaining a foothold in organizations. They provide the opportunity needed to help build intrapreneurship in organizations.

Intrapreneurship is a work in progress for many organizations. Like the corkscrew pin – it is simple, yet complex. Here are a few reasons why.

1. Most executives understand the need for intrapreneurship but many underestimate what is required to successfully implement it. It touches all aspects of the business, strategy, structure, systems, processes, policies through to execution. *It requires a system's view.*
2. It is not a silver bullet. It takes time and experience to develop the entrepreneurial capabilities that are needed to support and sustain intrapreneurship. Being entrepreneurial is a way of thinking and acting that is foreign to the rest of the organization. *It needs to be learned.*
3. It challenges existing business practices. Many of the things that are needed to support the core business are just the opposite of what is required to build a new business. *It is a different business model.*
4. Organizational obstacles can get in the way. Some are obvious others are hidden. You won't know what they are until you encounter them. It's what you do with them that matters. *Managing and overcoming obstacles.*
5. There is no roadmap or guidebook for organizations to follow.

Implementing intrapreneurship will vary depending on the organization. *Context matters.*

6. Leaders, who have succeeded in the past, have achieved their success by exploiting the core business not building a new one. Now they need to do both. Few know how. *Develop entrepreneurial leaders.*
7. Existing mental models used to evaluate ideas are often grounded in the past not the future. They can marginalize ideas and stifle innovation. *New thinking is required.*
8. Most employees will play by the rules. You need individuals that will step on toes and break rules to get things done. Intrapreneurs respect authority but are willing to challenge and question them. *Focus on driving change.*
9. People and cultures are resistant to change. They are more willing to see a project fail than succeed. If it succeeds, they will have to change. *Integrate people into the process.*
10. Although the overall end goal of intrapreneurship is new business growth short term financial pressure does not always provide adequate time to develop or demonstrate success. *Need a balanced investment portfolio.*
11. Standard metrics used to measure success may eliminate opportunities with higher longer-term potential. New metrics are needed to evaluate and monitor progress and success. *Tangible and intangible metrics.*

These are a few of the things can get in the way. They are also the building blocks for building intrapreneurship. On the surface they are simple but in reality, they are much more complex.

The ability to blend entrepreneurial pursuits within the context of an existing organization provides benefits for both the individual and the organization.

How would you evaluate your organization on these dimensions?

Chapter 1: Intrapreneurship/Corporate Entrepreneurship

- Intrapreneurship
- Corporate Entrepreneurship is the Catalyst for Growth
- Innovation versus Corporate Entrepreneurship
- 5 Reasons Why Intrapreneurship is Important
- ROI on Intrapreneurship
- Corporate Entrepreneurship: New Role for Leaders
- Corporate Entrepreneurship: A Strategic Priority
- 10 Reasons for Intrapreneurship – Fad or No Fad

Intrapreneurship

Entrepreneurship inside of established organizations is called Corporate Entrepreneurship or Intrapreneurship.

All companies want organic growth, but few organizations have a process in place to support and sustain growth over time. *An innovation process alone is not enough.*

Organizations need to build a framework to support innovation and new business growth.

Intrapreneurship is a process used to develop new businesses, products, services or processes inside of an existing organization to create value and generate new revenue growth through entrepreneurial thought and action.

Intrapreneurship sets the context for innovation and growth. It provides a system's view of the resources, processes and environment that are needed to support, motivate and engage the organization in entrepreneurial thinking and action.

Organizations with strong entrepreneurial orientations statistically perform better. They achieve higher levels of productivity, innovation, growth, employee engagement and financial returns.

Although business growth is the overall end game, intrapreneurship is difficult to achieve. It challenges traditional organizational practices. Many of the things needed to support the core business are just the opposite of what you need to do to build a new business.

There is no perfect way to implement intrapreneurship. There are however three components that enable intrapreneurship: people, process and place.

- People – leaders that possess a core set of action-oriented competencies and behaviors
- Process – systems and processes that support entrepreneurial thinking and action
- Place – an environment conducive to entrepreneurship, learning and growth

It is well known that internal champions (mavericks) can be effective in bringing new ideas to market. It is well researched that having the right processes can help facilitate entrepreneurship. It is well documented that creating an entrepreneurial culture can direct organizational behavior toward more entrepreneurial pursuits. *But....*

What is less understood is that all three of these elements are needed for intrapreneurship to be successful and sustainable over time.

The goal of intrapreneurship is to build capabilities that enable organizations to accelerate new business growth. That's why 65 percent of the top 100 most innovative companies are implementing intrapreneurship or corporate entrepreneurship.

What about your organization? Are you reaping the benefits of intrapreneurship?

Corporate Entrepreneurship is the Catalyst for Growth

Corporate entrepreneurship/Intrapreneurship is a business process that transcends all aspects of the core business and serves as the catalyst for business growth.

Institutionalizing entrepreneurship can be an effective way to gain a competitive advantage and being more entrepreneurial will help you attract and retain highly talented knowledge workers. Corporate entrepreneurs or Intrapreneurs are the engines of growth. They provide the energy, drive and motivation to help your organization grow. They possess a unique combination of competencies, enabling them to work effectively in an entrepreneurial environment.

Innovation is seen as the springboard to business growth. Despite the hype about it, the failure rate of innovation remains high. Innovation alone is not enough. Corporate entrepreneurship provides the necessary infrastructure for successful innovation. Higher levels of innovation yield greater market share, new product revenue, improved profitability, technical dominance, improved process and cost control, and greater shareholder returns.

The term "corporate entrepreneurship" is an oxymoron. Unlike an entrepreneurial start-up that is created as a stand-alone entity, corporate entrepreneurship is created inside an existing organization. It challenges traditional organizational practices and forces the organization to hold a mirror up to itself to see what it has become. You will find that embedding corporate entrepreneurship into an existing organization requires a major transformation.

Corporate entrepreneurship requires managing the inherent tension between maximizing economic value and developing human capital. Resources and control systems will have to be realigned to support corporate entrepreneurship. You will need to develop new practices for evaluating opportunities and managing risk. Customer intelligence will be more tightly integrated into your decision-making process. There will be a shift in traditional and rational approaches to hiring. You will need to find new ways to maintain the entrepreneurial behavior needed for competitive success.

Corporate entrepreneurship is not included in most of the theories, models or frameworks that have been developed to guide managerial practice. There is a limited understanding of the relationship of entrepreneurship to change, creativity, and innovation -- the building blocks of corporate entrepreneurship.

Leaders typically find themselves in uncharted waters and lack the guidelines on how to direct or redirect resources toward entrepreneurial strategies. Traditional management practices don't apply. Entrepreneurial leadership requires a shift in thinking and behavior. There is often a lack of entrepreneurial role models at the senior management level to provide direction. It is not a lack of talent but a lack of experience with these types of entrepreneurial endeavors that is missing.

Entrepreneurship can be extremely threatening to the people that do the work. Most of the research on individual characteristics and behaviors has been done on start-ups and independent entrepreneurs. There is currently no consensus in the academic and business world about what makes a good corporate entrepreneur. Corporate entrepreneurs and entrepreneurial leaders are a hidden talent in many organizations.

Corporate entrepreneurship will vary depending on the type of initiative, new business, product or service, or process. You will be developing the process as you move forward. There are a number of different obstacles and hidden barriers you will encounter along the way. You will have to find ways to work with and around existing systems and processes. No two initiatives will be the same.

The research conducted to date has identified some of the more pervasive constraints on corporate entrepreneurship. They include everything from an absence of innovation goals, lack of commitment from senior executives, no entrepreneurial role models, and misdirected reward and evaluation systems to long and complex approval cycles, lack of consensus on priorities, and a resistance to change. These issues provide a starting point for understanding some of the obstacles and barriers you will encounter along the way.

Many corporations are not prepared to institutionalize corporate entrepreneurship. There are no benchmarks, metrics or performance criteria for corporate entrepreneurship. Many executives do not know why new initiatives succeed or fail. A failure rate of fifty percent for new initiatives is deemed acceptable. The reasons behind success or failure are often unique to each institution. Understanding the fundamentals around project and program management can go a long way in helping to set up the infrastructure and discipline for tracking and measuring progress.

If you want to create an environment to accelerate business growth, corporate entrepreneurship is one way to accomplish that. It takes a commitment of time, resources, and experimentation. You must be willing to live with ambiguity and tolerate failure as part of the learning process. You cannot become entrepreneurial overnight; it takes practice and having the right people, processes and infrastructure to support and sustain it over time.

Corporate entrepreneurship can be the catalyst for business growth, but only if there is a commitment to it. Those organizations that have been successful in building entrepreneurial capabilities have reaped the rewards and perform better.

Is your organization committed to becoming more entrepreneurial?

Innovation versus Corporate Entrepreneurship

According to the Conference Board's CEO Challenge Study, innovation is one of four top priorities along with human capital, customer relationships and operational excellence. Not surprisingly, organizations are repositioning themselves for growth after a period of volatility and slow growth.

Experts from Drucker to Hamel to Christensen agree that *"Innovation is the key to the success of modern corporations."* Innovation is seen as the springboard to business growth. Higher levels of innovation yield greater market share, new product revenue, improved profitability, technical dominance, improved process and cost control, and greater shareholder returns. *But...*

Innovation alone is not enough. The context must be right for innovation to be successful.

Corporate entrepreneurship sets the context for innovation by providing the infrastructure needed to support and sustain innovation over time - continuous innovation.

Many executives ask me, what is the difference between Innovation and Corporate Entrepreneurship? The lines between them are blurred. According to Michael Morris author of Corporate Entrepreneurship and Innovation, *"There is a general lack of consensus surrounding an agreed upon meaning for both concepts."* They are so entwined that is difficult to see daylight between them.

One way to look at this is to think of Innovation as a *process.* Most organizations have an innovation process - a series of steps that take an idea from concept through to commercialization. It is a process that takes hundreds of ideas and narrows it down to a handful of potential candidates that are tested and eventually brought to market. There are mechanisms in place to support the front end and back end of innovation.

Each part of the innovation process is characterized by its own requirements - creativity, iteration, design, co-creation, disciple, structure, process, analysis, and control. Organizational systems, policies, procedures, and metrics are used to guide the innovation process, like stage gate systems, that ensure that various thresholds are met before moving forward to the next phase. The desired *output* is a new product or service.

In this way, "*Innovation is defined as a systematic, purposeful activity, planned and organized, with high predictability.*"[1]

Even though most organizations have an innovation process - failure rates are still high.

According to Relentless Innovation, "*One of the real challenges is that business as usual isn't simply accepted, it is defended and strengthened by management tools like Six Sigma, outsourcing and lean. While these help an organization become more effective and efficient, they also build greater resistance to innovation, especially sustained innovation.*"

Corporate entrepreneurship on the other hand sets the *context* for Innovation. It encompasses the innovation process. Corporate entrepreneurship requires a more holistic, systems approach to innovation. It provides the foundation. It is a complex process that touches all aspects of the organization including strategy, structure, policies and procedures, systems, culture, people, and customers. Unlike other business processes that might follow a standard work process, corporate entrepreneurship is less structured, it's more organic. It is an attitude, a competence, a way of thinking and acting. You are asking individuals to shift their attitudes, change their beliefs, and learn new skills. It requires managing the inherent tension between maximizing economic value and developing human capital. The focus is on *outcomes*, the business value you want to deliver to customers and the organization.

Corporate entrepreneurship is a change process or transformation that pushes the existing boundaries and tests the limits of organizational systems and processes. You develop the process as you move forward.

1. Bhattacharyya, 2006

This is just one way to think of the differences. You need to define what these concepts mean for your organization.

Innovation and corporate entrepreneurship are inexplicably tied together. They need to co-exist and work together to accelerate new business growth. A structured innovation process may work well for incremental and adjacent innovations but be less effective in transformational or blue-sky innovations. An innovation process might work best for new products but less so for business model innovation. An innovation process might work better in one industry than a totally different one. But setting the context for innovation establishes a foundation for continuous innovation – no matter what type of innovation you are developing.

Corporate entrepreneurship is designed to enable your organization to become more entrepreneurial. There is no silver bullet for becoming more entrepreneurial; it takes practice and having the right people, processes, and environment to support and sustain it over time. Those organizations that have been successful in building entrepreneurial capabilities statistically perform better.

The interesting thing is that corporate entrepreneurship touches every aspect of the Conference Board's CEO Challenge Study - innovation, human capital, operational excellence, and customer relationships.

If you want to harness the full potential of your organization and accelerate business growth through innovation, corporate entrepreneurship is one way to accomplish that.

Let us know how you differentiate between innovation and corporate entrepreneurship!

5 Reasons Why Intrapreneurship is Important

Intrapreneurship is entrepreneurship in the corporate world.

There are lots of reasons why Intrapreneurship is important. Here are 5 reasons why.

1. **Growth:** During the economic downturn most companies stopped investing in the future. Now they are sitting on piles of cash. They know they need to grow; they just aren't sure how. Intrapreneurship answers the question of – HOW!

   The goal of Intrapreneurship is to create the entrepreneurial mindset and infrastructure needed to support growth. It takes a system view of growth. It is a framework for transformation.

   Intrapreneurship helps organizations generate new business growth.

2. **Innovation**: Innovation is the key element in providing aggressive top line growth. But doing one or two innovation initiatives a year will not support or sustain innovation. Organizations need to be innovating all the time. Failure rates for innovation are still high, 50% to 90%.

   Innovation alone is not enough. Organizations need to set the context for innovation, the right people, the right processes and the right environment. Innovation and intrapreneurship are entwined, they are tied together. You need both to be successful.

   Intrapreneurship provides an environment to support and sustain innovation over time.

3. **Leadership**: Research has identified leadership as the key predictor of innovation success. Yet most CEOs to not feel like they have the capabilities inside their organizations to achieve their growth agenda. The skills and capabilities that propelled most executives to the top in the past are not the skills required to build new growth businesses. Only 4% of leaders are intrapreneurial.

   Intrapreneurship requires a new set of competencies and behaviors. Intrapreneurial leaders think and act differently, they have different motivations and aspirations, and they prefer working in different work environments. It is this differentiation that makes them the perfect candidate to lead new growth initiatives.

   Intrapreneurship is the one of the best ways to attract and retain your most entrepreneurial leaders.

4. **Change:** Change is one of the least understood and underdeveloped management disciplines. Most studies report a 60% – 70% failure rate when it comes to change initiatives. Risk adverse cultures and resistance to change impede an organizations ability to grow.

   Intrapreneurial leaders are change agents. They blaze new trails. They become the very change they wish to see. Not just driving change, but modeling change so others can change as well.

   Intrapreneurship enables organizations to effectively accelerate and manage change.

5. **Engagement:** Gallup Research estimates that disengaged employees cost US organizations over $450 billion in lost productivity. In 2018, only 30% of American workers were engaged and committed to their workplace. Lost productivity translates to slow or no growth.

   Intrapreneurship provides a platform to engage employees in work that is challenging and meaningful. Intrapreneurs are highly engaged in their work. Their passion and determination inspire others to get involved and try new things. As they grow, the organization grows.

   Intrapreneurship helps employees stretch and grow while keeping them engaged.

   Intrapreneurship has become a critical imperative for all organizations and a survival strategy for others. Organizations that have embraced Intrapreneurship have achieved higher financial returns, increased productivity, more innovation and higher levels of employee engagement.

Isn't it time you took a closer look at Intrapreneurship and what it can mean for your organization?

ROI on Intrapreneurship

Recently a colleague said that there was no return on investment (ROI) for Intrapreneurship for large organizations. The financials did not justify the investment. He is both right and wrong.

It depends on your perspective.

1. Are you looking at the traditional ROI when 80% of assets were tangible and most of the percent increase in GDP was from tangible assets or are you looking at the new reality where 90% of organizations assets are now intangible?

   According to the U.S. Bureau of Economic Analysis (BEA) "*intangible assets drove 90% of GDP growth.*" Intangible assets include investments in research and development, design and development and human capital.

2. Are you looking at human capital as an expense or an investment? Employee salaries make up close to half of many company's operating expenses. Investors have been evaluating the worth of companies based on intangible assets for years. They know human capital drives financial success.

   In his article Return on Intangibles, Jay Cross says, "*Instead of relying on expectations for a stable past, investors began betting on the future.*" They are placing bets on human capital – "*the know-how and abilities of an organizations people*".

3. Are you focused on developing people that can be effective in the core business or those that can build new growth businesses? A high potential in the core business is not necessarily a high potential when it comes to building a new business.

   In his article The Entrepreneurial Employee, Steve Strauss reminds us that, "*The growth of many corporate giants has been achieved by the entrepreneurs within. Think Apple, Google, Intel, Lockheed-Martin and many more.*"

4. Are you investing in transformational innovations or product line extensions and enhancements? Most organizations have spent the

last decade investing in products and services that were mature or at the end of their life cycle.

According to Accenture, "*Fully 64% of the 591 companies - are still focusing largely online extensions*" which translates into low returns and little business value. "*Only 20% view their innovations as game changers.*"

5. Are you making a distinction between the types of innovations you are developing, and the resources needed to support them? The type of innovation impacts key elements of Intrapreneurship - the type of resources, the types of leaders, systems and processes, environment, risk taking and metrics.

   Organizations often fail to understand the distinction between different types of innovations and why each of them requires a different set of skills and capabilities.

6. Are your leaders talking about Intrapreneurship but not actually doing anything about it? Intellectually executives understand the importance of being more intrapreneurial but emotionally they have not bought in. They do not have an experience base they can relate to, so they fall back to what they know.

   In the article It Sound Great in Theory, Susan Mazza says "*It is only when you take action that you can begin to observe the gap between what you think you know and understand and what you actually know.*" Intrapreneurship is an intellectual and emotional experience. You can't be an Intrapreneur until you are an Intrapreneur. It's all about the experience.

Is there an ROI for Intrapreneurship? The academic world says yes, higher levels of productivity, engagement, innovation and financial performance. The business world is more skeptical.

Many organizations are concerned that the risks of implementing Intrapreneurship outweigh the benefits. Financial risk is the most obvious but perhaps the bigger risks are not so obvious. There is the risk of losing some of your best and brightest employees, a risk to your reputation and competitive position in the marketplace, the very things that create value today.

Intrapreneurship is a way of thinking and acting. It's a mindset, a competence, a way of being. It's how you see the world – the old world and the new world. It really depends on your perspective.

What do you think! Is there an ROI for Intrapreneurship?

Corporate Entrepreneurship – New Role for Leaders

Not surprisingly there has been little attention paid to the role of senior management where it comes to corporate entrepreneurship*.

According to the article, The Future of the Corporation, "*The strategic decision for entrepreneurial activities is not well understood, and particularly poorly conceived is senior executive responsibilities in the corporate application of entrepreneurship.*"

In the past senior leaders were responsible for strategy formulation, policy setting, and directing organizational resources toward strategic objectives. Their focus was on optimizing the use of existing resources, while controlling and managing the use of strategic assets. Operational efficiency and risk avoidance were paramount. Traditional roles included the oversight of innovation efforts at lower levels within the organization. Efforts constrained by existing organization systems and practices resulting in incremental innovations, providing lower financial returns and growth. The focus was on the exploitation of the core business.

In the future the senior management team will be directly involved in the generation of innovation ideas that are more strategic and will have a greater impact. Senior executives will be actively engaged in innovation and the change process. They will participate by becoming role models for the change and leading the change effort. Demonstrating through their actions what is required to instill and drive entrepreneurial thinking and action. Fostering an environment that encourages employees to take risks, be more proactive and innovative. Efforts that will transform the company while generating new levels of financial performance. The focus directed on the exploration of new businesses.

The challenge for leaders is operating in both worlds simultaneously. Managing the core business at the same time they are building a new one. Many of the things that are required in the core business are just the opposite of what is required in a new business venture. The policies, practices and systems that support the core business get in the way. They create barriers to growth and stifle innovation. The skills and capabilities required to lead in the core business are not the same skills required to build a new one. Leaders will find themselves having one foot in both worlds; the core business and the new business they are building.

According to research only one percent of senior executives in large organizations can lead an existing business at the same time they are building a new one. The true entrepreneurial leader is rare.

Corporate entrepreneurship requires an environment that most leaders are not accustomed to dealing with. Leaders must be highly adaptable, flexible, and responsive to a rapidly changing market environment. They will now be competing for the same resources used to support the core business. There will be new issues and conflicts to deal with. There will be systems and processes that need to be changed or replaced, existing policies and procedures that no longer make sense. There will be resistance to change, controversial decisions to make and risks to take. They will have to capture knowledge and lessons learned to embed them into the memory of the organization.

Formulating a strategy is one thing, implementing it is another. These are two distinct disciplines that require different know-how. Active involvement in the entrepreneurial process is the best way to learn what it takes to be an entrepreneurial leader.

In most organizations' innovation is a bottom's up approach taking place at lower levels in the organization. This is a problematic. According to the authors of The Future of the Corporation, *"Individuals at lower organizational levels are more likely to limit innovations to those of incremental nature entirely within the strategic context of the organization."* These individuals perceive organizational boundaries as being fixed. They think that proposing a radically new idea would not be welcomed. That stepping outside the boundaries of acceptable behavior is not something worth risking. This approach results in fewer high growth opportunities and lower financial returns.

That's why senior management needs to take an active role in innovation and entrepreneurship. Senior management has a view of the organization that few others share. They can see strategic opportunities when they arise. They know which ideas will fly and which ones will not. They can look at every decision from a strategic perspective. They have the experience to know how far they can push organizational boundaries. They can influence and negotiate for resources not readily available. They have the political clout to get things done.

The lack of entrepreneurial role models in most organizations is something that can be fixed. It is not a lack of talent but a lack of experience that is the problem. Leaders must become adept at both exploitation and exploration. That is the paradox of entrepreneurship. It is a two-way street.

Is corporate entrepreneurship a strategic leadership role in your organization?

Corporate Entrepreneurship: A Strategic Priority

Corporate entrepreneurship begins and ends at the executive suite. It requires strategic oversight and involvement. If the chief executive officer and board don't fully understand or commit themselves to corporate entrepreneurship it will not fly.

According to Shaker A. Zahra, "*corporate entrepreneurship is a set of activities to enhance a company's ability to innovate, take a risk, and seize the opportunities that are allocated in the market.*"

In many organizations corporate entrepreneurship is being set up to fail because it is not a strategic priority. There is a deep divide between strategic management of the existing business and corporate entrepreneurship. The two collide – one is about exploiting the core business, the other about exploring new businesses.

Corporate entrepreneurship impacts executive responsibilities, strategic decision making and the allocation of resources. It shifts the balance of power and changes the political landscape. It raises new questions and challenges long held beliefs. It can create conflict and be divisive. It can turn the organization upside down.

In the article The Relationship between Corporate Entrepreneurship and Strategic Management, the author states that, "*Corporate entrepreneurship requires integrating the seemingly opposing activities of preserving the existing business and stimulating change through innovation.*" These are two different types of activities that require two different types of capabilities, resources, and cultures.

Now more than ever organizations are faced with the challenge of leveraging innovation to accelerate growth to emerge out of the current crisis. According to the article Strategic Resilience During the Covid-19 Crisis by McKinsey, "*As companies start to prepare for post-pandemic world, those that have fallen behind more resilient players will need to take fast, bold action to make up for lost ground.*" This requires a concerted effort to shift the focus from exploitation to exploration. A key driving factor behind corporate entrepreneurship.

Corporate entrepreneurship needs to be an explicit process articulated by the senior management team, based on an assessment of core competencies, and competitive position of the organization consistent with the strategic direction. There needs to be a specific corporate strategy for entrepreneurship.

A strategy that includes many of the following things:

1. A distinct vision with clear objectives of what the organization wants to achieve.
2. Identification of internal constraints, external influences, and competitive forces.
3. A process for allocating resources; funding, leadership, sponsorship, and workers.
4. A clear articulation of decision-making rights, authority, responsibility, and accountability.

5. A plan to develop the entrepreneurial competencies of individuals and the organization.
6. A change effort designed to create a culture of risk taking, pro-activeness and innovation.
7. A definition of the types of innovation initiatives the organization intends to pursue.
8. An innovation process used to discover, design, develop and implement ideas.
9. An investment portfolio over various time horizons to manages risk and reward.
10. A policy to tolerate failure, learn from the experience and capture lessons learned.
11. A definition of the metrics used to measure success, tangible, and intangible.
12. A direct channel of communication to and from the senior management team.

Instituting corporate entrepreneurship in an established organization isn't easy but establishing corporate entrepreneurship as a strategic priority is one place to start.

Corporate entrepreneurship is a major transformational effort that must be guided by the vision and strategy articulated by the senior management team. A vision that describes what needs to change and how that change will happen. Ensuring that the systems and processes are in place to enable and support corporate entrepreneurship. Aligning the resources and metrics needed to drive growth. Allowing managers to step up and outside the boundaries of traditional management practices. Enabling employees to think and act entrepreneurial. Setting aside notions of what is not possible and believing anything is possible.

According to the Model for Corporate Entrepreneurship by Covin and Slevin, "*Strategic variables such as the mission statement, business practices and competitive tactics all impact a firm's ability to adopt an entrepreneurial posture.*" Corporate entrepreneurship is not something that can be delegated – its success depends on the active involvement of the senior management team. Not on an ad-hoc basis but emersed in the process.

Understanding the nuances of what it takes to identify, develop. and deliver innovations into a rapidly changing environment. Strengthening relationships with customers. Seeing first-hand the barriers and obstacles that can get in the way. Making decisions without having all the data. Feeling the resistance and reluctance to change the status quo. Experiencing the emotional roller coaster that inevitably exists in these types of efforts. Dealing with uncertainty, ambiguity and the unknown. Only then will senior management be better able to refine their thinking, sharpen their focus and integrate innovation into the fabric of the organization.

This was reinforced in the study Nurturing the Corporate Entrepreneurship Capability, "*Without strategic commitment and support from top management, there is little incentive for traditional organizational systems to change and support existing and future corporate entrepreneurship initiatives.*"

If business model innovation has become the post-pandemic model for success. Perhaps corporate entrepreneurship is the best way to go about building that new model.

Is corporate entrepreneurship a strategic priority in your organization?

10 Reasons for Intrapreneurship – Fad or No Fad

A question that many executives ask me; "*Is intrapreneurship just the latest management fad.*" Fad or no fad the real question is why now!

Read 10 reasons why intrapreneurship and intrapreneurial leadership is needed **now.** Then let us know if you think intrapreneurship is a fad or here to stay.

1. **Inadequate Growth**: The current reality is that most organizations have spent the last decade investing in existing or mature products that are not providing adequate growth.

2. **Failure Rate**: The failure rate for new business initiatives remains high for new product and service innovations and greater than ninety percent for transformational efforts.
3. **Lack of Capabilities**: A majority of CEOs do not feel like they have the skills or capabilities inside their organization to achieve their growth agenda, they are probably right.
4. **Few Role Models**: Only four percent of executives in large organizations are entrepreneurs or entrepreneurial, most executives have achieved their success by managing the core business not building new ones.
5. **Major Barriers:** After a decade of cost cutting and streamlining operations, organizations have created rigid and inflexible systems that have created roadblocks and barriers to growth.
6. **Inability to Change**: Risk adverse cultures, resistance to change and fear of the unknown are impeding an organizations ability to respond to a rapidly changing world.
7. **Reliance on the Past**: Increasing uncertainty, complexity and ambiguity are putting pressure on organizations to rely on practices that worked well for them in the past but may not work now.
8. **Poor Execution**: Three out of five organizations say they are weak when it comes to execution and they see corporate entrepreneurship as a way to close the gap between idea generation and execution.
9. **Business Benefits:** Corporate entrepreneurship is linked to higher levels of productivity, engagement, growth, innovation and financial returns. It is also linked to intangible outcomes like knowledge, skill development and job satisfaction.
10. **Accelerate Growth:** Sixty five percent of the top one hundred innovative companies are instituting intrapreneurship as a way to increase their ability to deliver new business growth.

Is intrapreneurship the latest management fad or a business imperative? You decide!

Chapter 2: Force Behind Intrapreneurship

- Adoption of Intrapreneurship – Crossing the Chasm
- Intrapreneurship – Let's End the Debate
- Individual and Organizational Commitment to Intrapreneurship
- Great Divide that Derails Intrapreneurship
- Solving the Paradox of Intrapreneurship
- 9 Ways to Foster Entrepreneurial Behavior
- Are Intrapreneurs the New Silver Bullet for Organizations?
- Impact of Intrapreneurs on Organizations
- Accelerating Growth - Speed and Direction

Adoption of Intrapreneurship – Crossing the Chasm

The evolution of intrapreneurship has progressed from its inception, but the adoption of intrapreneurship is still far from complete. It reminds me of Geoffrey Moore's book 'Crossing the Chasm'. Although Moore talks about the traditional Technology Adoption Life Cycle, it is safe to say that ideas or concepts like Intrapreneurship go through their own adoption cycle.

Much like the adoption curve for new technology highlighted in Moore's book, 'innovators and early adopters' are engaged in some form of intrapreneurship. We see pockets of intrapreneurship sprinkled throughout these organizations, but it is far from being integrated into the fabric of the organization.

There is also a gulf between those organizations that are engaged in intrapreneurship and those that are still sitting on the sideline. A huge chasm exists between the 'early adopters and the early majority'. Moore describes the early majority as 'the pragmatists' who wait until things have been established before they buy into a product or concept like Intrapreneurship. This reluctance to adopt intrapreneurship is happening in some of the world's largest organizations. It is especially true when it comes to social intrapreneurship.

Unlike a technology that is gradually adopted by more and more companies Intrapreneurship is a behavioral and cultural movement. It has its roots in the hearts and minds of employees. It is an attitude, a competence, a way of thinking and acting that is not something you can buy. It is something you need to cultivate and develop.

It is employees that are the force behind intrapreneurship. They are the ones that are creating, building and delivering new value and growth in their organizations. Often it is small pockets of employees that band together for a common goal based on a core set of beliefs that anything is possible. They ignore and work around organizational obstacles that get in their way. They push forward despite setbacks that would discourage or dissuade others from moving forward.

Intrapreneurs are the force that will help drive Intrapreneurship across the chasm. They are the individuals who are currently working in those organizations that Moore calls 'early adopters. It is there that they are learning and developing their entrepreneurial skills. They are proactively developing the competencies that are and will be needed to thrive and succeed in a new world economy. An economy that is dominated by individuals and organizations that are entrepreneurial. Organizations that cannot only generate social and economic value but can effectively manage the core business as they transition to a more entrepreneurial orientation.

That is what intrapreneurship is all about. Building an entrepreneurial set of capabilities that will enable organizations to generate social and economic value for their clients and aggressively pursue an entrepreneurial mindset and actions. Unfortunately, intrapreneurship is not something that is easily measured in the short term, it takes time, patience and practice for it to be perfected. Only in hindsight will organizations see the value of their investments in Intrapreneurship. Those organizations that don't pursue it now will fall further behind.

Given my work with intrapreneurs and social innovators they prefer to build not manage, so once they have completed their work, they will look for new opportunities. Most of those opportunities will be in the 'early majority' companies – across the chasm. This is fertile ground for intrapreneurs to further refine their skills and deliver greater value to these organizations.

Intrapreneurs are not content unless they are doing something new, in a new way, for a new purpose that makes a difference. The biggest impact intrapreneurs will have on business will be showing organizations what it takes to develop intrapreneurship in their organizations. That will be their mission, it is what motivates them and what drives them. It is what will transform the current way we do business.

Intrapreneurship is a movement that has momentum because it is driven by workers. Workers intent on making a difference for themselves, their organizations and society. There is no turning back. There are too many workers. Too many factors that are aligned for intrapreneurship to be the catalyst for change. Too much pressure to revitalize our largest organizations, energize workers, solve social problems and build a better future for the next generation.

Intrapreneurs will be the ones that build that bridge across the chasm.

But will they find it more challenging, more difficult to convince the 'early majority' across the chasm that Intrapreneurship is the way to go. This group is more skeptical, wants references, relationships, they want to know that you are experienced, established and can deliver what you promise. Will intrapreneurs have enough experience to show that they are capable? Enough of a proven track record of success to convince them that they can be trusted. Will they have enough proof that their way is the best way?

Yes, this is the new frontier for intrapreneurs. It is the next step in their own evolution. It is the next big challenge, the next big opportunity for them. Intrapreneurs are not content to wait for an opportunity, they actively seek them out. Why do you think so many Intrapreneurs are willing to leave their job and start a business or are electing to be self-employed? They would tell you that there are not enough challenges or opportunities for them where they are. Better to take the risk and find a new challenge, then to languish where they are.

Crossing the chasm is the next big challenge for Intrapreneurs. It is the also the next step in the evolution and adoption of Intrapreneurship into a new group of organizations.

Intrapreneurship – Let's End the Debate

The ongoing debate in the business and academic world is whether people, process or culture is most important when it comes to intrapreneurship. Isn't it time we end the debate?

It is well known that internal champions can be effective at bringing new ideas to market. It is well researched that having the right processes can help facilitate intrapreneurship. And it is well documented that creating an innovative culture can direct organizational behavior toward more entrepreneurial pursuits. But…what is less understood is that all three of these elements are needed for Intrapreneurship to be successful and sustainable over time.

Champions and mavericks are known for their ability to push their ideas through to implementation. Their raw determination can make the impossible, possible. It is their belief in what they are doing; their commitment to the project, their ability to be independent, deal with ambiguity, navigate obstacles and bring things to closure that makes the difference. They provide the energy, motivation, and drive. It is their actions that move the project and the organization forward.

Seventy percent of organizations think that process alone will drive Intrapreneurship. Think again. Most organizations have an innovation process, yet most new innovations fail. A process can provide discipline and structure, but it can't anticipate or navigate obstacles. It isn't until you are into a process that you understand what needs to be tweaked or replaced. It isn't the process but the people behind the process that make the difference between success and failure.

Creating an entrepreneurial culture lays the foundation for changing organizational behavior. Change however takes time, energy and commitment that most organizations don't have. More than seventy percent of all large cultural change initiatives fail. Change requires a shift in thinking and behavior, a role model to guide the way. Not just modeling change but leading change and enabling others to change. It is the people that drive change by becoming the change they hope to achieve.

All three of these elements are important for Intrapreneurship, but the common thread that runs through all of them are people. Organizations need to identify the right people with a core set of entrepreneurial competencies to lead and participate in these new business initiatives.

Over the last several years Corporate Entrepreneurs LLC has been researching corporate entrepreneurs, intrapreneurs and entrepreneurial leaders inside organizations to figure out who they are, why they are different, and what distinguishes them from others. The research confirmed that these internal entrepreneurs are in fact a 'distinct' group of professionals.

These individuals possess a unique combination of competencies that set them apart from others.

The research showed that Intrapreneurs have many of the same competencies as senior level executives and managers, but it was the depth of competency that distinguished Intrapreneurs from their peers and senior executives. Intrapreneurs outperformed their peers and senior executives in ten of the seventeen core competencies. Not by a small margin but by a wide margin. This was the big ah hah!

It was this gap that soon brought to light why Intrapreneurs were different.

Intrapreneurs consciously or unconsciously take positions that enable them to build and develop these competencies at a much deeper and richer level. It is the type of experience that is important. It is the combination of competencies that set them apart. The breadth and depth of competencies enable them to operate effectively in the core business at the same time they are building a new one.

As organizations come to understand the tremendous impact that intrapreneurship can have on the performance of their company, the more important intrapreneurs will become. That's why we developed the Corporate Entrepreneur Profile™. Individuals, innovation groups and executives that take the profile can see if they have the competencies and behaviors needed to be a successful entrepreneur inside an established organization. The Corporate Entrepreneur Profile™ helps you activate this critical resource and the engine of growth that they represent.

Organizations that have identified and developed their intrapreneurs have achieved higher levels of productivity, engagement, innovation and financial returns.

Let's end the debate.

Individual and Organizational Commitment to Intrapreneurship

According to the Hay Group, intrapreneurship is the new "buzz" word. It has finally reached a level of acknowledgement, acceptance and adoption. As Intrapreneurship takes on greater prominence in organizations it is important for you to ask if the commitment is there to support, develop and integrate it into the culture of the organization. You need to ask yourself the same questions. Are you committed to intrapreneurship and what that entails?

For many organizations intrapreneurship is a response to a number of factors including a slow-down in growth, demands to increase levels of innovation and productivity, a shortage of qualified candidates for new positions, a new set of work demands from the Millennial generation, the need to improve levels of engagement, and pressure to retain existing employees who are no longer challenged or interested in climbing the traditional corporate ladder.

These are all solid reasons for engaging in Intrapreneurship but beware that organizations have been enamored with other "buzz" words and management practices before that never actually got integrated into the fabric of the organization. Intrapreneurship is not the next management fad – it is a business transformation. Not something that can only be part of this year's strategy, but an integral part of the way organizations do business now and into the future. It is a behavioral change that takes place at the individual and organizational level.

Organization must demonstrate their commitment to intrapreneurship by developing new policies, procedures and practices that enable intrapreneurship to thrive. It must become part of the corporate strategy, new management practices must be put in place, different metrics and measurements are required, creating a learning environment is important, and developing entrepreneurial competencies is critical. Having the right people in place to lead, support and direct resources toward entrepreneurial pursuits is required. Leveraging resources across organizational boundaries, collaborating with external partners and integrating customers into the development process.

These are things that organizations can start doing without disrupting the organization. It's not a revolution but an evolution of transforming the company to be more entrepreneurial.

It isn't something that can be taken lightly, once your organization starts down this road there is no turning back. Jumping in with both feet can be a trap that creates chaos without much progress. Engaging too slowly may discourage and disappoint those who are eager to drive the change. It may raddle the nerves of some of your most loyal leaders and employees. There are hidden obstacles and roadblocks that can easily derail it and leave things worse off than they were before the organization started down this path. It may set a precedence on changing how work will get done that you may not be able to undo or turn back from. That's not to say that it isn't important or worthwhile doing. Its exactly what organizations need to do to redesign, reinvent themselves to adjust to this new economy.

My concern is ensuring that you as an Intrapreneur are committed to this role and aligned with the organization. Like an organization once you start down this professional path it is very difficult to turn back.

The freedom and flexibility that comes from being an intrapreneur is what keeps you energized and engaged. The excitement of working on the most difficult problems and challenges is what inspires and motivates you. Dealing with ambiguity, uncertainty and complexity enable you to adapt more readily to a rapidly changing environment. Testing your own skills and capabilities enable you to see what you know and don't know about yourself. Learning to live with success and failure provides insight that can only be learned by experiencing it. Building a portfolio of intrapreneurial experiences lay the foundation for success now and into the future. This type of experience changes you personally and professionally. There is no turning back.

Going back to business as usual will no longer cut it. You've changed even though the organization and your peers may not have. You see the organization in a new light. You've found out what you do well and not so well. You now know what you like to do and not do. You've pushed the boundaries of what you thought you were capable of doing. You stepped outside your comfort zone and survived, even thrived. You see yourself for who you are at the core. You now understand what you need to be satisfied and fulfilled at work. You see what it takes to be true to yourself. These are valuable lessons learned but they are also requirements you will need moving forward. They define you and define what you will want and need in the next opportunity.

These are also the things that leave intrapreneurs out of sync with the rest of the organization. After an intrapreneurial experience you may feel like you no longer fit. This is especially true if there isn't another challenging opportunity for you to pursue. Many intrapreneurs get discouraged, disengage and leave the organization. They have seen what is possible, but the rest of the organization may not. They see opportunities that others do not.

This was something that happened to me while building a new business for a Fortune 100 company years ago. Most of my team were existing employees who'd been with the company for years, in one case over 20 years. We were creating a new business, a new product, and a new entrepreneurial culture. Just as we were getting ready to launch this new business, the division we were in was sold which orphaned our business and left all of us without a job. Although everyone was offered an opportunity to stay within the core business, thirteen out of the fourteen people on my team decided to leave and pursue other more entrepreneurial roles. None of them could see themselves going back to the core business. They had all changed, but it was clear that the core business had not. The company was not committed to becoming more intrapreneurial, they had seen our new business as an investment not a way to transform the business.

That's why it is important to understand not only your commitment to intrapreneurship but your organizations as well. In order for Intrapreneurship to work you and your organization must be aligned and committed to it.

Great Divide that Derails Intrapreneurship

The 2018 Deloitte Millennial Survey paints a realistic picture of the challenges that organizations face as they deal with the impact of Industry 4.0 and the growing unrest of millennials and Gen Z in the workplace.

Not only are millennials disappointed, they are discouraged with the lack of support and professional development by their organizations to prepare them for the future. Those individuals who plan on staying more than five years with their current employer say that part of the reason is their organizations commitment to helping them better prepare for Industry 4.0. The rest are open to jumping into the Gig economy to take control of their own destiny.

The news however is not all negative. It points to an opportunity for organizations to reinvigorate, re-energize and redesign their organizations to take advantage of this new world. The report touts the value of Industry 4.0 in freeing up routine work for more creative, more value based, socially conscious work that is aligned with the needs and desires of millennials and Gen Z.

The roadblock seems to be more clearly at the top of organizations. Beyond all the rhetoric the main focus of many organizations remains profit. According to the Deloitte Survey there is a wide gap between the priorities of millennials and those of the organization. Although millennials and Gen Z understand the value of profit to the organization, they also realize the value that business can bring to solving some of society's pressing problems.

Intrapreneurship can help organizations achieve both these goals. There is no question that Industry 4.0 will impact every company, industry and country in the world. Organizations that realize this will thrive, those that don't will eventually wither away. That's not to say that Intrapreneurship is the answer, but it is a mechanism for helping organizations change, adapt and create not only a profitable future but an impactful one.

That said it will not happen just by adopting Intrapreneurship as the latest management fad. It must be integrated into the fabric of the organization and into the hearts and minds of the executives at the top of organizations. Too often executives support these intrapreneurial efforts only to sit on the sidelines and watch from a distance. That doesn't work. Executives need to not only support it; they need to be engaged in the process. Seeing and doing are not equal. What has been missing in many organizations is more relevant, experienced based and entrepreneurial professional development. Plus, an understanding of the Industry 4.0 elements that are impacting business.

Professional development is required up and down the organization. This is especially true when it comes to Intrapreneurship.

Over the years we have seen executives in organization after organization fund and promote professional development of Intrapreneurial efforts without being part of that process. They ask their subordinates to assess, build and develop the capabilities that are needed to be intrapreneurial, but they are often not willing to do it for themselves. This is the great divide.

Not only are these executives missing the opportunity to build the capabilities that are needed to be an intrapreneurial leader. They are unable to effectively contribute to closing the gaps that surface between the core business and the new businesses that their organizations are developing. It is often these types of issue that stall and derail intrapreneurial efforts. Many executives are unable to bridge the gap between these two worlds. Two worlds that will inevitably collide. Not only do executives lose because of this, the organization loses as well.

We can appreciate the inherent feeling most of us go through when beings assessed for capabilities we may or may not possess. It can be unnerving. Yet, we are talking about a new set of capabilities that have not always been part of the core set needed in the existing business. So, it is not surprising when we hear executives decline to assess themselves or look at their own capabilities. Perhaps they think they won't fair as well given their work in the existing business. This is a false belief.

It's a false premise because what we found is that most executives possess the key capabilities, it is just the degree to which they possess it. The depth of a capability is often a reflection of their experience or the types of projects these executives have worked on throughout their career; strategic initiatives, stretch assignments, cross-functional leadership roles, special projects with high visibility, customer facing endeavors or new business ventures. Aspects of these types of experiences provide a starting point for developing many of the capabilities that are needed to be an effective intrapreneur or intrapreneurial leader.

It is like a muscle, the more you use it the stronger it becomes. You may not even think you have it in you until you flex your muscle. That is exactly what we found in our work with senior executives across a wide spectrum of companies and industries. The most effective intrapreneurial leaders had selectively and proactively raised their hands for assignments that were outside the norm of the existing business. Assignments that were strategic, future oriented, needed cross-functional collaboration, required a deeper understanding of customers, presented the toughest challenges, the hardest problems to solve or risky decisions to make etc. This was one part of their professional development roadmap.

These intrapreneurial leaders also wanted to understand their starting point in terms of intrapreneurial capabilities. They wanted to know: Where they were now? Where they need to go? How they could get there? They welcomed getting a more comprehensive assessment of their current capabilities. They were open to seeing themselves in a new light; their strengths, areas needing development and ways on how to proceed. It gave them a baseline to work with, a plan to move forward and a measurement to evaluate their progress down the road. This was the other part of their professional development roadmap.

Yet it was this second roadmap where we see the most resistance from senior executives. They are willing to hold a mirror up to others but not to themselves.

We applaud those organizations that are taking their executives through the same rigorous professional development programs as their potential intrapreneurs. These executives have a richer understanding of the nuances that are required to support, engage and lead intrapreneurial efforts in their respective organizations. They can more clearly see both sides of an issue, understand the impact any one decision can have on the business and are better able to deal with roadblocks they encounter along the way. In doing this they gain respect from their employees, their peers, the CEO and Board.

Executives that walk this professional development roadmap bring years of wisdom from the past and new learnings from the present to help create a future that helps integrate these two worlds. The ability to bridge the gap between the core business and the new business they are building highlights the real value that executives can bring to Intrapreneurship. They join the ranks of the one percent of leaders inside organizations that can truly be called Intrapreneurial Leaders.

Solving the Paradox of Intrapreneurship

Intrapreneurship is a two-way street. It is not a binary choice. It's not an either-or but an and-also. You need leaders that can manage the core business at the same time you need leaders that can build new ones. This is the paradox of Intrapreneurship.

Intrapreneurship is all about finding the right balance between the core business and the new businesses that you are building.

It's not a switch that you can turn on or off. It requires a deeper understanding of the nuances that influence and support Intrapreneurship. The correct allocation of resources, the right mix of innovations, the right people to drive it and the right culture to support it. These are distinct and different requirements. They represent a startup.

At the same time you need to keep the organization moving forward, enhancing existing products and services, leveraging new technology, engaging employees in challenging work, managing a balanced portfolio of investments, driving incremental change in core systems and processes and being responsible to shareholders. These are the fundamental principles that drive and sustain established organizations. They are the foundation.

The paradox is that you need to do both things simultaneously. One view represents the past and the other the future but they both help us see that what is needed is something in the middle. A bridge from one to the other. A process that leverages the best of both. A roadmap for evolving the core business to the new business model. That bridge today is intrapreneurs.

Intrapreneurs are the ones that can bridge this divide and help transform their organizations. They can operate effectively in both worlds. But it is leaders in the core business that must set the stage.

The question for leaders is whether or not they will embrace Intrapreneurship as part of their overall strategy. Recent studies suggest that leaders are looking at Intrapreneurship as a way to generate new business growth. The question is their commitment to it. What level of commitment are they willing to make? Is it a matter of just adapting to the new business reality or adopting it as viable alternative growth strategy or integrating it into the organization?

Despite their similarity, adapting and adopting have totally different meanings. When you adapt to something you are willing to change your idea or behavior, so it is easier to deal with a particular situation. When you adopt something, you take something and make it suitable for a new purpose. Integration takes it a step further. When you integrate something, you combine something into an integral whole.

Where your organization fits on this spectrum of commitment will determine how big, strong and durable that bridge will have to be between the core business and the new business you are building.

It is also a signal to intrapreneurs the level of influence, persuasion and motivation that will be required to push things through. The amount of collaboration, leadership and political savvy that will be needed. The degree of risk taking, decision making and communication that will be required. The effort and energy required to bring skeptics on board, secure funding, and show results. The uncertainty, doubt and frustration that you will have to live with. The breadth and depth of capabilities needed to deal with roadblocks and obstacles that will get in your way. The amount of stress you will need to endure and the level of resilience you will have to have. These are only a few of the things that will be impacted by the level of commitment your organization makes to intrapreneurship.

The less committed they are the more committed you need to be. If your organization is adapting it will be incumbent upon you to move the organization forward to adoption and eventually integration. It's a transformation that takes time, patience and a lot of energy.

Keep in mind as an intrapreneur you have one foot in both worlds – the core business and the new business you are building. Your success will depend on how well you deal with the other side of the bridge, the core business. They will be quite happy to watch from a distance from the comfort of their offices. But it is incumbent upon you to open their minds, their perspective, and their beliefs of what is possible. To engage them and inspire them to want to explore new opportunities.

This requires having a deep understanding of how the core business operates and where it is flexible and where it is not. A network of people you can count on to support you. Resources that are available for you to leverage. Insiders who can provide assistance, direction, connections and technical support. An understanding of the political climate and key influencers. A sponsor that will pave the way for you with others. A CEO that is prepared to support you with the board. These are only a few of the things you will need to succeed.

Solving the paradox of intrapreneurship comes down to you, the intrapreneur. And it is for these reasons that having the right set of competencies and behaviors are critical. You must know how to operate effectively on both sides of the bridge. That's why you are hearing that what intrapreneurial leaders need is a strong set of soft skills; self-awareness, influence, collaboration, communication, listening, motivation, negotiation, delegating, emotional intelligence, empathy, creativity, flexibility, resilience, etc. These are important no matter what side of the bridge you are dealing with.

The key challenge for organizations is identifying and developing intrapreneurs that can work effectively in both the core business and the new business they are building. But this is not an easy task because what is required in the core business is often just the opposite of what is required in a new business. It is not that one way is better than the other it is just that you need someone who can work effectively in both. Working in and between these two different types of environments is not easy, it is stressful and requires a great deal of stamina, finesse and competence.

The key challenge for individuals is demonstrating through your actions and your experience that you have what it takes to operate effectively in both worlds. Being an intrapreneur is not an intellectual exercise it comes from the experience itself. You need a solid understanding of the core business and you need to build a portfolio of entrepreneurial experiences. It is only then that you can appreciate, compare and contrast how different these two different sides of the bridge really are.

How many times have you seen your organization put someone who has been successful in the core business on a new entrepreneurial project, only to see them fail? Or they acquire a startup company and see the leadership team from the startup eventually leave.

The only way to solve the paradox of intrapreneurship is identifying and then developing professionals that can operate effectively on both sides of the bridge. Then move the organization from adapting to adopting and eventually integration.

Integrating intrapreneurship into the fabric of the organization will only happen when there is a clear understanding of the steps, the processes and the people that are needed to move from one side of the bridge to the other side.

9 Ways to Foster Entrepreneurial Behavior

Corporate entrepreneurship is vital to the future of every enterprise, but it presents difficult challenges for companies and their entrepreneurial employees. Our research suggests that success comes from managing these unique relationships differently. Nowhere is this more important than when it comes to the entrepreneurs inside your organization.

Corporations and executive recruiters are usually quick to screen out job applicants who they suspect are mavericks—no matter how exceptional their credentials. Fitting well with the prospective employer's corporate culture has long been a guiding principle of hiring; but does it always serve the best interests of organizations and employees? And, should senior executives use the same management approach for every employee?

Such doubts arose early in my career and grew stronger as my work at various industry-leading organizations increasingly put me in contact with individuals who, like me, were entrepreneurially inclined. I soon discovered that individuals charged with developing new ventures within established organizations have widely divergent levels of talent, job satisfaction, and success.

To better understand the factors that determine success or failure of new ventures in large organizations, we designed and implemented abroad cross-industry study. What we learned from that inquiry is that developing corporate intrapreneurs is increasingly critical to growth, yet companies know very little about how to develop and harness their capabilities. Our findings shed new light on an opportunity too often overlooked—and even more often misunderstood.

True innovation is essential to every organization's long-term vitality. To grow their business, attract new talent, and compete effectively, leading companies continually dedicate key resources to develop new products and services to replace those they will one day lose. Given the critical importance of innovation, then, it is only prudent for management to commit significant resources to the task, and to manage them in ways that will produce the best outcomes.

As logical as this seems, many companies and organizations fail to provide enough management attention to the people involved in their innovation endeavors. Instead the focus is on the systems and processes that support innovation, not finding the right people. Such short sightedness, however inadvertent, places their organization's long-term future at considerable risk.

Management development programs and career tracks can also work against an organization's best interests when applied to entrepreneurial individuals. We found that once management deems a corporate venture to have either failed or achieved long-term viability, the individuals driving the venture are often expected to join, or rejoin, the core business—typically in line positions where rigid procedures, tight budgets, and predictability are the norm.

Or, when a venture succeeds management sometimes leaves them to lead what has become an established enterprise in its own right. This leaves many corporate entrepreneurs unhappy and in want of fresh challenges that will capitalize on their entrepreneurial skills— whether in the present organization or another.

People frequently refer to corporate entrepreneurs as intrapreneurs. We think that management's preference for this term is evidence of the paradox of being an entrepreneur in an established organization. For many managers the term entrepreneur strongly connotes a maverick, a radical individual, or even the proverbial loose cannon—someone disinclined to adhere to policies and procedures. The term intrapreneur, therefore, may help to distinguish internal entrepreneurs from the more familiar self-employed variety.

One of the difficulties encountered in studying intrapreneurs is a broad lack of understanding about them. There is no common definition or consensus within the academic and business communities about whom they really are. Instead, we found that organizations frequently apply the attributes of external entrepreneurs to their own intrapreneurs. This is a mistake.

Although entrepreneurs and intrapreneurs share many of the same skills and capabilities, they are different. Intrapreneurs possess a unique combination of competencies that distinguish them from entrepreneurs and more traditional employees. They have different motivations and aspirations. They think, act and make decisions differently. It is these differences that set them apart.

Comparing companies that have a history of success in new venture development with those that have fared less well reveals that a major determinant of success is how management regards and acts toward its entrepreneurial personnel. The management support they give them, the level of work autonomy, the time available to pursue ideas, how they measure and reinforce innovative behavior and to what extent they provide role clarity.

Our analysis of the attitudinal and behavioral differences of these employees suggests there are several changes organizations can make to more effectively foster entrepreneurial behavior. These include the following:

1. Recognize the unique qualities that intrapreneurs bring to the organization and value them every bit as strongly as you do line managers. In a very real sense, intrapreneurs hold the keys to the company's long-term success.
2. Give intrapreneurs the freedom to experiment and recognize that frequent trial and error is an inherent part of discovery. Moreover, the freedom to experiment should not be reserved for new ventures and R&D departments but cultivated throughout the organization—great ideas can emerge from the most unexpected places when given enough freedom.
3. Assign intrapreneurs to your organization's biggest and most challenging problems—problems with a capacity to truly affect its future.
4. Encourage innovative and entrepreneurial behavior by financially supporting projects knowing that some of the projects will fail.
5. Ensure there is role clarity, that expectations are clear and unambiguous with defined outcomes.
6. Provide decision-making latitude and freedom from excessive oversight by delegating authority and responsibility to intrapreneurs.
7. Help intrapreneurs to overcome organizational hurdles. They may be adept at navigating such obstacles, but some systems and processes occasionally might need to be altered, or rules bent, if the respective project is to have a meaningful opportunity to succeed.
8. Provide training and professional development opportunities in key areas of entrepreneurship, such as navigating amidst uncertainty and creative thinking.
9. Proactively recruit entrepreneurially inclined individuals.

The overarching finding of this study is that long-term success requires establishing corporate entrepreneurship as a core competency, then nurturing it with the same degree of commitment given to other core business elements.

In brief, this means providing full support that begins at the board and CEO levels. Without top-level support, intrapreneurs quickly become disenchanted, new ventures languish, and the company's future grows less certain.

Conversely, when senior management understands, values, cultivates, and manages the organization's entrepreneurially minded employees they also help assure its long-term vitality.

What is your organization doing to foster entrepreneurial behavior?

Are Intrapreneurs the New Silver Bullet for Organizations?

As Intrapreneurship captures the imagination of individuals and organizations alike you must ask yourself – why now. Is it the promise of new business growth, increased productivity, employee engagement, talent retention or something more strategic – *preservation?*

Are the hopes and dreams of workers based on the notion that being an entrepreneur in or outside of a company is the new path to personal and professional success or something more frightening – *falling behind?*

In either case Intrapreneurship is being seen as 'the silver bullet'. To protect, defend and revitalize the organization. To inspire, engage and make work meaningful for individuals.

The term silver bullet is often used as a metaphor for a simple, seemingly magical solution to a difficult problem. A simple remedy for a difficult problem.

Intrapreneurship represents a new direction for work that makes sense and has the best upside.

Organizations want to believe that there is a silver bullet that will solve their company's issues. The perception is that there is a solution out there if they can just find it. So, they latch on to the latest fad or management practice that seems to be the next thing. Today that is Intrapreneurship. But the business graveyard is filled with management practices that promised much but delivered little.

Intellectually these organizations are right that Intrapreneurship is the best way forward. What seems to be missing is the 'how'. Intrapreneurship is not something outside an organization it is part of the DNA of the organization. It is embedded in the people and culture. Looking outside for answers is ignoring the fact that the resources are already within their grasps. They just need to find a way to identify, leverage and organize these resources. The proliferation of incubators, accelerators and corporate VC's is seen as the answer. This is taking a process approach.

In turn employees are looking for more meaning at work and want the freedom and flexibility to explore the breadth and depth of their own capabilities. They believe that being an entrepreneur or intrapreneur is the best way to do that. They read articles from experienced entrepreneurs who tell them that 'we all need to be entrepreneurs now'. That the traditional career ladder is dead. That the future of work is being an independent consultant, free agent or self-employed. That being an intrapreneur is the best way to achieve professional growth in an existing company.

Intellectually these individuals are correct. What seems to be missing is the understanding that intrapreneurship is not an intellectual exercise it is grounded in experience. You can't be an entrepreneur or intrapreneur until you are one. Thinking you are one is not the same as being one. What about the thousands of entrepreneurs that didn't make it? Why is there a lack of stories about successful intrapreneurs? Why are intrapreneurs frustrated with the slow progress of intrapreneurship in their own organizations and looking to leave? This is looking at it from a people perspective.

The question that organizations must ask is how to best leverage both process and people to achieve their goals. The question that individuals must ask is do they have capabilities and competencies required to be effective and successful as an entrepreneur or intrapreneur. Intrapreneurship requires both. Many organizations focus on process without giving enough consideration to the human element.

Process helps provide structure, discipline and a set of practices that enhance intrapreneurship. It provides a roadmap, a new way forward and a defined approach. Process alone however is not enough. It is the people that provide the energy, motivation and effort required to achieve challenging goals. They are the catalyst that drive change, manage it and create change. It is also people that create the culture needed to sustain change.

In her article Talent Data Creates a High Performing Culture, Pamela Walter states that, "*The currency of our times; talent, data and attention have impacts on organization, team and individual effectiveness. How well do you know the team, i.e. individuals and aggregate strengths that could be fully leveraged to achieve breakthrough levels? How well do you know yourself?*" These are questions that organizations and individuals should be asking themselves.

There are no silver bullets when it comes to solving complex business problems. It takes hard work and preparation that too often is missing when it comes to intrapreneurship. That preparation comes in having the right people and processes in place to support and sustain intrapreneurship. Although the concept behind intrapreneurship is clear, the context in which it is implemented will vary substantially. Therefore, there is no cookie cutter solution to intrapreneurship. Intrapreneurship must be customized to the unique and diverse culture and operating environment of each organization.

It is for this reason that people are the key to intrapreneurship. They can effectively navigate their way around the organization. They learn which processes need to be changed, tweaked or replaced. They can deal effectively with organization obstacles and roadblocks that get in their way. They know how far they can push the boundaries of what is acceptable behavior. They can unlock the entrepreneurial talent within their team. They are willing to challenge and question authority. They are willing to make unpopular decisions that move their project forward and so much more....

Are Intrapreneurs the new silver bullet? It is not clear that they are, but the potential is there.

We will only find out if the organizations in which they reside give them the freedom to explore the breadth and depth of their own capabilities and those of the organization. It is about exploring what is possible. It is only then that an organization will understand what needs to be done to effectively and successfully institute intrapreneurship. You don't know what you don't know until you explore the unknown. That's what intrapreneurs do.

When a new internal venture falls short of expectations it is often easier to write it off rather than figure out the what, the why and the how that weren't done for it to be successful. Having one or two ventures a year is not enough to institute and transition an organization to a more entrepreneurial culture. You don't know what is possible until you try different things. You don't learn to be entrepreneurial by playing it safe. You don't know why you fail until you do. You don't know how to succeed until you've had success. It is a learning process that takes time and patience.

The simple truth is that every individual, executive and organization wants to believe that there is a silver bullet out there. The question is will Intrapreneurs become that silver bullet or must we realize that there are no silver bullets in life.

Impact of Intrapreneurs on Organizations

Are intrapreneurs having an impact on organizations? That is a question that is being raised at the highest levels of organizations. Although many organizations are embracing intrapreneurship there is an underlying skepticism about exactly what is the contribution of intrapreneurs to the organization or what are they doing to move the organization forward.

Traditional metrics are not enough to measure success. Organizations need to look at the impact that intrapreneurs are having on the organization itself. Not just in the numbers but in the way they are changing the business model.

1. They are bringing new thinking to the organization.
2. They are dealing effectively with ambiguity and uncertainty.
3. They are energizing and engaging co-workers.
4. They are helping shape and change the culture.
5. They are modeling a new type of leadership.

6. They are finding new ways to execute with precision.
7. They are building strong relationships with customers.
8. They are redefining how work gets done.
9. They are creating new systems and processes.
10. They are helping attract and retain employees.
11. They are re-branding the organization to be more entrepreneurial.
12. They are making the organization more responsive to market changes.
13. They are leveraging new technology in new and creative ways.
14. They are creating value that has a social and environmental impact.
15. They are leading their companies into the future.
16. And yes, they are having an impact on the bottom line.

These are some of the impacts that intrapreneurs are having on organizations.

These impacts are not always bold and forceful, they are often subtle and hidden. The impact itself may not be felt right away but can be far reaching. It may not be obvious to the leadership team until it has been integrated into the fabric of the organization. It may not be acknowledged until something goes right or wrong with an intrapreneurial initiative. It may not take on meaning until it can be measured and quantified. But keep in mind that these things are having an impact none the less.

Never before have we seen a shift in power from the organization to the individual. As Intrapreneurship takes hold in organizations it is not only transforming organizations it is disrupting them. But this disruption is not destructive it is constructive. It is transformative.

It is not only an operational shift; it is a behavioral shift that is taking place. A shift that by its very nature is changing the culture of the organization, the way work gets done and the way the organization operates.

Thanks to the efforts of intrapreneurs that are driving change not because they feel they want to but because they know they need to. They see a very different way of operating then past generations of workers. That's why these subtle shifts aren't always as obvious to the rest of the organization.

It is not something that can easily be measured at a point in time but over time. It is not something that you can assign a high or low value until you see the full impact of it on the organization. It is not something you can label disruptive if it moves your company forward.

Perhaps if we started measuring some of these impacts, we would start to see the positive benefits that intrapreneurs and intrapreneurship bring to organizations more clearly. That aggressively embracing intrapreneurship and encouraging intrapreneurs would accelerate this transformation and minimize the disruption so that organizations can more quickly adapt and respond to market changes.

There are a number of organizations that are already doing this and in doing this they are reaping the benefits listed above and achieving the financial goals that have always been the measure of success.

What about your organization? What is the impact that intrapreneurs and intrapreneurship are having on your organization?

Accelerating Growth – Speed and Direction

When we think about April in Boston, we think about Patriots Day and the running of the Boston Marathon.

Two separate events, one that honors the past, the battles of Lexington and Concord and the other that celebrates the present – a personal challenge to run 26 miles requiring incredible endurance.

Unfortunately, the pandemic has put the marathon on hold this year but that has not stopped runners from practicing with the hope that the event will be held this fall.

During the running of the last Boston Marathon a reporter said "*that we are seeing younger runners in the race whose motivations are different. They are running to beat their best time, not beat other runners.*" For them it is all about increasing their own speed. Breaking their own barriers.

These runners realize that running fast is not enough, they need to be increasing their speed to stay ahead of their own personal best. The same is true for organizations.

All businesses are being impacted by the accelerated pace of change. It is no longer enough to keep pace with a rapidly changing and dynamic business environment. The rapid pace of change makes acceleration a critical part of everything we do. Like a runner, it is not enough to be running fast, we must be running faster over time. Organizations need to be moving faster in a world that is increasingly more complex and uncertain.

Acceleration is an event that occurs when something moves from one state or phase to another. It shows the change in speed in a unit of time. The concept of acceleration is often misunderstood. You may have heard someone observing a runner say, "They are moving fast." A runner can be traveling fast and still not be accelerating.

Acceleration is all about changing how fast an object is moving. If the runner is not changing the speed, they are not accelerating. But acceleration is not enough. You need more than speed to succeed. Acceleration is a vector that can change in two ways – a change in speed and change in direction. Like individuals' organizations must not only be moving faster, they must be moving in the right direction.

On a road trip a couple of years ago my husband said he would take over driving while I rested. When I woke up, he said that we were making good time, but I noticed that we were heading south not east. In fact, we had lost a good half hour. The speed was great, but the direction was off. His decision to take the bypass to avoid going through the city and maintain our speed was fine. It was missing the turnoff that messed us up.

We see similar things happening in organizations. Most organizations spent the last few decades streamlining operations to make them more efficient and effective. This has enabled them to operate at maximum speed to support their core business, but these efforts have hampered their ability to create new businesses. Streamlining systems and processes to support an existing business is great in a more stable, steady growth economy but doesn't work in one that is constantly changing.

The accelerated pace of change is impacting every aspect of your business. There is more complexity, ambiguity, and uncertainty than ever before.

Globalization and technology have leveled the playing field. Employees are less engaged; they want to be challenged and they want to do something that has meaning. Customers and clients are more knowledgeable, have more choices and are less loyal. The world of business is being transformed. Entire markets are being restructured.

According to a recent article titled The Need for Speed in the Post Covid-19 Era, "*speed is an essential ingredient for outperformance in times of unprecedented change.*" The article goes on to say that during the pandemic, "*executives and directors say their organizations are making extensive changes with one overriding goal: to increase the speed at which they adjust strategic direction, make and implement tactical decisions, and deploy resources.*" These are positive signs that organizations are adjusting to a new normal – creating a new way forward.

Yet, we continue to see organizations struggle with their ability to change, let alone accelerate the speed in which they change. Change is the biggest obstacle and the biggest opportunity for most organizations. In fact, many organizations report that given the volatile market things have slowed down, risk is avoided, decisions take longer, and growth has stalled. All of this is happening at a time when most organizations are under pressure to generate new growth. It's not only speed but a change in direction that is required. One that enables organizations to be more flexible and adaptable.

A key to enabling organizations to increase their speed is their ability to adapt their strategies to this new environment. This has not been easy. Although many organizations have demonstrated their ability to adjust their strategies, others have not fared as well. According to the article, Strategic Resilience During the Covid-19 Crisis, "*Roughly half of executives reported that the crisis exposed weaknesses in their company's strategic resilience, defined as the extent to which an organization's business model and competitive position prove resistant to disruption.*" Not surprisingly, the article reported that the most important "strategic lever" used during the crisis to address this issue was business model innovation.

It was not just business model innovation but innovation in general that has kept businesses thriving and growing during the pandemic. Thanks in part to the individuals inside these organizations that didn't see a problem but an opportunity, found a better way to get work done remotely, and challenged themselves and their organizations to address new and unmet needs in the market. despite this major disruption. These individuals – these intrapreneurs – need to be recognized and acknowledged for stepping up and making a difference at a time when it was easier to sit behind your computer screen on a Zoom call rather than acting. Both speed and direction attributed to the success of those organizations that thrived.

In order for organizations to increase the speed in which they respond to change and achieve business growth they are turning to intrapreneurship. The goal of intrapreneurship is to build the capabilities that enable organizations to quickly change direction and accelerate growth. Organizations that have successfully implemented intrapreneurship statistically do better. They tend to attract and retain the best and brightest. They have higher levels of employee engagement, innovation, and growth.

It's not just about speed – intrapreneurship helps you move your organization in a new direction.

Chapter 3: Nuances of Intrapreneurs

- Intrapreneurs are Entrepreneurs Inside
- Unraveling the Mystery of Intrapreneurs
- Nuances of Identifying Intrapreneurs
- Intrapreneurs Have a Key Differentiation
- 3 Types of Intrapreneurs
- Living in a World of Contrasts
- 10 Perception of Intrapreneurs – Negative or Positive
- Corporate Entrepreneurs and Intrapreneurs – No Such Thing

Intrapreneurs are Entrepreneurs Inside.

Last week I was reminded that not everyone understands the term Intrapreneur or how it is different from being an entrepreneur. While being interviewed about my book *Intrapreneurs* I was asked how I would describe an Intrapreneur to someone not familiar with the term. This interchange made me realize that we still have a way to go in letting people know what it means.

For those of us that are intrapreneurs, we may have forgotten that there was a time when we too did not understand the term. Many individuals performing this role had never heard the word. They never thought of themselves as an Intrapreneur. They had a title and a well-defined job description – or so they thought. It wasn't until they took a deeper look at their work that they began to understand the implications of what they were doing. It was a gradual awakening – an evolution.

They had never seen themselves in this way before. No one had brought it to their attention. They pondered it, explored it. and then began to experiment with it. The result was an acknowledgement of their differences, their capabilities, and the secret behind their success. It was only then that they began to believe that anything was possible. That no problem was too big, no challenge was too difficult. They went on to build a career - they did it their way.

These intrapreneurs were able to unravel the mystery of who they were at the core and explore the depth of their own capabilities without the aid and assistance of their organizations. In doing this they are more self-aware, more present, and more enlightened about what it takes to succeed as an Intrapreneur. It was not about climbing the corporate ladder but climbing the ladder of self-awareness. It is a journey of self-discovery.

One of my favorite Intrapreneurs seems to have floated through her career in a Fortune 100 company. Not only did her organization not understand what she did, they didn't know how she did it. Yet her success, time after time, spoke volumes about her capabilities. There was a time when she had to write her own job description because the organization was unable to put into words what she did. To this day she continues to break new ground, find new solutions, solve pressing problems, and contribute to society. She has endured because she keeps learning.

It was not by accident that my first book was titled *Entrepreneurs Inside*. Originally it was titled to denote the difference between entrepreneurs outside an organization and those inside. Over the years the term Intrapreneur has taken on a new and more important meaning. It is not just about being an Entrepreneur Inside an established organization. It is being an Entrepreneur Inside yourself – your mindset, thinking, perspective, behavior etc. This is the true essence of being an Entrepreneur Inside.

Back then it was clear that educating individuals and organizations was the key to unlocking the mystery behind the term Intrapreneur. Although the term had been around for decades there was still a large percentage of organizations that were struggling to understand what it meant. We were often invited into organizations to brief the executive team. It was usually someone in the organization that got the concept and wanted us to educate the rest of the organization. You could tell right away if the executives and employees understood by the questions they asked.

Even today we see that there is a large percentage of the population that does not grasp the concept behind Intrapreneurs and Intrapreneurship. So, we may need to step back and remember that we need to educate first before asking organizations to sign on to this concept. Especially today when organizations are reluctant to make new investments in ideas that are not fact based or proven by past experience. This has raised the stakes on whether Intrapreneurs will be embraced in this new normal or take a back seat.

The McKinsey & Company article, Innovation in a crisis: Why it is more critical than ever - stated that "Pausing innovation efforts until the world has stabilized is a short-sighted view – and one that may have lasting consequences for companies' ability to grow in the years to come." The article goes on to say that "Prioritizing innovation today is the key to unlocking postcrisis growth" but the article also states that "Few executives feel confident that they are prepared to capture new growth opportunities."

Intrapreneurs are needed to help prioritize those innovation efforts and unlock that growth.

The challenge for intrapreneurs will be articulating the value that intrapreneurs and intrapreneurship bring to organizations especially now. Here are five reasons why each are important and are linked together.

Intrapreneurship – *What!*

1. Growth – helps organizations generate new business growth.
1. Innovation - provides an environment to support and sustain innovation over time.
2. Leadership - best ways to attract and retain your most entrepreneurial leaders.
3. Change - enables organizations to effectively accelerate and manage change.
4. Engagement - helps employees stretch and grow while keeping them engaged.

Intrapreneurs – *How!*

1. Growth – develop new Ideas that create value and generate new revenue growth.
2. Innovation – build new systems and processes to support innovation over time.
3. Leadership – effectively navigate and lead through uncertainty and the unknown.
4. Change – intrapreneurs are the catalyst for change, they model and drive change.
5. Engagement – they inspire, motivate, and engage workers to exceed expectations.

Intrapreneurship is not something that everyone will grasp right away. It often takes time and experience for individuals to see what you see, do what you do and appreciate the value you bring to organizations. Keep this in mind when you are advocating for Intrapreneurs and Intrapreneurship.

Now it is more important than ever to promote intrapreneurs and intrapreneurship. Recognizing that you may need to educate first and then show them the way forward through your work. It may not be easy, but it will be worth it for you and the organization.

Intrapreneurs are entrepreneurs inside (inside organizations, inside themselves) building new businesses, products, services, and processes.

As intrapreneurs it is incumbent upon us to continue to push forward by educating others on the value that Intrapreneurs bring to organizations to push through the roadblocks and barriers that you will inevitably encounter in this new environment.

The bottom line is that organizations that implement Intrapreneurship statistically perform better. They achieve higher levels of productivity, innovation, growth, employee engagement and financial returns but it is Intrapreneurs that make that happen.

Unraveling the Mystery of Intrapreneurs

Ten years ago, I set out to understand who corporate entrepreneurs and intrapreneurs were, how they were different and why it was important.

At the time there was no empirical data that adequately described who these individuals were. There was no consensus in the academic and business worlds. Attributes of external entrepreneurs were randomly applied to these individuals. It was clear that nobody really knew.

So, it became my mission to find out.

My hypothesis at the time was that I would find a few key attributes that would distinguish intrapreneurs from more traditional employees. That women were more successful intrapreneurs given their collaborative and relationship-oriented styles. The goal was to define the characteristics and capabilities of successful intrapreneurs.

Along the way I met a Senior Vice President of a major New England Bank who was an experienced intrapreneur and together we set out to unravel the mystery of who these individuals were. In order to do this, we first had to find them. Given the high failure rate of new ventures

(90-95%) inside organizations our task was to find those few individuals and projects (5-10%) that were successful.

We thought we would start by asking C-Level executives in large organizations if we could talk to their entrepreneurial leaders. They scoffed at us and told us they didn't have any of those types of people. Needless to say, we had to find another way. It took us six months to find these internal entrepreneurs, but it was worth the wait.

Most of the individuals involved in our research had built million-and billion-dollar businesses for their organizations. They didn't think of themselves as internal entrepreneurs. They told us that they didn't feel like they fit. They said that their organizations did not understand them or appreciate them for who they were, what they did or how they did it. So, they were more than happy to help. They wanted their organizations to know what it was like to be an entrepreneur inside an established organization. They knew our research would help do that.

Together we worked with them to define who they were at the core and what made them intrapreneurs.

Earlier research had been conducted using the Big Five Personality to try to determine if these five factors adequately characterized intrapreneurs. The research was inconclusive. One researcher that we spoke to said that the Big Five was too high level to accurately distinguish intrapreneurs from more traditional employees. We realized at this point that we needed to dive deeper. We decided to look at behaviors and competencies to see if we could differentiate intrapreneurs from others.

In order to conduct our research, we needed to build a tool to do our research. We worked with a behavioral assessment vendor who had over thirty years of experience in developing successful profiles for specific job functions. We worked collaboratively with them to identify the behaviors and competencies that intrapreneurs needed to be successful and effective in that role. Then we created a new success profile designed specifically for intrapreneurs called the Corporate Entrepreneur Profile™. We used the profile to conduct our research and refine the tool along the way.

We were excited about having a tool that would accurately predict which capabilities were critical for the role of intrapreneur. The intrapreneurs we worked with were equally excited to better understand themselves and why they felt like they didn't fit in their organizations. Looking at their results made it clear why they felt that they didn't fit. If they fit, they wouldn't be intrapreneurs.

The research also helped us answer the key questions we asked in the beginning. Was there a small set of capabilities that distinguished intrapreneurs from more traditional employees and were women more successful intrapreneurs. Neither of these things wound up being true.

What we did learn that was more insightful and valuable was that it wasn't a few key capabilities, but it was the breadth and depth of those capabilities that was the key differentiation. Intrapreneurs possess a unique combination of behaviors and competencies that distinguish them from others. It is the breadth and depth of those competencies that distinguish them from their peers and more traditional leaders.

We also found that the women and men intrapreneurs are equally successful. That is because they both possess the same breadth and depth of competencies across the spectrum of competencies required for the role of intrapreneur. Men and women were equally collaborative and relationship oriented. What we did find was that the top six competencies were the same for both men and women – Independent Thinking, Navigating Uncertainty, Engaged & Thriving, Driving Change, Leadership Effectiveness and Execution.

Every few years we update our research and over the years we continue to see the same top six competencies at the top of the list. Last week I updated the research again and found that after ten years the most important competencies for intrapreneurs are these top six. Although the scores for women have increased slightly over men in that same time frame, they are tracking very closely. We've also learned that intrapreneurs think, act and make decisions differently. They have different motivations and aspirations and much more……

What we find most rewarding is to see those intrapreneurs that have retaken the Corporate Entrepreneur Profile year after year showing significant improvement. Enhancing their own skills and capabilities. Being more engaged and motivated in their work. Making a bigger contribution to the organization. Building a portfolio of intrapreneurial experiences. Taking on bigger and more challenging opportunities. Resulting in more successful intrapreneurial efforts inside their respective organizations.

Finding your inner entrepreneur is a journey of self-discovery. It begins and ends with you. It makes you look at who you are, who you think you are and who you need to become. It requires an honest assessment of your own strengths and weaknesses. A deep look inside your own values and beliefs. Your attitudes about work and life. Your goals, ambitions and aspirations. The lessons you've learned from your experiences.

It isn't something you are given; it is something you develop. It's not an intellectual exercise but something you acquire through experience.

Nuances of Identifying Intrapreneurs

An executive recruiter told me that now that the market is heating up for intrapreneurs, growth leaders and entrepreneurial leaders, more and more professionals are claiming to be one. *The reality is that few individuals fit this role.*

Research has found that only a small percentage of individuals in large organizations are entrepreneurs or entrepreneurial. The statistics are stacked up against all those professionals claiming to be intrapreneurs. *They are hurting themselves and the real entrepreneurs out there.*

A few *nuances* that may help you identify intrapreneurs:

1. They think, act, and communicate in ways that are just the opposite of what is expected. They make the rest of the organization very uncomfortable. *These individuals are viewed with suspicion.*

2. They are transparent and open about who they are and what they do. Everyone thinks they are trying to hide something. Just the opposite, they are letting everyone know who they are, how they operate and what they need to be successful. *Their honesty is unsettling.*

3. They have a breadth and depth of experience that enables them to see problems as opportunities, uncertainty as a challenge and ambiguity as a game to be played and won. They calculate the upside and downside of every decision. They take risks based on what they can afford to lose. *Their actions are unnerving to others.*

4. They are not afraid to fail. They are more concerned if they don't try. Ask them how many times they have failed. Then ask them to tell you about a time when they failed and what they learned from the experience. *They see failure as a step to success.*

5. They do not conform to the corporate model. They don't fit. This is the number one issue that we hear from intrapreneurs all the time. *If they fit, they wouldn't be entrepreneurs.*

The lack of understanding about intrapreneurs is creating havoc in the market and putting pressure on organizations to be more cautious. It is also prompting individuals to claim that they are something they are not, intrapreneurs. *There is a cost to all this confusion.*

It is becoming more difficult for organizations to find intrapreneurs and more difficult for intrapreneurs to distinguish themselves. *The cost is progress, growth and renewal for both organizations and individuals.*

Now that the word is out that intrapreneurs are in. What are you doing to identify them?

Intrapreneurs Have a Key Differentiation

After years of working with corporate entrepreneurs, Intrapreneurs and entrepreneurial leaders it has become very clear that these individuals have a key differentiation.

They are in alignment with who they are not what the organization wants them to be.

By being true to themselves they are more productive, more engaged and better employees.

They are not content to sit on the sidelines and wait until things get better. They take steps to make things better. They create the future through their actions. They move themselves and their companies forward.

They see the world with a fresh perspective. They don't let old mental models or past experience get in their way. They create new mental models that adapt to a rapidly changing world.

They look at every problem as an opportunity. They know that there is a solution to every problem. They just need to find it. They search for new and creative ways to solve problems. No problem is too big.

They deal effectively with complexity. They do not try to simplify things too quickly. They know that simplifying things narrows their choices. They keep their options open until they no longer make sense.

They don't let uncertainty stop them from deciding. They collect enough information to make an intelligent decision. They know that nothing happens until you make a decision. No decision is a decision.

They play by a new set of rules. They know that the old rules are no longer effective. Playing it safe gets you more of the same. New rules are needed to deal with a very different business environment.

They know that the only way to make progress is to make change happen. They become the change they hope to achieve. Not just leading changing but modeling change. Making others comfortable changing too.

They are not afraid to fail they are only concerned if they don't try. They know that failure ultimately leads to success. If you aren't failing, you aren't learning and growing. The only way to get better is to experience both success and failure.

They see potential in every individual, and they encourage them to reach for something bigger, better and more challenging. They inspire them to become the best of who they are. By motivating others, they are motivating themselves. They know it takes a team to succeed.

Many of the things that corporate entrepreneurs do are just the opposite of what you see with more traditional employees and leaders. It is what differentiates them from the rest.

Progress can only be made by individuals who are willing to lead through difficult times and challenge traditional beliefs and practices.

3 Types of Intrapreneurs

A key contributor to intrapreneurship success is having the right skill sets and competencies to drive things to completion. As the entrepreneurial leader, you will need three types of people on your team to be successful: *creators, doers, and implementers.*

Our research showed that there are subtle differences between intrapreneurs that distinguish one from another. This wasn't the focus of our research, but it surfaced after looking at the results. We saw that intrapreneurs exhibited different clusters or groupings of behavior, they performed different roles and leveraged certain competencies to accomplish their work.

The creator is the person with the innovative ideas. The doers are task-oriented individuals. The implementers are the individuals who bring things to closure. No matter what you call them – there are three types of intrapreneurs you will need on the team. Each requires a slightly different set of competencies and behaviors. This may seem like a simple way to view your team, but all three of these roles are important when it comes to intrapreneurship. It is rare to find all three of these types of intrapreneurs in one person, although we have. They are among the most effective and successful intrapreneurs.

Creators may be easier to spot. They are the idea generation people (the discovery phase.) They see possibilities. They are high on learning and love change. They are always looking for ways to do things better. They are big-picture thinkers and often can see the gestalt. They are independent and prefer to work in less structured environments. On the downside they can get bored easily and find it difficult to stay focused on the details because they are always thinking of the next idea. *Creators develop the ideas that fuel innovation.*

Doers are focused on achieving objectives. They are the task-oriented individuals (the incubation phase.) They understand the big picture and can get involved in the details when they need to. They are assertive and take responsibility for their actions. They have good communication skills and are effective in instructing others. They are not afraid to stand up to authority or challenge the status quo. They are less concerned about structure and organizational obstacles that get in the way. They know what needs to get done. They just go it. *Doers are task-oriented and dedicated to their work.*

Implementers are the individuals who make things happen. They are focused on closer (the execution phase.) They know how to get things done or figure out how to get them done. They are goal-oriented, creative, and competitive. They have good planning and negotiating skills. They work well in high-pressure situations. They are good at taking the initiative, negotiating, and motivating others. They have the execution skills required to drive projects to completion. They don't let anything get in their way. *Implementers are high on closure.*

Use these descriptions as an initial filter when you are developing your team. Take a moment to mentally separate your team into these three categories. Once you've done this, you may want to use a behavioral assessment tool to get a better understanding of individual styles and work practices. They help you identify the specific behaviors that separate the creators from the doers and implementers. They can also help you identify those one or two individuals that can do it all.

Ask yourself: What are the strengths and weaknesses of everyone on the team? What about the team as a whole? How do you leverage everyone more effectively? Who are the most creative people on my team? Who are the individuals you can rely on to get the work done in a timely fashion? Who do you need to help bring things to closure? Asking these questions is a good way to ensure that you have the right mix of people on the team.

Intrapreneurship requires having the ability and skills to establish and achieve challenging goals. It means having the right set of behaviors and competencies. You must be able to identify and develop the right mix of people and then organize work to best leverage their talent. Not everyone is suited for this role.

Intrapreneurship is a mindset, a set of competencies, a way of thinking and acting. It is how one looks at things and what actions they take a result of that thinking. That is what is key.

Who are the creators, doers, and executors on your team?

Living in a World of Contrast

Entrepreneurs inside of existing organizations live in a world of contrasts, where two worlds collide. The core business and the new business they are building.

Many of the strategies, structures, policies, procedures and culture required to support the core business are just the opposite of what is required to build a new one.

Organizations know a lot about what it takes to maintain and grow the core business, less so when it comes to new growth businesses. The processes and practices that support the core business are often the very things that get in the way of new growth initiatives, impeding progress.

It is up to the entrepreneur to find a way to navigate these obstacles. They must co-exist in both worlds.

One internal entrepreneur said, "*She felt like she was playing chess while everyone else was playing checkers.*" It wasn't that one game is better than the other. It is that she and the organization are playing two different games. She told me that she would have to stop and shift to the other game when dealing with her peers and boss. Then shift back when working with her team. It is a balancing act. The entrepreneur is forced to operate in both worlds simultaneously. They must be loyal on one hand and independent on the other, poised and passionate, analytical and intuitive, collaborative and competitive. It is up to the entrepreneur to shift gears not the other way around.

What kind of person would want to operate this way? Why set yourself up for working this way? It sounds chaotic, even a little schizophrenic.

Who would subject themselves to this if they didn't have to especially given the current economic climate? Many workers are sitting on the sidelines, keeping their heads down waiting for things to turn around. Not internal entrepreneurs, they see opportunity in good times and bad. They are willing to take on the toughest challenges, step up to the most difficult assignments. They thrive in an environment full of complexity, ambiguity and the unknown. They are not afraid to fail. Win or lose they learn and grow from the experience.

Internal entrepreneurs possess a unique combination of competencies and behaviors that set them apart from others. They don't fit the traditional profile, the company man or woman that has come to personify the business landscape. Therefore, they are often overlooked or worse they are invisible. These internal entrepreneurs are part of a small percentage of individuals in organizations that are actively engaged at work. According to a study by Towers Perrin only twenty one percent of employees are engaged in what they do. Of those engaged only a few individuals have the entrepreneurial skills to work effectively in the core business at the same time they are building a new one.

Internal entrepreneurs are the pioneers, builders and change agents that are moving their companies forward into the future. Yet, many organizations don't understand who they are, why they are different or even why it is important. Look at any organizational website or job posting. Where do you see it listed - *Wanted Internal Entrepreneurs*? Perhaps at Google this is the norm, any place else it is an anomaly. The time has come for organizations to recognize that internal entrepreneurs are and will continue to be the most sought-after professional in the new economy. *Internal entrepreneurs live in a world of contrast, the place where the old world and new world collide.*

10 Perceptions of Intrapreneurs – Negative or Positive

As organizations embrace corporate entrepreneurship, they are beginning to understand the magnitude shift that is required to implement it successfully. At the same time, they are beginning to look at corporate entrepreneurs and Intrapreneurs in a new light.

Many executives have a negative perception of Intrapreneurs. They can't relate to them. Yet, many of the perceptions about Intrapreneurs are exactly the things that organizations need. These perceptions define who these individuals are. They are both negative and positive. *It's how you look at them.*

These are just a few of the perceptions of Intrapreneurs we've heard about:

1. **Hard to Control**. Entrepreneurs are difficult to manage. That's true because they don't need to be managed. They manage themselves. They are self-motivated, highly engaged and willing to do what it takes to make things happens. *They are leaders not followers.*

2. **Challenge Authority**. Entrepreneurs are not afraid to question authority or challenge the status quo. That's a good thing. They know that unless things are done differently nothing will change. *They lead change.*

3. **Take Big Risks**. Entrepreneurs weigh the upside and downside of their actions. They know in advance the tradeoff between acting and not acting. *They take calculated risks.*

4. **Lack Data**. Entrepreneurs are decisive. They will collect enough information to make an intelligent decision. They know when to bring data into the equation. *They balance intuition and data.*

5. **Don't Fit**. Entrepreneurs don't fit. They are not your typical employee interested in climbing the corporate ladder. They are less interested

in being part of the core business. They want to build the growth side of the business. *They are focused on the future.*

6. **Disrupt the Organization**. Entrepreneurs make waves. Existing structures, systems and processes get in their way. They find new and creative ways to solve problems, deal with barriers and resistance to change. They shake things up. *They lay a foundation for growth.*
7. **Not as Loyal.** Entrepreneurs are loyal. They are loyal to their project first, and then the company. They are also willing to put their job on the line for the organization and what they believe. Very few employees can say the same. *They are your best employees.*
8. **Stubborn**. Entrepreneurs are hardheaded. They have strong beliefs in what they are doing. They are not easily deterred. It enables them to achieve goals that others think are unachievable. *They are persistent.*
9. **Transparent**. Entrepreneurs are transparent. They wear their heart on their sleeve. You always know where they stand. They are open, honest and speak the truth. *They are self-confident.*
10. **Difficult to Retain**. Entrepreneurs are hard to retain. They are more likely to leave if they are not given opportunities to stretch and grow. That's not their fault. They need to be challenged and working on something of value to the organization. *They are value creators.*

Corporate Entrepreneurs and Intrapreneurs are your best bet for building a sustainable environment for innovation growth.

Corporate Entrepreneurs and Intrapreneurs – No Such Thing

In the last several years there have been suggestions that there is no such thing as a corporate entrepreneur or intrapreneur.

No evidence that they exist. No clear definition of who they are. No consensus in the academic and business. Comments stating that they only exist in our imagination.

Tell that to all the individuals in organizations currently engaged in that role. They would beg to differ.

After decades of hearing the term corporate entrepreneur and intrapreneur being tossed around there is still confusion and a lack of understanding about who these individuals are. Attributes of external entrepreneurs are randomly applied to these individuals. Broad concepts like the Big Five Personality are used to try and define them. Descriptors are used that are related to process and results not behaviors and competencies. No wonder there is a lack of understanding.

What does this tell us about the status of Intrapreneurs in the business and academic world – a lot.

It tells us that the role of corporate entrepreneur and intrapreneur are not taken seriously. If they were, they would be called out in job descriptions, performance reviews and competency models that are used to describe other important roles in the organization. Although many organizations excel at building competency models for the core business, they fall short when it comes to creating one for intrapreneurs. Intrapreneurs are on their own.

It tells us that business is not ready to fully accept or embrace intrapreneurs. That they are an overlooked and underutilized resource. Their ideas and suggestions often dismissed as being too radical, too risky, and too far from the core. They challenge the status quo and their questions are often out of line. These are key deterrents for individuals that are inclined to be more entrepreneurial. Intrapreneurs are left wondering if they will ever be able to utilize their entrepreneurial capabilities.

It tells us that executives think innovation and growth will come from existing leaders. Only a small percentage of executives participate in innovation efforts. As a result, there is a lack of entrepreneurial leadership at the top of most organizations. And there is very little evidence that organizations are developing intrapreneurs to fill the void of leadership when it comes to innovation efforts. Intrapreneurs must take responsibility for developing their own leadership competencies.

It tells us why most of the innovation taking place inside organizations is incremental not disruptive. That there is still a low tolerance for risk and failure. That stepping outside the boundaries of acceptable behavior is frowned upon and discouraged. That individual initiative is not always appreciated or rewarded. That dissent is not tolerated. Intrapreneurs and their ideas are often sidelined for more traditional approaches.

It tells us that organizations think that having an entrepreneurial mindset is the answer. But the desire to instill an entrepreneurial mindset in employees is not enough. Thinking like an intrapreneur is not the same as being one. Without the opportunity to be an intrapreneur in action it only serves to accelerate growing disappointment among internal entrepreneurs. It's a negative factor in retaining your entrepreneurial talent. Intrapreneurs find creative ways to demonstrate their value by being action oriented.

It tells us why so many workers are disengaged and eager to find the next new opportunity that offers them a challenge. That there is growing frustration among workers looking to engage in entrepreneurial pursuits within their organizations. Leading to the migration of workers to become self-employed and look for projects that are meaningful, create value and can make a difference. Intrapreneurs are finding that some organizations are willing to supplement their current staff with consultants, free agents and the self-employed to get access to entrepreneurial talent.

These are some of the signs that there is not a serious commitment to understand, recruit and develop intrapreneurs in many organizations.

In turn we are disappointed to see that the academic world has not advanced the discussion and research about intrapreneurs.

It tells us that the academic world has not come to terms with the differences between entrepreneurs and internal entrepreneurs. Most of the research is focused on external entrepreneurs and results are often applied randomly to internal entrepreneurs. It does a disservice to both. The research to date has not been able to show a correlation between individual characteristics and innovation success. Due in part from not having the right characteristics to measure.

It tells us that there is no benchmark for establishing a baseline for research about the individual characteristics of intrapreneurs. Therefore, it is up to researchers to choose tools frequently used to describe characteristics of other groups, functions, roles or capabilities. Some of these tools add dimensions to the discussion but do not zero in on the specific capabilities of intrapreneurs. Standard tools are good for placing individuals in broad categories common to many different roles.

It tells us that the research to date has only provided a high-level assessment of the capabilities that are aligned with being an internal intrapreneur. That the results from this work are not conclusive and too general to be applied specifically to intrapreneurs. Resulting in a lack of empirical evidence to accurately or adequately define who intrapreneurs are at the core. The academic world continues to use anecdotal data to describe intrapreneurs.

It tells us that there is no common foundation for identifying and developing intrapreneurs. No terminology to help guide organizations in determining who is a good fit to be an intrapreneur. No way to measure and track them to see if they are fulfilling the role other than through process and results but how they get to those results depends on how they think and act.

This is exactly what we found over a decade ago and not much has changed. Although the business and the academic world have advanced our ideas about what it means to be an intrapreneur we have made little progress in understanding who they are and what it takes. That's because most of the business and academic community have missed the obvious.

It's not about personality, social styles, emotional stages, life stages or communication styles, it's about behaviors and competencies. Behaviors required to be an effective and successful intrapreneur. Behaviors that have been exhibited by serial intrapreneurs and executives that have been successful in the role of intrapreneurs inside their organizations. Individuals that have built million-and billion-dollar businesses for their companies.

That's not to say that the other predictive tools are not important they are, in fact they help paint a complete picture. But they are not the starting point for understanding corporate entrepreneurs or intrapreneurs. It's all about the behaviors and competencies that lead to entrepreneurial thinking and action.

Behaviors that when combined identify a combination of competencies that have shown time after time to be critical factors in an intrapreneurs success. Behaviors and competencies, you can identify, develop and measure over time. Competencies that consistently get better as intrapreneurs gain more experience. Competencies that enable intrapreneurs to lead and inspire others to become intrapreneurs. Competencies that distinguish intrapreneurs from their peers.

We believe that corporate entrepreneurs and intrapreneurs are real. They are thriving in organizations that have recognized and learned that certain behaviors and competencies motivate, engage and energize intrapreneurs. It's what makes them corporate entrepreneurs and intrapreneurs.

Intrapreneurs are in alignment with who they are not what the organization wants them to be. Being in alignment with one's true nature makes them more productive, engaged and innovative. Intrapreneurs are an enigma to the rest of the organization.

Let us know if you think corporate entrepreneurs and intrapreneurs are real or only a figment of some people's imagination.

Chapter 4: Intrapreneur Profile

- Do You Want to Be an Intrapreneur?
- Intrapreneurs Thinking Process
- Navigating Uncertainty
- Intrapreneurs – Engaged and Thriving
- Intrapreneurs – Driving Change
- Extraordinary Leaders
- 5 Ways Intrapreneurs Excel at Execution
- End of Being Average
- Operating System that Powers Intrapreneurs

Do You Want to Be an Entrepreneur?

The current economy has a lot of employees thinking that when things get better, they want to get out from under their employers and take control of their own destiny. Beware of what you ask for.

Being an external entrepreneur isn't easy. Keep in mind that there is no safety net when you step out on your own. Yet, if you don't try it sometime in your career you are missing a great opportunity.

Why not test your entrepreneurial capabilities where you are now? All you need to do is step up to the challenge within your own organization. The fact is that over fifty percent of new business initiatives start inside of existing organizations. These entrepreneurial opportunities are likely to increase over the next decade as organizations reinvent and redesign themselves for the new economy. Why not flex your entrepreneurial muscle while you have the chance.

Recently, I heard Alan Weiss author of Million Dollar Consulting talk about trends in the next decade. He indicated that *"there will be more reliance on transient talent."* The media has been talking about the future of work for years but suddenly the reality that work is changing is here. Those who will succeed will be those who have the entrepreneurial skills to take on project work and translate what they know into customer value, inside or outside of an organization.

Being an entrepreneur takes time and it takes practice. The best way to become an entrepreneur is to be an entrepreneur. Those individuals that recognize that having entrepreneurial skills will enable them to navigate the future will be better prepared for the road ahead. Key competencies for internal entrepreneurs are:

- Independent Thinking – You rely on your own knowledge and experience to guide you.
- Navigating Uncertainty – You proactively deal with ambiguity and uncertainty.
- Engaged and Thriving – You are driven by the excitement of a challenge.

- Driving Change – You are willing to change and effective at driving change.
- Leadership Effectiveness – You effectively manage and integrate limited resources.
- Execution – You establish and achieve challenging goals.

Internal entrepreneurs know that what they learn from these experiences enhance their capabilities as well as the organizations. So, the question is not *do you want to be an entrepreneur*. The question is *can you afford not to be an entrepreneur*. Both external and internal entrepreneurs are the key to growth.

The sooner you accept this reality the sooner you will begin to see the value of building the entrepreneurial skills needed to succeed and thrive in the new work environment.

Intrapreneurs Thinking Process

A key distinguishing attribute of Intrapreneurs is that they think differently. *So, what does that really mean?*

Keep in mind that our traditional thinking methods have not changed for centuries. For over 2000 years we have used logic, reason and argument as a basis for thinking. Yet argument lacks creativity. It is based on the premise that there is a winner and loser, *"I am right you are wrong."*

Intrapreneurs understand the limitations of logic, reasoning and argument. They use different techniques to focus their thinking, be more creative, and collaborative.

Intrapreneurs see the world through a different lens.

Intrapreneurs are independent thinkers. They rely on their own observations and experience to guide them rather than depend on the word of others. They proactively challenge and question the status quo. They believe that there is different and better way to get things done. They are confident in their abilities.

Intrapreneurs are willing to explore the unknown. They see the unknown as a field of possibilities. They understand that creativity comes from exploring the unknown and integrating it with what they already know. They don't let not knowing something stop them. They consistently push the edge of their own knowledge.

Intrapreneurs are whole brain thinkers. They effectively leverage both sides of their brain. They are both analytical and intuitive. It is their ability to know when to use intuition and when to use analytics that sets them apart from others. They can evaluate a situation from both perspectives.

Intrapreneurs are integrative thinkers. They can hold two totally opposite concepts in their mind at the same time. Instead of choosing one over the other they create a new creative solution from both. They realize that answers are not always an either/or but can encompass both. Abstract thinking comes naturally to them.

Intrapreneurs use trial and error to guide their thinking. They use experimentation to test assumptions and to challenge traditional approaches. They know that nothing new can be learned without experimentation. Experimentation is how they learn. They experiment intelligently.

Intrapreneurs embrace complexity. They don't try to simplify things too quickly. They know that complexity provides more possibilities, new avenues to explore. Cutting off these options too early may narrow their options down the road. They linger longer in complexity than others.

Intrapreneurs take a holistic or systems view of the world. Everything is a puzzle to them. They can take things apart and put them back together in a new way to form a new picture. They are good at analyzing and synthesizing large amounts of information. They can see patterns and linkages that did not exist before.

Intrapreneurs balance thinking and action. Intrapreneurs are more likely to act on an idea before it is clearly developed. They learn from taking action and take new actions to move the idea forward. They use more of an iterative approach to thinking and action.

It was Albert Einstein that said that" *Everything has changed accept the way we think.*" Isn't it time we looked at how we think to see if it is getting in the way of moving our organizations forward?

Intrapreneurs are already thinking differently and changing the way their organizations look at the world.

Navigating Uncertainty

In a volatile and rapidly changing world we must learn to navigate uncertainty. Those that do will thrive and those that don't will have to learn how to survive. As harsh as that may seem it is our current reality. That's why Intrapreneurs are needed more than ever.

What does it mean to navigate uncertainty? That was a question we sought to answer many years ago when we first started working with Intrapreneurs.

We defined Navigating Uncertainty as the ability to deal proactively with ambiguity, uncertainty and the unknown. It is the ability to steer a course forward during a period or state of being uncertain.

In the article Leadership in Midst of Crisis, "*73% of executives said that their ability to deal with ambiguity and uncertainty was the most important attribute of dealing with the current economic climate.*"

What does it take to be proficient in navigating uncertainty? We just need to look at Intrapreneurs to understand what it takes.

Navigating Uncertainty is the one of the top six competencies exhibited by Intrapreneurs. They deal effectively with uncertainty. It is part of what drives them, excites them and challenges them. It is what makes them Intrapreneurs.

Intrapreneurs are pioneers, builders and change agents. They blaze new trails, turn ideas into businesses, and seek out opportunities to stretch and grow.

Intrapreneurs embrace the unknown, they see it as a field of possibilities. They deal with uncertainty by acting not sitting back and waiting for things to become clearer. They don't try to predict the future they shape the future. They don't wait until they have all the resources they need to proceed; they leverage what they've got. They don't let structures get in their way. They make decisions without having all the information. They have a high tolerance for risk. These are attributes that distinguish Intrapreneurs from others.

They do these things because they are creative, goal oriented, decisive, take initiative, are good short-and long-term planners, balance data and intuition, motivated by learning, effective in instructing others, respond well to change and have a healthy ego. These are the underlying behaviors that enable Intrapreneurs to be effective at navigating uncertainty. But It is their self-confidence, motivation, experience, breadth of knowledge, tolerance for failure and risk profile that propel them to act.

Unlike more traditional workers, intrapreneurs are willing to step-up, speak-up and stick-out even in uncertain times. The question is why everyone else is not willing or able to do the same.

In her TEDx talk, How to Navigate Our Uncertain Future, Anne Rinne spoke about why we find it difficult to navigate uncertainty. "*We're trapped in our own experience, grasping to a reality that no longer exists.*" She went on to call it a state of 'permanent impermanence'. A time when it is hard to keep up and the fact that we are less equipped than ever to deal with the pace of change. She says we are in a time of flux.

Rinne provides two key points worth noting. One is that we are often trapped in our own past experience that no longer exists. Second, we are dealing with a permanent and accelerated pace of change.

Many of us rely on our past experience to guide us into the future. That made sense in a world that was stable but today we are faced with just the opposite. What worked in the past may no longer work in the future. That's one of the reasons Intrapreneurs are willing to explore the unknown. They know that we can't solve today's problems with solutions from the past. The sheer complexity, ambiguity and uncertainty that we face are issues that we have not been faced with before.

Intrapreneurs understand that an organization's past experience can get in the way and slow down progress. That's why Intrapreneurs use exploration and experimentation to test new ideas and create new experiences. Experiences that inform the future, not impede its progress.

Navigating uncertainty is difficult enough without the fact that the speed of change makes it more uncertain and complex. Intrapreneurs must deal with uncertainty and the rapid pace of change at the same time. These are two things that they do very well. Driving change is another top competency of Intrapreneurs.

Intrapreneurs are willing to take on the toughest challenges. They look at every situation as an opportunity to grow. They are flexible, adaptable and open to change. They see the world as it could be not as it is. Intrapreneurs create the change the hope to see, not just adapting to change but driving change through the decisions they make and the actions they take.

It is the combination of these two competences, navigating uncertainty and driving change that enable Intrapreneurs to be effective in navigating uncertainty. Together these two competencies ensure that Intrapreneurs proactively deal with uncertainty by leaning into it not bending under its weight. They do this by exploring the unknown and seeing new opportunities and then responding quickly to take advantage of those opportunities.

The key to navigating uncertainty is understanding the underlying behaviors that enable you to effectively deal with uncertainty. Here are a few of the behaviors you will need:

- Creative – Generates new and creative ideas that defy convention.
- Competitive – Exhibits courage and confidence when competing.
- Decisive – Quick to make decisions based on available information.
- Healthy Ego – Copes well with adversity and puts things in perspective.
- Goal Oriented – Sets realistic goals that are aggressive but achievable.
- Initiative – Anticipates the need for action and responds quickly.
- Instructive – Effective at instructing and engages others to take action.
- Learning – Seeks opportunities to learn and grow from experience.
- Planning – Balances short-term demands and longer-term needs.
- Response to Change – Takes on new challenges with energy and drive.

Being competent at navigating uncertainty requires that you exhibit many if not all these behaviors. Only then will you be able to see what opportunities exist or emerge in these uncertain times. It's all about getting in front of the curve.

Navigating Uncertainty is grounded in how you react in an uncertain world.

How would you rate yourself and your organization on navigating uncertainty?

Intrapreneurs – Engaged and Thriving

Two reports last year talked about the dismal state of employee engagement in the workforce with no signs of improvement.

The current economic climate has contributed to an unhealthy work environment where employees are stressed and totally disengaged.

Intrapreneurs on the other hand are not sitting around waiting for things to get better. Many have left the corporate world to start new ventures or they are making the most of where they are. They have a deep desire to stay active and connected. Even incremental improvements can have an impact in a slow economy.

Intrapreneurs are highly engaged in their work. They love the excitement of challenge. They don't wait for opportunities they create them. Their passion and determination inspire others to get involved and be engaged. They are self-motivated and good at motivating others. Plus, they have a high tolerance for stress.

Intrapreneurs thrive in different work environments because they want to stretch and grow. It's in their nature to be curious and that leads them to explore new things. They are active learners.

On the other hand, the 70% of employees that are disengaged or highly disengaged at work are doing a disservice to themselves and their organizations. According to Gallup over $450 billion is being lost in productivity. The pressure to do more with less is at a breaking point.

Reports by Gallup and Towers Watson state that engagement is an organizational responsibility, one that organizations are not doing very well. It is easy to point to the economy as the main reason for low engagement levels, but it goes beyond that. According to Towers Watson, "*Companies are running 21st-century businesses with a 20th- century workplace practices and programs.*"

The only way out of the economic mess is getting the economy growing again. That is what Intrapreneurs and entrepreneurially minded people are all about – generating new business growth.

So, it was surprising to read a report that some companies that have started actively recruiting again are hiring far fewer self-employed individuals. "*That's ironic*, says Vickie Elmer, *because company executives and human resources say they want self-starters, innovative hires, a certain entrepreneurial spirit.*"

No wonder companies are struggling. No wonder that employees are not engaged.

Intrapreneurs are the very people that organizations need to turn things around. They take initiative, find opportunities, don't let barriers get in their way and get things done.

Organizations that see the value of hiring intrapreneurs and individuals who were forced to jump into self-employment during the economic downturn will have a bright future. Those that don't will continue to live in the dark ages.

Intrapreneurs – Driving Change

The accelerated pace of change is putting pressure on organizations to transform themselves and generate new business growth. Leaders are struggling to do both well.

Keep in mind that growth is all about change and change is all about people. People and organizations are resistant to change. It is a failure to change that is impeding growth.

Change is one of the least understood of the management disciplines. Leaders are not adequately trained or equipped to deal effectively with change. They continue to rely on traditional management processes and practices to guide them.

Change has always been a soft skill. It is not something that organizations have embraced. Now it is taking center stage. The rapid pace of change has made change a critical success factor. Either '*change or be changed.*'

Organizations are responding to this challenge by identifying and developing their top talent – their high potentials. Yet, most high potentials are selected because of their success in the core business not growing new businesses. That's a mistake. Research shows that a different mindset is needed. A distinct set of capabilities are required.

Intrapreneurs have that mindset; they have a distinct set of capabilities. They not only drive change; they break down resistance to change. In the article To Change A Company, You Need Intrapreneurs, Jennifer Silberman, states "*It's the efforts of courageous Intrapreneurs that change their (organizations) trajectory.*"

Intrapreneurs have an innate curiosity to explore the unknown which makes them great change agents.

- They love a challenge. They are consistently building their capabilities by challenging themselves. No challenge is too big.
- They take responsibility for their own growth and development. They proactively seek out opportunities that enable them to stretch and grow. Personal growth is what motivates them.
- They embrace change. They know that nothing happens until someone takes action, takes the lead and creates a new path for others to follow. Intrapreneurs take the lead, they make change happen.

Intrapreneurs are the key to growth, the catalyst for change. Being a change agent is a skill that will only increase in value over time. Intrapreneurs know this.

They are building the skills that will help them take control of their own destiny. They are creating a brighter future for themselves and their organizations.

Extraordinary Leaders

Entrepreneurial leaders have a breadth and depth of experience that often transcends that of those who followed traditional career paths.

They understand their companies' overall goals; they know where the corporate boundaries are unyielding and where they can flex. They are passionate about creating new opportunities that fit the business strategy, and they can ably marshal and energize resources to create those opportunities. *These individuals have a unique combination of competencies.*

These individuals are not always the inventors of new products, services or processes, but they are very often the team builders who turn those ideas into profitable businesses. They are seen as the business architects who design the work environment, create informal controls, provide the discipline, and drive the change by promoting entrepreneurial behavior in others. They open channels of communication, and establish clear roles and responsibilities, goals and measures.

Entrepreneurial leaders are change agents; they have a high tolerance for ambiguity, prefer autonomy, have plenty of perseverance, and are committed to making a difference. They are goal-oriented, self-motivated and decisive. They are willing to push the limits of what is acceptable behavior to get things done. Their motivation and behaviors mean that they inevitably run up against entrenched bureaucracies. They face plenty of resistance, isolation, lack of encouragement, and issues of control. They are often forced to challenge policies and procedures.

Their leadership style lends itself to networking, building relationships, and empowering employees to achieve results. They encourage diversity, promote collaboration, and strive to empower individual team members. They are also emphatic and attuned to the individual and collective needs of team members. They are often independent thinkers and have strong opinions and belief in what they are doing. They are committed to the task and dedicated to completing the mission.

In light of the above traits, there are many who say that anyone can be a corporate entrepreneur or entrepreneurial leader but there is little evidence to prove that one way or the other. There is, however, evidence that certain behaviors and competencies can determine success. These are often better indicators of who is best suited for the role of entrepreneurial leader. Traditional leaders thrive in environments that support the core business, but entrepreneurial leaders relish the opportunity to create something new. They languish, however, when it comes to maintaining or sustaining a business.

The real difference between traditional leaders and entrepreneurial leaders may be in the experience itself. An entrepreneurial leader will encounter new hurdles along the way, including hitting the wall, traversing the valley of despair, or flying blind. These experiences will bring profound changes to the individuals involved. It will change who they are and who they have become. They will have a hard time stepping back into old roles or behaviors.

Entrepreneurial leaders make the transition to a new way of working that is foreign to the rest of the organization. Asking them to go back to the core business will be unsettling. Asking them to help institutionalize what they've learned will inspire them.

Not only are these leaders' good entrepreneurs, they are also good employees. They are committed to serving the company and the new initiative. They must live in two worlds at the same time: the entrepreneurial venture and the core business. It is as if they have one foot in one boat and one in another. They must find the right balance when organizational pressures, resource constraints and funding issues of the existing business come in conflict with the new initiative.

Who are the entrepreneurial role models in your organization?

5 Ways Intrapreneurs Excel at Execution

Execution is a competency needed to effectively leverage your organizations investments in innovation. That's why Intrapreneurs are important. Execution is a core competency of Intrapreneurs.

Execution is a learned experience. It is a process that is driven by the decisions and actions that are taken to move a project forward. The measure of success of is not whether it was delivered on time or on budget but whether it delivered value – to your customers and the bottom line.

Execution is not something that you think about at the end of the project, but throughout the project. It is an attitude, a competence, and a set of behaviors that motivate people to bring things to a successful conclusion.

Execution requires clarity of vision, an iterative process to get there, and the ability to deliver business value. It also requires having the right skills and expertise, someone able to simplify the complex. These are things that Intrapreneurs do and capabilities they've acquired.

1. Clarity of Vision

   Clarity of vision is one end of the spectrum; execution is at the other. As the project evolves the vision will shift and so will the process for getting there. Most entrepreneurial efforts never actually wind up where they initially intended because they cannot account for all the variables that will eventually get in the way. It is not until you move forward that you begin to see what an idea really is or what it can become. The original idea can morph into something bigger, bolder or different. Environmental, organizational, technical and competitive factors need to be continually integrated into the plan. Planning becomes an iterative process. Keeping everyone on the same page will be important in laying out a roadmap for implementing it. Intrapreneurs consistently align vision with execution even if the target has changed. They communicate plans clearly, effectively and often.

2. Iterative Process

   Execution is not an event but an integral part of the development process. Iterative plans require an iterative development process. As customers begin to see what you are building, they will begin to see more clearly what they really want. Requirements will change many times during the duration of a project. More time will be spent testing, anticipating potential hurdles, dealing with new threats and risks to project plans. Activities that require the strategic allocation of resources, assigning responsibility and accountability, instilling discipline and taking calculated risks – things Intrapreneurs do well. Intrapreneurs understand that there must be flexibility to change course when it is necessary. They look at execution as a series of decisions. They know that every change provides an opportunity to increase the business value of an idea. They effectively manage the development and change process.

3. Business Value

Intrapreneurs create value because they have an unrelenting focus on customers. One takeaway from the Lean Startup Conference was "*Know exactly what your customer values. The customer rarely buys what the company thinks it sells.*" That's why Intrapreneurs engage customers in dialogue and discussion. They are good listeners. They build strong working relationships with customers to better understand their needs and what benefits they hope to achieve. Before they execute their ideas, they test and validate them in the marketplace. In turn they understand the limits of their organization's capabilities. They know what is possible and what is not. They are content to work with what they've got. They leverage existing resources to build solutions that provide both social and economic value. Intrapreneurs are effective at integrating opportunity with capability to deliver value.

4. Execution Skills

Execution requires having the ability and skills to establish and achieve challenging goals. There are certain individuals who excel at execution. They know how to get things done, tear down barriers and push through obstacles. They are strategic and analytical, goal oriented, creative, and decisive. They are good negotiators, deal well under pressure, and manage time effectively – all attributes of Intrapreneurs.

Identifying and leveraging their skills throughout the process will ensure that tasks are completed. Intrapreneurs are high on closure and will do whatever it takes to get things done. They will step on toes and break rules if necessary. Intrapreneurs are willing to work until they find the best solution. They take full responsibility for delivering results.

5. Simplify the Complex

   Execution is a complex set of interrelated variables that must come together perfectly to achieve precision. The conventional approach is to build the simplest map, disregard as many things as possible, as soon as possible. Intrapreneurs on the other hand like to linger in complexity. They embrace complexity. They don't try to simplify things too quickly. They take a more holistic approach. They keep the entire problem in mind while they work on various parts. They look at linear and non-linear relationships, multi-directional paths, things that might not initially make sense. They know that truly creative solutions spring from complexity. Intrapreneurs can take a set of complex interrelated variables and translate them into a simple solution. Then communicate them in terms that others can understand. They simplify the complex.

In his article 5 Must Have Skills of Intrapreneurs, Dan Toma says *"A successful Intrapreneur runs successful projects – it's as simple as that."*

Intrapreneurs know that delivering business value is the end game but executing with precision maximizes the value that is delivered to customers and the organization.

End of Being Average

In a speech to a local college, New York Times columnist, Tom Friedman proclaimed that "*average is officially over, in a hyper connected world; we must adjust to it before the global economy passes us by.*" This coming from the author, who told us years ago that, the world is flat.

Organizations have been dealing with this for several years. Redesigning their business models and changing how they operate. Now the focus is on the individual.

Only now are individuals feeling the impact of Friedman's words. The very essence of work is changing. The social contract between employer and employee is broken. Many professionals are unemployed or underemployed. Graduates are finding it difficult to secure jobs that leverage their education. The world of work has been turned upside down.

According to Friedman, "*Employers will no longer pay you for what you know, but only for what you do with what you know.*" This is the great divide between success and failure in the 21st century economy.

It is also part of the reason why entrepreneurship and intrapreneurship are on the rise. There is a growing need for entrepreneurial thinking and action. This is good news for intrapreneurs. It is the very essence of who they are.

Entrepreneurial thinking and action alone are not enough, intrapreneurs need more in their tool kit to be effective and successful. It is a combination of competencies, knowledge and experience that are needed. Intrapreneurs possess a distinct set of competencies that set them apart from more traditional employees. Everyone has these competencies. It is the breadth and depth of these competencies that distinguish the intrapreneur from others.

Intrapreneurs exhibit superior performance in key competencies that are needed to perform this role. On average Intrapreneurs exhibit superior performance in fifteen of seventeen competencies identified for this role. When compared to C-level executives, Intrapreneurs had greater depth in ten out of the seventeen competencies. Not just by a little but a wide margin. * There is nothing average in that.

How can this be! Well, most executives have achieved their success by exploiting the core business, not building new businesses. Just the opposite of what intrapreneurs do. Intrapreneurial initiatives provide a depth of knowledge and understanding that can only be gained through the experience itself – building a new business. It is the experience that provides a deeper and richer understanding of the nuances of building something new inside an established organization.

That said, understanding the core business is an important part of being an Intrapreneur. Most intrapreneurs start their careers in the core business, learning what works and what doesn't work. They experiment, test assumptions and look for possibilities. They push on organizational boundaries to see where they are flexible and where they are not. Eventually they will want something bigger, more difficult and more challenging to take on. Their previous successes (and failures) have propelled them to this moment. It is then when they know they are ready. They don't sit around and wait for the organization to hand them an opportunity, they proactively find one. That's not being average.

Intrapreneurs will raise their hands for the toughest challenges, biggest problems. Not because they know the answer, but because they know that they will learn from the experience. Win or lose they will grow from the experience. They will do what it takes to get things done, even if it means stepping on toes or breaking rules. Nothing comes from playing it safe but playing it smart provides new insight, new knowledge that moves the organization forward. There is nothing average in that.

Intrapreneurs are totally engaged and energized by the work they do. They are highly motivated and good at motivating others. Intrapreneurs believe in what they are doing. In many cases it turns into a cause. That's why most Intrapreneurs are loyal to their project first, then the organization. This runs counter to what most organizations would like to see but it illustrates the commitment that intrapreneurs have to what they are doing. Workers that are engaged are more productive, innovative and help their organizations achieve higher financial returns. These workers are anything but average.

It was Gifford Pinchot that gave us the Intrapreneurs Ten Commandments. The first one being "*Come to work each day willing to be fired.*" Intrapreneurs are willing to put their job on the line for what they believe. How many employees in your organization are willing to do that? There is nothing average about that.

Perhaps Friedman is right, being average is not good enough in today's rapidly changing environment. According to Friedman, "*Companies are looking for people who can invent, adapt and reinvent their jobs every day.*"

That's what Intrapreneurs do. That's who they are. They are not afraid to lose they are only concerned if they don't try. They look at every opportunity to make a contribution to themselves and their organizations. It's a two-way street. As they grow, so does the organization.

Being average is not something intrapreneurs are willing to accept. The intrapreneurs that I've met have helped their organizations build million and billion-dollar businesses. They have helped propel their organizations into the future.

It's time to end being average.

Operating System that Powers Intrapreneurs

Like organizations we each have our own internal operating system (IOS) that is unique to us. Your own personal IOS powers you to operate in a certain way. It is how you are programmed. Much like the operating system (OS) in your computer or phone.

Exploring your own IOS is the key to understanding your inner intrapreneur.

Thinking you are an intrapreneur is not the same as being one. You need to ask yourself who you are at the core. It is not just what we see on the surface that matters. It is the internal operating system that is driving you in one direction or another.

Why is that important?

The future of work is at stake. According to Tom Friedman, in his article After the Pandemic, A Revolution in Education and Work Awaits, "*The reality is that work is broken.*" It has become a blank slate.

It is not just the advent of a digital technology that is changing the nature of work, it is the human element that is shaping the future. Technology can solve a lot of problems, but it is talent that will direct the use of that technology.

The path to growth and renewal is igniting the Intrapreneur inside of all of us. It is only through human ingenuity and self-less commitment that Intrapreneurs can recreate, re-invent and drive change for the better.

Normally we would hope our organizations would take the initiative to identify and nurture its own intrapreneurs. The truth is that most organizations do not know who they are or even how to find them. So, it is up to you to find your own inner intrapreneur and demonstrate your value through your actions.

Understanding your own internal operating system is the key. Everyone has the potential to be an intrapreneur. You just need to explore the breadth and depth of those dimensions that drive you to be an intrapreneur.

Your IOS includes your motivations and aspirations, professional toolkit, and portfolio of experiences that influence and often control your actions. How much do you know about yourself? Ask yourself the following questions:

Motivations and Aspirations

- What excites you about your work?
- What motivates you to take-action?
- What inspires you to work harder, smarter, faster?
- Are you restless and easily bored?
- Are you willing to explore the unknown?
- Are you interested in making an impact?
- Do you find yourself questioning the status quo?
- Do you want to work on the biggest, most challenging issues?
- Do you take responsibility for your own growth and development?

Professional Toolkit

- What are the tools, techniques, and models you use at work?
- What are the theories and processes you rely on to do your work?
- What are the rules you live by and those you are willing to break?
- How do you approach problem solving, making decisions, taking risks?
- How do your beliefs, values and habits influence your actions?
- How does your attitude, expectations, and behaviors impact others?
- Do you take shortcuts to leverage what you have already learned?

- Do you convey a high level of passion and conviction for your work?
- Do you motivate and inspire others to express themselves freely?

Types of Experiences

- What types of work experiences appeal to you?
- What kind of experiences do you learn from?
- What experiences have challenged you the most?
- How many strategic initiatives have you worked on?
- How many new business ventures have you been involved with?
- How many of your projects have been stretch assignments for you?
- Which projects required you to take a cross-functional leadership role?
- Which projects had high visibility and attention of the board?
- Which projects have been customer facing endeavors?

The answers to these questions are building blocks that direct you to be more traditional or intrapreneurial. They not only influence what you do, they influence how you do them. They are the internal control system that powers your thinking and actions.

The foundation for these building blocks is grounded and informed by the types of experiences you choose.

Like the OS in your mobile phone the more applications (or in this case experiences) you have the bigger and more diverse your toolkit. The more difficult and challenging your experiences the greater your motivation and aspirations. They evolve together, build upon one another, and increase your capacity to do more, be more and achieve more.

Let's face it. The handwriting is on the wall. The concept of a career ladder is gone. According to Reid Hoffman, Co-Founder of LinkedIn "*The old paradigm of climb up a stable ladder is dead and gone. No career is a sure thing anymore.*" That means that you are on your own. You must create your own path forward.

That is fine with Intrapreneurs. They are not interested in a traditional career path. Intrapreneurs want to be challenged and stretched beyond the boundaries of what they know.

The career path for an intrapreneur is not linear or sequential. It is a series of starts, stops, exploration, discovery, roadblocks, dead ends, reflections, and learnings. It is not something you plan for it is something that evolves. It might manifest itself as a new opportunity, an unsolved problem, a new insight, or addressing an unanswered question.

The more you do, the more you learn, the more value you provide. These are things that you take with you no matter where you go or what you do. It is your own internal operating system (IOS) and like any system it gets better over time.

Today, being an intrapreneur is the key to self-preservation and survival. It is no longer a nice to have but an imperative.

Isn't it time you explored who you are at the core? Start by looking at your own internal operating system.

Chapter 5: Success Factors

- Deciding to Be an Intrapreneur
- Two Things Intrapreneurs Need for Success
- Unlocking Your Inner Intrapreneur
- Relying on Intuition
- Finding the Right Balance to Be an Intrapreneur
- How Intrapreneurs Unlock Leadership Potential
- Intrapreneurial Roller Coaster
- Intrapreneurs - Commitment, Conviction and Courage

Deciding to Be an Intrapreneur

Understanding what it means to be an intrapreneur is one thing but having what it takes is something entirely different. There is a growing temptation to want to be an intrapreneur without understanding the implications of taking on that role. The decision to be an intrapreneur, especially in a large well-established company should not be taken lightly.

One millennial seemed to understand this and decided to prepare herself for the journey.

Despite the fact that intrapreneurship is gaining traction as a growth strategy in some of the largest organizations, and that there is growing recognition that intrapreneurship is a factor in attracting and retaining talent, there is less focus on developing the individual capabilities that are required for Intrapreneurship. The focus has been on building organizational capabilities with the intent of changing individual behavior. Perhaps we need to turn this around and look at how individual behaviors build organizational capabilities.

Being an intrapreneur is not a destination, it's a journey. It is a process of learning and self-discovery. This is the story behind one individual who did just that.

It was over a year ago now that Megan accepted a job with a major consulting firm. Even before joining the company she had decided she was going to be an intrapreneur in her new role. Although she had never been an intrapreneur before she felt that she was destined to be one. With that in mind and before stepping into her new role she contacted us to take the Intrapreneur Scorecard. It was clear from her results that Megan had many of the capabilities that would be needed but she wanted to know more.

So, she reached out again to us to get a more in-depth look by taking the Corporate Entrepreneur Profile. The profile provided a detailed assessment that looked at the seventeen competencies and thirty-three behaviors that are needed for intrapreneurs to be successful in that role. Once Megan completed the profile, we went through the results in detail which helped her to see where she was strong and which areas needed further development. The profile enabled her to realize that she had the capabilities to be an intrapreneur in a large organization. The real proof would be demonstrating her intrapreneurial capabilities in her new role.

Armed with this knowledge Megan moved forward. It was a new position in the company, one where she was responsible for identifying new opportunities and services. Her confidence had been boosted by the knowledge that she had what it took to be an intrapreneur. She was also aware of those areas that needed further development, so it was easier for her to focus on improving them.

Megan said that, "*during the first year I was constantly aware of identifying new opportunities and suggesting new service products.*" Even though she worked in the lower ranks within the company she didn't wait for instructions from her superiors but kept pushing forward – some things worked, others did not. She remarked how many people complain about the lack of opportunities and interest in large organizations. That was not the case with Megan. She used her creativity and took the initiative to create opportunities. It was what kept her motivated.

Part of her challenge in her first year was learning about the culture of the company and how to fit in as an intrapreneur. It was clear that what she was doing and how she was doing it was different than business as usual. By understanding this and knowing what it takes to be an intrapreneur she didn't settle in or act as a typical employee. Instead, she demonstrated through her actions what it took to be an intrapreneur. To her surprise she said, "*I managed to transfer this way of thinking and acting to my manager.*" Megan was creating a new way of working not only for herself but the company.

Well, it has been over a year now and Megan is totally engaged in presenting new service opportunities to the company. Although the past year has presented a number of challenges, Megan always looked at them as opportunities to learn more about herself and the company. In doing so, she has a deeper and richer understanding of what it takes to be an intrapreneur in an established organization. She can look around and see other employees who are not motivated, not engaged because they have been doing the same thing for years.

Now that Megan has settled into her new role, she is taking the time to reflect on the past year. She can see how the Corporate Entrepreneur Profile gave her the confidence to be an intrapreneur and transfer that same intrapreneurial spirit to her team. Plus, it helped her in being fully satisfied with her job. But is also made her realize that by taking the profile other employees like herself can realize their own entrepreneurial potential and will be able to change. That they too can have a more meaningful career while at the same time supporting the growth strategy for the company.

So, it wasn't surprising when Megan contacted us and wanted to take the Corporate Entrepreneur Profile again to look at her progress over the last year. Megan had started this journey with a clear understanding of both her strengths and weaknesses as an intrapreneur. Plus, she knew that the work experience itself had helped her grow into the role. Megan felt she had made progress but thought it was important to see if and how things had changed. So, she took the assessment again.

It was clear right away that Megan had made significant progress. The results were impressive. The overall increase in her competency scores was forty plus percent. Her total score was higher than the average for all the intrapreneurs in our database. Her behavior scores remained solid and showed several areas of improvement. In some cases, the results showed that Megan did better than she would have rated herself. She commented on the results. "*I am really happy with the results and more confident in my job. Having already worked in a large organization for a year I was really surprised to find out how accurate these results were especially regarding areas that I need to improve.*"

Megan's desire to take responsibility for being an intrapreneur should be applauded. She set out to be an intrapreneur and made sure she knew what she needed to be successful in that role. This was not something her company did, it was something she did on her own. With a solid year of experience behind her and a significant increase in her capabilities Megan can continue to influence and drive the change that is needed within her organization to become more intrapreneurial.

It wasn't an organizational capability that changed Megan, it was Megan that changed an organizational capability.

Two Things Intrapreneurs Need for Success

My grandfather was an apple and cherry farmer in upstate New York. After high school he went to work with one of the prominent apple farmers in the area to learn about the business. He was an apprentice, a student, an intrapreneur whose practical ideas were used to help his boss build a thriving and successful business.

Eventually he set out on his own buying parcels of land in the area and built his own successful apple and cherry business. His products were sold to large companies like Motts and Comstock that turned those apples and cherries into some of the same products we have today. He had learned the business by doing the business and then took what he learned and set out on his own. So, by the time he died he had become the prominent farmer he had started out working for those many years before. He learned to be an entrepreneur by being an intrapreneur first.

Although his business would compete with his former employer, they remained friends and shared techniques, tools and new approaches that changed how they both farmed. The apple and cherry orchards that he planted are still there today. A tribute to the energy and passion of one man who like many intrapreneurs set out to build a business in and then outside of an established one.

Intrapreneurs are not born they are made through their own sheer will and determination. Like my grandfather, today's intrapreneurs must find their own way. They must learn, do and learn some more. They are in charge of their own destiny. There is no job security, no job for life anymore. We must build the skills and capabilities that will enable us to create our own future in or outside of an organization.

As the world around us speeds up it has become increasing clear that by the time a person gets out of college the things, they learned may be obsolete. There is a significant shift going on in education, book learning is not enough. Experiential learning is key. We see this in the adoption of entrepreneurship in most college and universities. The creation of incubators and venture groups on campuses.

According to Dick Resch, "*Schools should put more emphasis on teaching entrepreneurship skills that students thrive in an economy that rewards people who are flexible and resourceful enough to adapt to the changing nature of work. The future of work is not predictable. That's why students need transferrable, creative skills and competencies. No matter where the future takes us entrepreneurial skills will never be obsolete.*"

Like students, today's workers need the same entrepreneurial skills. They key is learning to be an intrapreneur inside an organization, so you build the skills and competencies that are transferable no matter where you go or what you do. It's why you hear so much about creating an entrepreneurial mindset. A way of thinking that enables you to be creative, innovative and entrepreneurial. But thinking alone is not enough. It's the doing that builds the skills and competencies that are needed. It's about taking action. Thinking and action are two bookends that you need for intrapreneurial success.

These are a few of the ways that Intrapreneurs Think and Act.

Intrapreneurial Thinking:

1. Independent Thinker – you rely on your own knowledge and experience to guide you.
2. Explore the Unknown – you challenge what you've always know to be true.
3. Whole Brain – you rely on both the analytical and intuitive side of your brain.
4. Integrative Thinker – you are able to hold two diametrically opposite concepts in your mind at the same time to create a new solution.
5. Pattern Recognition – you see patterns and relationships that form new concepts and ideas.
6. Synthesizer – you are able to analyze and synthesize large amounts of data to make decisions.

7. Experiential – you do not rely on past experience; you evaluate ideas by experimenting.

Intrapreneurial Action:

1. Inherently Creative – you develop creative ways to leverage existing resources to solve complex problems and explore new opportunities.
2. Iterative Planning – you find iterative planning more useful because things are continually changing and so are your options.
3. Leverage Contingencies – you can't eliminate variability, so you explore contingencies to see if there is a better way.
4. Take Calculated Risks – you look at the upside and downside of a risk before making a decision.
5. Embrace Surprises – you embrace surprises because it refines your thinking and your actions.
6. Control Uncertainty – you control uncertainty by acting on it not sitting back to see what happens.
7. Focused on Execution – you take action and get things done; execution is not a goal but a process.

It is not surprising that the number one competency of intrapreneurs is thinking – independent thinking – and the number sixth competency is taking action – execution. Intrapreneurs are effective in putting their thoughts into action. We've seen an increase in the number of individuals that are being trained to be independent thinkers, but execution is still one of the weakest competencies within organizations.

In between Thinking and Action you will need to be able to deal with uncertainty, ambiguity and the unknown. You need to be fully engaged, self-motivated and able to motivate others. You will need to drive and model the change you hope to achieve. Plus, it requires effective leadership – the ability to leverage existing resources in new and creative ways. These are the competencies that separate the true intrapreneurial leader from more traditional leaders.

If thinking and action are bookends then the competencies listed above (navigating uncertainty, engaged and thriving, driving change and leadership effectiveness) enable leaders to be effective in their role. Of course, there arc handful of other competencies you will need but our research shows that these are the top, most important.

A competency is a set of abilities, capabilities, proficiency, expertise and mastery that one needs to do a specific job (intrapreneur) successfully and effectively. A competency is developed through action and experience.

In the Reflective Practitioner, Donald Schon looks at "*knowing in action – a form of acquired tacit knowledge – and reflection – the ability to learn through and within practice. The basic idea is that through reflection-in action which responds to the belief that our knowing is in our action; we can gain verifiable insight into our thought processes. It is the practice by which professionals become aware of their implicit knowledge base and learn from their experience*."

Just as my grandfather did so many years ago, Intrapreneurs can develop the critical competencies they need to lead, drive growth and transform their organizations by doing. As their actions evolve, so does their thinking. Intrapreneurs put their thoughts into action and their actions inform their thinking. As a result, they become better intrapreneurs and more effective leaders.

Thinking and action are intertwined. It is the interplay between these two that build entrepreneurial muscle and the competencies Intrapreneurs need to succeed.

Unlocking Your Inner Intrapreneur

Intrapreneurship is not an intellectual exercise it is an experiential one. It's not just about thinking like an intrapreneur, it's about acting like one.

Entrepreneurs must not only 'think and reason' about opportunities they must 'act on them'. Opportunities are often created by the entrepreneurial process itself – it is the interaction across stakeholders where value is created. It is a co-creation process. Creating new markets, new businesses, new products and services.

Having an intrapreneurial mindset and thinking like an intrapreneur is one side of the equation. The other is being decisive and then putting your thoughts into action. You cannot be an intrapreneur until you have mastered both.

We call these Intrapreneurial Attributes. These attributes reflect how Intrapreneurs see and respond to the external world. It is your outward expression of your inner intrapreneur, Thoughts (mindset, thinking methods) and action (decision making, taking action.)

- Mindset – How you perceive the world.
- Thinking Style – How you process information.
- Decision Making – How you approach decision making.
- Taking Action – How you put your thoughts into action.

It was Peter Drucker that said, "*You must not only think but act like one entrepreneur.*" According to Drucker, "Intrapreneurship is something that can be taught and learned." It's about learning to be an intrapreneur. Developing the skills and competencies needed to be an intrapreneur. It's a journey of self-discovery. It's a deliberate choice.

We have found that many people have an intrapreneurial mindset and thinking but fall short when it comes to decision making and taking action. This is often a reflection of the processes and practices within an organization as well as the reluctance of the individual to step outside the bounds of what is acceptable behavior. This prevents individuals from taking the necessary steps to turn their ideas into products and services.

So, what does all this really mean and how do you know if you measure up. Based on research and numerous studies we've compiled a list of attributes that support each of these.

<u>Mindset</u>: Intrapreneurs make significant leaps in thinking that are not always linear, or fact based. They connect seemingly unrelated dots, leverage what they have, rapidly test and refine their ideas, embrace complexity, learn as they go, abandon an activity when it no longer makes sense and fail quickly and recoup quickly.

<u>Thinking Methods</u>: Intrapreneurs challenge what they have always

known to be true. They are integrative thinkers, analytical and intuitive, see patterns and relationships that form new concepts, they can analyze and synthesize large amounts of data, evaluate ideas by experimenting, and resist relying on past experience to guide them.

Decision Making: Intrapreneurs do not wait until everything is perfect before they are willing to make decisions. They resist diving into the data to early, make decisions without sufficient data, exercise good judgment and risk taking, willing to shift gears or shut a project down when presented with new data, and they seek to understand complexity, not simplify things too quickly.

Take Action: Intrapreneurs are inherently creative and action oriented. They find iterative planning more useful, embrace surprises to refine their thinking and action, look at all the options and leverage those that push them further, take calculated risks, deal with uncertainty by acting and are totally focused on execution, getting it done right.

A study was done at the University of North Carolina, looking at how successful serial entrepreneurs think and act. The study showed that entrepreneurs define the future by their actions. According to Professor Sara Sarasvathy, University of Virginia, Entrepreneurial Thought and Action is about the following things:

- Action vs Analysis – entrepreneurs have a bias toward action.
- Make vs Find – they define the future through their actions
- Means vs Ends – it is about the process not the ends

We've found that the same is true with Intrapreneurs, so we've incorporated questions into our Intrapreneur Scorecard that get at the essence of what it means to think and act like an intrapreneur.

More recently we have seen a shift in how intrapreneurs think and act. A majority continue to have an entrepreneurial mindset and thinking but are now more decisive and action oriented. We attribute this to the growing abundance of educational programs on Intrapreneurship and the commitment by many organizations to develop intrapreneurship as a core competency.

Even though Intrapreneurship is becoming a strategic priority for many organizations. According to a recent PWC report on the future of work, "*Only 56% of respondents say they have avenues present for employees to offer innovative ideas and support them in turning ideas into action.*"

The article To Drive Innovation, Focus on People, Not Technology states that the missing ingredient in most organizations is a: "*Focus on the Innovators, not the innovation.*" In other words, businesses must invest more in their people. In the article A Road Map to Success as an Intrapreneur, Tony Holbrook states that; "*Not nearly as much attention is given to the traits necessary to be a successful intrapreneur*".

Many organizations are realizing that talent is the limiting factor in intrapreneurship. That identifying and developing intrapreneurs requires understanding first who intrapreneurs are, how they are different and what skills and capabilities they need to succeed. Then providing talent development through experiential learning. Experiences that are not grounded in the past but represent the new digital technology and entrepreneurial skills needed for the future.

Until organizations step up to this challenge, you must invest in yourself, develop your own skills and capabilities.

Unlocking your inner intrapreneur is a state of mind, a shift in thinking, being curious, embracing complexity, dealing with ambiguity, facing the unknown, seeing patterns, synthesizing data, experimenting, testing your ideas, prototyping, taking risks, being willing to accept responsibility for your decisions, involving customers in the experience and a willingness to fail. These are all intrapreneurial attributes you will need to be successful in the role of Intrapreneur.

It's not enough to think like it intrapreneur, you must act like one.

Relying on Intuition

An important attribute of being a corporate entrepreneur is being able to rely on intuition. A new venture often faces a number of issues where there isn't always a clear-cut answer. Relying on intuition is often the only way to make a decision.

Having a can-do attitude refers to believing that something is possible, but intuition is about going with your gut. It is more of a feeling about something, an internal guidance system that points you in one direction versus another. There are some individuals who possess an uncanny ability to interpret situations by relying on their gut.

Sometimes intuition will have to do.

Relying on intuition is unnerving for many, especially those who are grounded in facts and figures. Management especially may be uncomfortable about these decisions. Any doubts they may have had about the venture going in are often magnified when they hear decisions are being made by relying on someone's gut feeling. Yet it's often these decisions that make the difference and provide another avenue for exploration.

Many corporate entrepreneurs have good influencing skills and are very convincing in their arguments. They can make a solid case for their decision without all the facts and figures, relying much more on intuition. Often it is their belief in what they are doing that enables them to win others over to their point of view.

A decision based on gut is one thing, making a commitment to that decision is another. Corporate entrepreneurs will take the initiative to make unpopular decisions when they feel they are right. They will accurately assess the risk and take the appropriate action when needed. They are not risk takers; they are *calculated* risk takers. Once they make the decision, they commit themselves to it.

Decisions based on intuition should be vetted by testing assumptions about the gut feeling. Often the team's collective wisdom provides enough input to reinforce or dismiss the feeling. Corporate entrepreneurs take responsibility for their decisions, right or wrong. They have confidence in their own abilities to make decisions based on their gut. They are decisive.

A Fortune 100 company decided to invest in a new product line. The company had conducted extensive research to better understand the market need and define the product requirements. They had a solid business plan and were ready to build the team. The entrepreneurial leader, who had not been involved in the initial market research, was concerned about the viability of the business plan. The leader had a nagging feeling that something was missing, and that the product design was not right.

Determined to dismiss their own gut feeling, the team began to dig deeper into the research, went outbound to speak with prospective clients, interviewed internal sales people, and concluded that the product as currently defined would not meet the needs of the target market. By going with their gut feeling, they were able to refine the business plan and readjust expectations to reflect the true reality of the situation. Of course, this increased costs and pushed out delivery dates, but it was better to catch it before the product was further down the development cycle.

Relying on intuition is an under-utilized and underdeveloped skill that organizations must begin to understand. Accepting it will likely be the most difficult part.

How comfortable are you in making decisions based on intuition?

Find the Right Balance to Be an Intrapreneur

Intrapreneurship has been an evolution not a revolution. As it has matured so has our understanding of the nuances, contradictions and conflicts inherent in the role of intrapreneur.

Intrapreneurs have been on their own trajectory. Evolving at their own pace, in their own way to achieve a deeper and richer appreciation for what it means and what it takes be an intrapreneur. The role has also evolved as organizations have started to adopt, embrace and integrate Intrapreneurship into their organizations.

For years the evolution of Intrapreneurs and Intrapreneurship have been out of sync, but things are coming into alignment.

At a time when much of the world seems out of balance, we find that Intrapreneurs are personally and professionally striving to find the right mix, the right balance, and path forward for themselves and their organizations.

Consciously or unconsciously Intrapreneurs have been moving their companies forward toward a more intrapreneurial orientation. They have been the pioneers charting a new course and exploring the depths of what is possible and not possible. It has always been a balancing act for intrapreneurs.

A key part of this is the energy and effort that Intrapreneurs have put into their work to learn the ins and outs of being an intrapreneur. Often, they have been on their own, learning as the go, testing ideas and experimenting with new ways of working. Pushing the limits of what is acceptable behavior and testing the patience of their bosses and the organization.

They now understand what it takes to be on the other side of the great divide between the core business and the new. They see the business more clearly through both lenses. These valuable lessons have given them the insight to understand the limitations of the core business and those of the new businesses they are building. These experiences have been invaluable.

The value lies in finding the right balance between all the potential conflicts that exist between these two worlds. For intrapreneurs it becomes a more personal and professional challenge or choice. They must decide where the stand and then work from that vantage point to address the issues inherent in their role. Every intrapreneur will have to find their own balance.

Here are some of things that intrapreneurs must come to grips with in their role. They represent both sides – the core and new business. Most of them are at odds with one another and create tension, conflict and division between people and in the organization.

Balance Issues Include:

1. Passion – Core versus New Business – Where is your passion?
2. Leadership – Traditional versus Intrapreneurial – What are your leadership traits?
3. Posture – Loyal or Independent – How do you relate to the organization?

4. Approach – People or Process – How do you approach work?
5. Goals – Profit or Purpose – What are you trying to achieve?
6. Priorities – Short versus Long Term – Where is your focus?
7. Results – Revenue versus Value – How do you define success?
8. Competence – Conformity or Differentiation – What makes you stand out?
9. Creativity – Incremental versus Disruptive – How visionary are your ideas?
10. Compassion – Tough Minded or Empathic – Are you realistic or compassionate?
11. Relationships – Competitive or Collaborative – How do you relate to others?
12. Presence – Poised versus Passionate – How do others perceive you at work?
13. Engagement – Direction or Autonomy – What keeps you engaged?
14. Self-Awareness – Confident or Competent – How well do you know yourself?
15. Motivation – Exploitation or Exploration – What keeps you motivated?
16. Mindset – Challenge versus Possibility – How do you see the world?
17. Thinking Process – Logical or Creative – How do you collect and process information?
18. Decision Making – Factual or Intuitive – How do you make decisions?
19. Taking Action – Task or Action Oriented – How proactive are you at work?
20. Influences – Knowledge or Experience – What inspires you take action?

Of course, there are other things we could put on this list, but these are some of the things that Intrapreneurs deal with every day. The list is not what is important or which side of the balance sheet you find yourself on. The list represents all the things that co-exist simultaneously. Things that by their very nature are out of balance.

The goal is not to be on one side or the other but to understand the dynamics that exist between them. Recognizing that many of the obstacles and roadblocks that Intrapreneurs encounter revolve around these differences. To know them you must first experience them and that is what Intrapreneurs have been doing over the last several years.

Only by knowing where you stand on each of these aspects of work will you be able to see them more clearly in others. Take a minute to go through this list, answer the questions and decide where you think you are.

When we think of Intrapreneurs, we think of them leaning more to one side than the other when it comes to this list but, we are seeing Intrapreneurs finding a middle ground that works for them and the organization. They are leveraging what they've learned and weighing the tradeoffs between moving forward and standing still. As a result, they are more effective in their role and able to move their projects forward more quickly.

The key to true intrapreneurial leadership is learning how to co-exist in both the core and new business at the same time and finding common ground that enables things to keep moving. It is a balancing act.

Not only for the intrapreneur but for the organization

How Intrapreneurs Unlock Leadership Potential

Intrapreneurs proactively take steps to learn, grow and change themselves to be better, do better and help others be their best. They are open to exploring who they are and what they are capable of becoming.

In doing so they are unraveling the mystery of who they are at the core and making adjustments along the way.

Intrapreneurs are not afraid to push the limits of their own knowledge and experience. They do it through their own thoughts, words and actions. They will expand their reach beyond what they know to be true to that which is still unknown. They will face adversity head on with an optimistic outlook. They will blast through barriers that get in their way. They will push the boundaries of what are sacred business practices. They will dispel fears by exposing the beliefs behind them. They will mitigate risk by managing the upside and downside of that risk. They will lead and motivate others into uncharted territory with a belief that anything is possible. They will stay the course despite the emotional toll it takes on them or their team.

To do this Intrapreneurs must first understand where they are, at a point in time and then use that as a benchmark for improvement.

When it comes to leadership the link between success and failure lies in self-awareness.

According to the definition, "Self-awareness is having a clear perception of your personality, including strengths, weaknesses, thoughts, beliefs, motivations and emotions." It is all about how you see yourself. It's your internal view of who you are and how you operate.

In the article How to Become a Better Leader in the MIT Sloan Management Review, "*Self-awareness has been cited as the most important capability for leaders to develop.*"

In a study of successful business leaders conducted by Green Peak Partners and Cornell University they found that "*A high self-awareness score was the strongest predictor of overall success.*"

In the book Hearts, Smarts, Guts and Luck, Anthony k. Tjan found that there is "*one quality that trumps all, evident in virtually every great entrepreneur, manager and leader. That quality is self-awareness.*"

Although most of us think we know who we are, in reality we may only be seeing a part of the picture. We tend to highlight the positive aspects of ourselves and ignore the negative. In the HBR article, What Self-Awareness Really Is, the author Tasha Eurich found that in 10 separate investigations with nearly 5,000 participants that "*even though people believe that they are self-aware, self-awareness is a truly rare quality. The researchers estimated that only 10-15% of the people that were studied actually fit the criteria.*"

In the Forbes article, Great Leadership Starts with Self-Awareness, "*One of the key indicators of low self-awareness is being unaware of personal blind spots – traits or aspects that may limit the way you act, react, behave, or believe, and in turn, limit effectiveness.*" This can be an issue especially for senior leaders who may have a strong ego or a heightened sense of self-confidence. According to the article, "*The more power a leader holds, the more likely they are to overestimate their skills and abilities.*"

So why is self-awareness so important for Intrapreneurs? It just may be the key to leadership success.

As intrapreneurs you have a key differentiation. You think, act, and make decisions differently. You have different motivations and aspirations. You see the world through a different lens. You are an enigma to many people in your organizations. They will not always understand you or appreciate you for what you do or how you do it. You will find yourself alone, isolated from others who align more closely with the core business and what it stands for. Being different is a curse and a blessing.

To that end it is incumbent upon you to understand that your differentiation is what makes you unique, complex and often misunderstood. You've got one foot in the core business and one in the new business you are creating. It is up to you to understand the difference and understand the gaps that exist between these worlds for you to be effective in both.

Self-awareness enables you to be more aware of those differences and to operate more effectively and successfully.

It helps you reconcile oneself as an individual separate from the environment and other individuals.

- It helps you better understand your behavior patterns. How your behavior affects you as a leader and its impact on other people.
- It helps you monitor your inner world – your thoughts and feelings. You can see where your thoughts and feelings are taking you.
- It provides insight into your beliefs and values. You gain insight into what you believe and value and how they influence you.
- It gives you the capacity for self-reflection and mindfulness. You are more conscious of yourself and those around you.
- It helps you understand what motivates you and influences your decision making. You see more clearly how you arrive at making the decisions you do.
- It makes you appreciate your openness, honesty, commitment and truth seeking. You understand why seeking the truth is important, both good and bad.

The value of self-awareness is in helping you focus your attention, your emotions, reactions, personality and behavior which determines where you go in life. According to Anthony K. Tjan, "*The best thing leaders can do to improve their effectiveness is to become more aware of what motivates them and their decision making.*" You cannot change something if you don't know it needs to be changed.

Often, we wait until a situation arises and deal with it at that moment. We don't take the time to reflect before we react. Self-awareness is developed through practice and self-reflection. It starts with assessing your own level of self-awareness and understanding those things that are impeding your ability to be effective. If you don't you are flying blind.

After years of working with Intrapreneurs and Intrapreneurial Leaders the link between success and failure lies in self-awareness. That's why we have included self-awareness in all of our assessment tools. The more you understand yourself, the more you understand others and you can lead, inspire and engage them in more intrapreneurial pursuits.

Perhaps that is the reason why only one percent of leaders are intrapreneurs or intrapreneurial. We continue to be amazed at how many leaders are eager to have their people assess themselves, but they are not willing to do it themselves.

Leaders that do look deep within themselves are able to understand those things they need to change in order to reach their full leadership potential.

One intrapreneur not only took the initiative on her own to assess her capabilities. She circled back the next year to reassess what she learned and how she had improved. She showed a forty two percent improvement in performance in the key leadership competencies she needed to be effective in her role. Not only did she work on things she needed to change she improved on those things she was already good at performing. In doing this she became a better leader and led her team to great success.

Intrapreneurs that want to unlock their own leadership potential need to become more self-aware.

Intrapreneurial Roller Coaster

As the need for Intrapreneurs grows so do the demands that are being placed on them.

Organizations are under pressure to be more innovative, generate new growth, provide social value, improve engagement and retain their best talent.

These are the same reasons why Intrapreneurs are getting the attention they deserve.

This in turn is placing increasing pressure on Intrapreneurs to deliver results that exceed expectations. It is not just about delivering a new product or service, business or process, but creating a new way of working, changing systems and processes, and building a new culture. The goal is to create value that is sustainable over time.

So, what is it like being an intrapreneur in this new environment?

It's a journey, not a destination. It is a process of learning as you go. Adopting what works and discarding what doesn't. Turning things inside-out and upside-down. Exploring the unknown, flying blind and walking a tight rope with-out a net.

It is a lot like riding a roller coaster. At times it can be exhilarating and at others it can plunge you into the depths of despair. There will be times when you find yourself in an endless loop. Once you are on the path there is no turning back. You want to go higher, faster. It's the thrill of the ride. The challenge for intrapreneurs is that the ride has no end. Until you decide it is time to get off.

True intrapreneurs love the highs, the lows, the long hours, the heated debates, and the pressure to deliver something new. They are motivated by the excitement of being part of the future and making a difference. If you decide to come along for the ride, you must be prepared to hold on to your hat, because it will be a bumpy ride.

Individuals who are eager to join an intrapreneurial initiative may not understand the demands that such an endeavor can place on them personally or professionally. It is incumbent upon you to set the proper expectations up front.

There will be long hours, extreme pressure, resistance and reluctance to change. As one intrapreneurial leader told me, "*There were times when I thought the whole team was coming unglued. They pumped themselves full of coffee or power drinks to keep themselves going. They were constantly explaining to their spouses why they wouldn't be home until late.*" It wasn't something any of them had thought about in the beginning.

Given the high failure rate of new innovations, there is also a high probability that the initiative you are working on may not be successful. Are you and your team members prepared to deal with the consequences of failure? Are you committed to putting in long nights and weekends? Are you willing to break rules and step on toes to get things accomplished? Can you deal effectively with uncertainty, complexity and the unknown? These are only a few of the things you will need to deal with.

Despite all the rhetoric about the need to have a tolerance for failure, many companies are still unwilling to acknowledge failure as part of the learning process. Those who join an intrapreneurial initiative must be willing to accept the consequences of failure. Depending on how your organization deals with failure, it can be career-limiting or career-enhancing. In most cases, it is not looked upon favorably.

One intrapreneur, didn't find out until after they were hired that the project they were asked to lead had already been tried once before and failed. Instead of letting that fact dissuade them from moving forward they took the time to explore why the last one failed. Ensuring that the same mistakes would not be repeated. This individual understood the risk and the potential for failure. Despite that they succeeded where their predecessor had failed.

The initial excitement of a new project can quickly turn into the harsh reality of aggressive timelines, resource shortages, and limited funding. The team doesn't always factor in the unexpected or think about backup strategies, which create anxiety when things go wrong. They neglect to think about their own ability to absorb the pressure or consider the toll that long hours might have on their health or family life. They try to work through lunch to pick up precious time when a ten-minute break or a breath of fresh air may be more effective.

Although the pressure to perform is often self-imposed, there comes a time in every project when the pressure seems unbearable. The team starts to get trapped in a negative cycle, things slow down, and progress stalls. Individuals make sacrifices that may jeopardize their personal well-being. Tradeoffs will have to be made between family and work. Some team members will self-select out of a project if the pressure becomes too great. Others will call it quits and leave the company. It is important to find ways to deal with individual and team stress.

Every project goes through its own up and down cycle. We call it going through the Valley of Despair. It's part of the change process. You will be personally and professionally changed by the process. Some of you will resist that change, others will thrive in it. You will have to let go of what is familiar, stable and grounded and move toward something that is shaky, unproven and foreign. That's the only way change happens by letting go of what you know and having faith in what you don't know yet.

Being an intrapreneur requires a certain degree of independence that often pits the individual against the organization. You are loyal to the organization but grow increasingly more loyal to the team and project. You find yourself torn between support for authority and taking measures into your own hands. The tug and pull are uncomfortable. You will be forced to make choices that are unpopular and politically incorrect. Those decisions can be gut-wrenching and threatening. You will want to find individuals who are not afraid to ask the tough questions and are willing to try new approaches.

Although intrapreneurs are willing to challenge and question authority they still maintain a healthy respect for authority. You will need people willing to challenge current thinking. Team players that can depend on each other and take responsibility for their actions. Individuals that are politically savvy, influential and effective at motivating others even when they have no control over them. It isn't positional power but personal power that makes the difference.

Politically you and your team are operating inside the core business. Team members must realize that they are still a part of a larger organization. They must learn to live with the values of the core business along with their own values. The team will build its own identity which will eventually separate them from the rest of the organization. This creates tension and conflict that can slow things down. You will need to find alternative paths forward and speed things up to make up for lost time. You are always working against the clock. Every minute counts.

Like an entrepreneurial start-up, intrapreneurs operate in a less formal way. The informal nature of start-ups is foreign to many people with experience in hierarchical organizations. Everyone will be asked to sign up to do things outside of their current responsibilities. You will want to be sure that everyone is comfortable operating in a less structured environment. That they are willing to perform tasks that may seem to be beneath them and tasks that stretch them outside the boundaries of their own comfort zone.

Stress is a normal part of work but is magnified many times over when it comes to working on these intrapreneurial projects. It is an inevitable part of the process and it separates those who have the physical and mental capacity to deal with large amounts of stress from those who don't. Being an intrapreneur requires a lot of energy and stamina to stay the course. It can help to find and identify, at the beginning, those individuals with high energy and a tolerance for stress. Individuals with a high tolerance for stress can deal with duress in a balanced manner. They will need every ounce of energy to endure the long days.

At the same time, intrapreneurship is exhilarating and a lot of fun. It is hard work that is extremely rewarding. There is a sense of pride and ownership. There is also the excitement of building something of value and making a contribution. It is a time of discovery and exploration. It is an adventure that you will treasure and look back on with pride.

If you like riding a roller coaster, then you know that it can be a bumpy ride. You will need to be able to deal with both the highs and the lows, the joy and frustration, success and failure, resistance and acceptance. But in the end, it will be worth it for what you learn along the way.

Set expectations that it will be a bumpy ride.

Intrapreneurs – Commitment, Conviction and Courage

An individual totally committed to their work must have the conviction and courage to act on their beliefs. It is not enough to advocate something you must act on it.

If you see that the corporation is headed in the wrong direction you must be willing to speak up and voice your opinion. If you think an executive decision is a mistake, you must defend your position and give them an alternative to reconsider their position. If you feel compelled to take a stand you must be willing to put your job on the line. A true intrapreneur will do just that.

What inspires intrapreneurs to speak up and speak out? What level of conviction do you need to be so moved that you are willing to go against the grain? What kind of courage does it take to face the consequences of what you believe? What level commitment do you need to sacrifice it all for taking a stand in what you believe to be the best outcomes for the business, irrespective of your own personal outcome?

Intrapreneurs feel the answers to these questions, they know when the time calls for their unique perspective to be heard, while others are closing the books on a project and thinking about their next career opportunity. One intrapreneur was contemplating these very same questions when she decided that a monumental strategic decision being made by her company was a mistake.

Strategic decisions are often made by executives who are far removed from the pulse of the market. They see a situation through their frame of reference. They make a rational decision based on the facts or what they perceive to be the true picture.

In reality, the decision may seem sound given the current economic environment but sacrificing the future for the present may not be a wise thing to do. Despite their best intentions, a series of obstacles and roadblocks can cause some of the most passionate executives to begin to let go of their large opportunities. They just cannot "see" the end game anymore.

Intrapreneurs who work closely with clients and customers have a different sense of reality. They understand the rational and emotional side of the market. New innovations require a lot more than a financial justification and process adherence to succeed. They require an emotional commitment by the company and potential clients. This type of emotional commitment can only be felt through consistent connections with these clients, and it can only be realized if the "feeler" stays open to the experience, allowing them to see the opportunity before them.

This intrapreneur knew both cognitively and emotively that the company's recent decision was wrong. She knew that if she did not stand up and say so, over a decade of work would become another graveyard internal startup project. She did not hold a position within the top level of senior management, but she had the day-to-day execution experience that this leadership team lacked. She jumped on planes when others stayed back, and she lived the strategic plan in multiple markets, across multiple countries. She coupled that with strong business acumen for delivering her message and sound rationale, and before long, the results of her initiative were making waves internally.

After a phone call and an executive summary email explaining why she felt the business was strategically headed in the wrong direction, she was summoned back to headquarters to justify her comments. She knew full well that she may have overstepped her authority and likely put her job on the line, but she was confident that what she was saying was right for the future of the business, whether she was a part of that future or not. If she did not voice her concerns now, she would be haunted with regret for years to come.

Putting together the business case for keeping the business going wasn't going to be easy. The executives were under a lot of financial pressure and had already formally announced the new strategic direction across the company. A change in direction would be "backtracking" at this point. She also knew that a rational explanation would not be enough. There had to be an emotional connection to drive the point home. Someone that is passionate enough about the investment to be willing to sacrifice themselves for the good of the company. In many cases it is the intrapreneur who takes on this role.

The senior executives were so impressed with her arguments and passion they accepted her proposal. She had successfully turned the strategy around and was told to make it happen. She wasn't fired but fired up to lead the charge.

It took commitment, conviction, and courage to do what she did to save a business that had a promising future.

Co-Authored with Sarah Fisher

Chapter 6: Aspirations

- The Intrapreneurs Quest
- Intrapreneurs – Fame or Fortune
- 2 Things Intrapreneurs Want at Work
- Internal Entrepreneurs – Earn the Right
- Are Intrapreneurs Crazy or Wired Differently?
- Finding Your True North as an Intrapreneur

The Intrapreneurs Quest

As the dynamics of work are changing so are the aspirations of millions of professionals around the world. It is no longer just about making tons of money or climbing the corporate ladder. It's about something far more important and far more valuable.

It's about reaching your potential. Expressing your true self. Taking advantage of your talents.

Intrapreneurs are leading the way. They are on a quest. A personal and professional journey that transcends work. It's not just about what they accomplish but who they are at the core.

Like the Knights in the Middle Ages that were in search of the Holy Grail, today's Intrapreneurs are searching for the answers to some of the biggest problems and challenges facing the world. And in doing so they are not only finding solutions to these issues; they are finding themselves. Their true nature and capabilities.

Research shows that when people live lives that are aligned with their true nature and capabilities, they are happy, productive and self-fulfilled. It is the desire to become everything that you are capable of becoming. It is not an end goal but a journey of self-discovery.

According to Kendra Cherry, "*People are motivated to achieve their full potential. This need for fulfillment and personal growth is a key motivator of all behavior. People are continually looking for new ways to grow, to become better, to learn new things, and to experience growth and self-actualization.*" Nowhere is this more evident than with intrapreneurs.

It was Abraham Maslow, who first coined the term 'self-actualization'. Self-actualization is at the top of the pyramid – Maslow's Hierarchy of Needs. The premise was that once lower needs (physiology, safety, love and belonging, esteem) were satisfied than individuals could become self-actualized. The textbook definition for self-actualization is "the full realization of potential and of one's true self."

Although I was familiar with the term 'self-actualization' it wasn't until looking it up again that it made me wonder if we were missing the obvious. Were intrapreneurs unknowingly becoming self-actualized just by the very nature of the role? Were they challenging the notion that you need to proceed in an orderly fashion to reach the top of the pyramid?

Digging deeper into the traits and characteristics of a person that is self-actualized a pattern emerged that illustrated how closely the competencies and characteristics of intrapreneurs are aligned with someone that has reached their potential. Here is a list:

- Inherently unconventional – being out of the ordinary
- Independent – rely on their own experiences and judgement to guide them
- Autonomous – do not rely on external authorities
- Embrace the unknown – deal effectively with ambiguity and uncertainty
- Motivated by growth not satisfaction of needs
- Socially compassionate
- Problem oriented rather than self-centered
- Creative – original and inventive
- Realistically oriented – efficient perceptions of reality
- Spontaneous in thought and behavior
- Enjoy the journey, not the destination
- Humble and willing to learn from others
- Deep relationships with a few
- Resist conformity to culture
- Have purpose, mission in life to fulfill
- Grateful and appreciate things, sense of wonder
- Acceptance of self, flaws and all
- Sense of humor is philosophical
- Values and attitudes are democratic
- Peak performance – transcendent experience
- Risk being vulnerable
- Real wish to be themselves

Many professionals possess a mix of these competencies and characteristics, but it is the breadth and depth of these that distinguish the true intrapreneur from others. They engage in experiences that expand and enhance these competencies. They step outside what they've always known to be true to test the waters, experiment, learn and grow. They push the boundaries of what is acceptable behavior. They explore the unknown.

Intrapreneurs are unconventional, independent and deal effectively with ambiguity and uncertainty. They are on a mission, with a vision and don't get bogged down with details. They are motivated by a challenge and the desire to grow. They are realistic problem solvers. They use their knowledge, intuition and creativity to find solutions. They are focused on the process not the destination. They approach each challenge with a sense of wonder. They are self-aware and leverage their strengths and accept their weaknesses. They resist conforming to the existing culture. They are fair in their dealings with others. They will risk being vulnerable to learn and grow. All of these align with the traits of someone that has tapped into their true potential.

It was Maslow that said that true state of self-actualization in society was rare. We find the same thing with intrapreneurs. The research has shown that only a small percentage of individuals are entrepreneurs or entrepreneurial.

Maslow also said that there are no quick roots to becoming self-actualized. The same is true with intrapreneurs. Intrapreneurship is not an intellectual exercise it comes from experience. It takes time and patience to be an intrapreneur.

Maslow used the term actualization to describe "*a desire that could lead to realizing one's capabilities. He felt that these people had somehow managed to find their core nature that is unique to them and is one of the true goals of life. The desire for self-fulfillment.*"

The ability to reach your potential as in intrapreneur is realized through a strong desire to find answers, solve problems, and develop new solutions that create value. You are stepping outside your comfort zone and creating something new, something that has never been done before.

Intrapreneurs are looking to solve the most difficult and challenging problems. In doing so they are not only finding creative solutions to pressing problems they are unknowingly exploring the breadth and depth of their own capabilities.

Are intrapreneurs helping us see a path to self-fulfillment?

It is something worth thinking about.

Intrapreneurs – Fame or Fortune

Last Saturday I attended a National Speakers Association meeting where the speaker talked about the need to decide if you want Fame or Fortune.

Do you want to be known for something that changes how people think about the world or do you want to build a business that generates lots of cash?

The speaker was focused on making a fortune.

It raised a number of questions in my mind. Did you really have to choose one or the other? Why not both? Was there more to being successful than fame or fortune. Was he an entrepreneur or a capitalist? Was he sincere in his efforts to help attendees find their own way to fame or fortune? Was he helping us understand the steps to being successful? Was his success a matter of drive, ambition, talent, networking or the right connections? Was it more important to make a difference or build an empire? Was the driving force behind him to be bigger and better than his peers?

Like others in the audience it was not clear what the real take-away was from his presentation. Clearly, he had found the right formula for his own success and we applaud and admire him for that. The real question was how we could use his success to enhance our own.

Although I got several good ideas from him the whole event left me still pondering the question of fame versus fortune when it comes to Intrapreneurs. Was this the great divide between entrepreneurs and intrapreneurs? Was there more than fame and fortune for intrapreneurs?

The literature says that entrepreneurs are motivated by money and intrapreneurs are motivated by creating value and generating new business growth. They aren't in it for the fame or the fortune because in most cases they are the unsung heroes, working behind the scenes, making things happen, taking personal risks, driving change, adding value and making a difference. It isn't about them, it's about what they can contribute to the organization, to the greater good, to society. Their own reward is the satisfaction in knowing they have done a job well done, that they had an impact and made a difference.

Looking at all the intrapreneurs and social intrapreneurs that I've met, my sense is that they would have difficulty choosing fame or fortune. Look at fame. If you ask someone to name, the top five Intrapreneurs you get a blank stare. Ask them to name a famous entrepreneur and they give you a list. The same is true when it comes to those who've made a fortune.

Most of us think of Art Fry at 3M who helped develop the post-it notes. When I show participants in my workshop a picture of Bill Gates and next to him is Art Fry everyone knows Bill but only one or two will guess who Art is. And that's because the wall behind Art is covered with post-it notes. It wasn't about fame or fortune for Art it was finding something to hold his place in his hymnal while at church on Sunday. Post-it notes were not a planned product. It served a purpose, solved a problem and leveraged a product that otherwise had little or no use at the time.

If we think about it Art eventually developed a bit of fame because he is now held up as an example of being a corporate entrepreneur or intrapreneur. Although the product he discovered created billions for 3M it is not clear that Art shared in the same financial fortune. The real fortune for him was knowing that he had discovered something that we see in just about every business environment today, that his idea contributed to the growth and success of 3M, served as an example to other employees that anyone can be an intrapreneur, that there is satisfaction in creating something that has value to you, your customers and the organization.

So perhaps we need to rethink this notion of fame and fortune as a choice. Not that these aren't important and nice to have but they may not be what drives and motivates intrapreneurs. The most successful intrapreneurs I know that have built million-and billion-dollar businesses for their company, but their names are not listed anywhere. They are widely recognized within their own firms but much less so outside their organizations.

Most however have done well financially. These individuals are handsomely rewarded for their efforts. The more successes they create the more money seems to come their way. But have they made a fortune; I wouldn't say so? A little bit of fame, a rewarding career and being financially secure have been and will probably continue to be the modus operandi for intrapreneurs.

Intrapreneurs want the freedom and flexibility to explore the unknown, create value and have an impact. They want to leverage their passion with purpose and meaning. They recognize that the world is rapidly changing, and they want to be a part of that change. Do they want fame and fortune as well?

Let us know what you think.

2 Things Intrapreneurs Want at Work

In last month's blog we talked about whether Intrapreneurs would choose Fame or Fortune. Since then I've met with several intrapreneurs who said that what they really want is freedom and flexibility. Not fame and fortune.

These intrapreneurs want the freedom to do what is needed to solve customer problems and create new services. It isn't about shining a light on themselves. They aren't looking at this as a win for them, they are looking at it as a win for the customer and the organization.

They want the flexibility to try new things independent of how things got done in the past. They aren't concerned about how to get it done they are interested in getting it done. The real reward is knowing that they were successful in achieving their goal.

All the intrapreneurs I spoke with were offered promotions in their own firms, but they turned them down. None of these individuals were interested in climbing the traditional corporate ladder. The thought of climbing higher in their organization was not appealing. Unless they would have the same freedom and flexibility that they now enjoyed. Many expressed concerns that they would eventually become part of the problem and not the solution. It would take them further away from the action.

Intrapreneurs prefer to work on the leading edge, exploring the unknown and creating value for their clients. Being closely aligned with customers and the markets is what makes their work so rewarding. It is what motivates them and keeps them engaged. It is also a key ingredient of their success. Not only engaging customers but integrating them into the process itself.

Most intrapreneurs are not interested in the political wrangling and power struggles that go on in the upper echelons. To them it is a waste of time and energy. It negates the real issues that organization's face in a world that is rapidly changing, where growth is harder to achieve, and competitive forces are consistently changing the playing field.

Intrapreneurs prefer to be as far away from the corporate politics as they can be. The thought of spending hours in meetings that never seem to accomplish much more than take up time is not what they want to be doing. They recognize that politics is a factor in all businesses, but they prefer to leave it to others to play that game. It's not that they don't engage in politics, much of what they are doing is politically charged. They just don't let it get in their way. They find sponsors who are more adept at organizational politics and will shield them from organizational distractions.

Intrapreneurs want opportunities that give them the freedom to cross organizational boundaries. They want the freedom to recruit and solicit help from those whose experience and knowledge are far greater than their own. They want the freedom to challenge traditional methods and practices that no longer make sense. The want the freedom to question decisions that may have made sense in the past but may not today. They want the freedom to partner with internal and external organizations that help further the cause even if they might eventually become competitors. They want the freedom to give customers a stake in the game by giving them a seat at the table to help shape and guide the project along the way. They do it because they want to expand their own knowledge and that of the organization.

Intrapreneurs know that flexibility is the key to dealing with complexity, uncertainty and the unknown. They want the flexibility to do what is right, not what is politically correct. They want the flexibility to change course or even kill a project when it no longer makes sense. They want the flexibility to create new processes and systems that support what they are doing. They want the flexibility to encourage workers to step outside their comfort zone despite the consequences. They want the flexibility to experience failure as part of the learning process. Intrapreneurs understand that being flexible is the best way to adapt, react and deal with a rapidly changing business environment. Being inflexible will do just the opposite.

The intrapreneurs that contributed their thoughts to this blog posting were fortunate, they had the freedom and flexibility they wanted and needed to stay motivated, engaged and productive. It wasn't something they were just given it was something they had earned. These individuals had demonstrated through their actions that being successful is not always about coloring inside the lines but stepping outside of them. Freedom and flexibility are achieved through superior execution.

Each of these intrapreneurs had been given more freedom and flexibility as they achieved more success. This in turn had increased their visibility and accelerated their potential within the organization. Just the opposite of what they wanted. Yet it gave them leverage in their negotiations and allowed them to more freely move around the organization looking for new and exciting opportunities.

What organizations often fail to understand is that freedom and flexibility is what is needed in today's business climate. What many organizations find hard to accept is that the traditional career ladder is not what employees always want? What many organizations fail to see is that existing structures and processes are stifling innovation and growth. What many organizations fail to acknowledge is that technology is transforming the way business operates in ways they can't even imagine. What many organizations fail to accept is that power has shifted from the organization to the individual. More and more employees are choosing self-employment as a career choice.

All these dynamics are creating a more uncertain, more complex and unpredictable world that many organizations are not totally prepared to deal with. Intrapreneurs thrive in this type of environment. They are after all pioneers. Charting a new course. Finding new and creative ways to get things. Discovering hidden needs that even analytics cannot predict.

They are the answer to this changing business climate. Yet, like traditional employees Intrapreneurs have wants and needs and freedom and flexibility are two of them.

Freedom and flexibility are key ingredients for intrapreneurial success. Not only for the individual but for the organization as well.

Intrapreneurs - Earn the Right

A question that is frequently asked is whether you must *earn the right* to be an intrapreneur.

In our work we have found that the most successful intrapreneurs are individuals who have achieved a certain level of success within their organization.

The success itself could be the launch of a new product or service, solving an organizational problem, creating a new process or opening a new market. The type of success doesn't really matter it is the visibility and recognition that one achieves from that success that gives these individuals the freedom to be an intrapreneur.

It is also the confidence that they acquire from their success which empowers them.

The fact is that most professionals do not think of themselves as intrapreneurs. The reason is that most organizations do not proactively identify or develop Intrapreneurs. As a result, individuals who are more entrepreneurial inclined will develop their own capabilities through their work. They are *unknowingly earning the right* every day to be an intrapreneur.

One executive vice president of a major financial organization said that she had never heard the term intrapreneur until someone brought it to her attention. The more she thought about it, the more it made sense. Of course, by then she had successfully built a multi-million-dollar business for her company. She had acquired the clout and political capital she needed to continue to develop her entrepreneurial skills inside the organization.

What about someone just starting out, must they earn the right as well?

That's a great question. Every intrapreneur must build a portfolio of skills and capabilities that enable them to be successful. It all depends on the work they sign up for and the challenges they take on. Playing it safe is not the way to build the skills that will be needed. What they need is an opportunity to develop and demonstrate their entrepreneurial capabilities.

According to Richard Branson, "*Virgin could never have grown into the group of more than 200 companies it is now, were it not for the steady stream of Intrapreneurs who looked for and developed opportunities, often leading efforts that went against the grain.*" He goes as far as saying that it is time for a major shakeup in organizations. They need to unleash the power of their Intrapreneurs.

Like Richard Branson, we believe organizations must "enable Intrapreneurship." It is the right time for organizations to proactively enable these individuals. In turn, these individuals must *earn the right* to become an intrapreneur. They must demonstrate it through their work.

It is only then, that they can *claim the title of intrapreneur*.

Are Intrapreneurs Crazy or Wired Differently?

Are you hardwired to be an Intrapreneur? That was a question that came up in a discussion at a luncheon of experienced women intrapreneurs.

All these women had successful careers, but they did it their way, on their terms. They didn't let organizational barriers or obstacles get in their way. They looked at everything with a fresh perspective, always asking if there was a better way.

They were willing to question and challenge authority and the status quo. Just because the organization did something the same way for twenty years didn't make it the best way, the most efficient way to do it. They would see an opportunity and go for it. They would identify a problem and find a solution. If they saw a need they created a service to address it. They took the initiative to do what was right.

When they were asked to explain why they did these things, a few of them said they were hardwired that way. "*Hardwired asked one of the participants. What does that mean*?" It means that you are conditioned to act in a certain way.

You look at everything as an opportunity to do something better, faster or more effectively. You are willing to experiment, test your ideas. You react to situations by keeping an open mind. You take a stand and stick out your neck for what you believe. Right or wrong you learn from the experience.

Your peers sit back and watch what you are doing. They think your ideas are crazy, impossible or will never fly. They may even ask you if you are crazy. Yes, it seems that being labeled crazy has become a rite of passage for Intrapreneurs.

One participant said that her organization thought that what she was doing was crazy. The rest of the group nodded and acknowledged the comment. They too had similar experiences. The group assured her that having that label was a good thing. What it meant was that she was different and making a difference in her organization.

All our lives we are programmed to fit in to a world that is stable and predictable, but the world is anything but that today. Growing up we are educated and guided to fit into a certain mold. Our institutions provide structures, processes, and practices to abide by that may have worked in the past but will fail in the future. Most individuals are ill prepared to deal with the new environment. Many will need to be reprogrammed to fit into the future.

Intrapreneurs on the other hand are wired for this new world. The way they think, and act are signs that they are hardwired differently. Something in their past, some experience enables them to look at the world through a different lens. They see possibilities.

There is usually something in their past, some part of their work experience or even their education that enables them to think and act differently.

One intrapreneur talked about her background in developing new products for a small startup firm. When the startup was eventually acquired, she left with a wealth of experience. Then she joined a large financial services company where she leveraged her entrepreneurial skills.

She wound up developing a series of new financial products and building a billion-dollar business for her company.

A second Intrapreneur started her career working for two of the most entrepreneurial companies at the time. Both companies left an entrepreneurial imprint that stayed with her throughout her career. Being entrepreneurial was the only way she knew how to work. It was the foundation for her success. Building multi-million-dollar businesses for the companies she worked for.

Another intrapreneur went to an innovative and progressive school that encouraged students to explore new things. There was no formal curriculum, the school allowed students to gravitate toward things that interested them. Working on new and creative projects is what motivated this Intrapreneur and made her a successful intrapreneurial leader.

A majority of Intrapreneurs develop their entrepreneurial skills by raising their hands to work on the most challenging problems and opportunities. No opportunity is too big to tackle, no problem too difficult to solve. Intrapreneurs use these types of experiences to learn and develop new capabilities. They are rewiring their brain to think and act differently.

What does it really mean to be hardwired? That was the question that the women intrapreneurs meeting that day had raised.

The term wired and rewired are terms that are often used as metaphors. We know that our brains are not made of wires, *"Doing something over and over again doesn't just make it easier. It changes the brain. That may not come as a surprise but exactly how that happens has long been a mystery"* according to Alison Pearce Stevens, in her article Learning Rewires the Brain.

Our brains contain about 100 billion neurons that store information and communicate between each other. When you learn something new, your neurons communicate with each other, making new connections. *"That means that when you learn something new, your brain physically changes."*

Nathan Spreng, neuroscientist at Cornell University wanted to know how the brain changes as we learn. *"At the beginning, you require a lot of focused attention. Learning to swing a bat requires a great deal of focus when you first try to hit the ball. But the more practice, the less you have to think about what you're doing.*"

The more something is practiced, the more connections are changed and made to include all elements of the experience (sensory information, movement, cognitive patterns). You can think of it as a Master controller" created for a particular behavior which allows it to be performed with remarkable facility and reliability over time, according to the article, 10 Fundamentals of Rewiring Your Brain.

Intrapreneurs unknowingly have been rewiring their brains through the entrepreneurial experiences and tasks they have been performing. "*As we learn something new, cells that send and receive information about the task become more and more efficient. In a sense, the neurons become wired together,*" says Alison Pearce Stevens. You are creating new neural connections, patterns and networks in the brain.

According to neuroscientists, when we learn and experience something new it creates a chemical reaction that creates a memory. When you apply learning – you change your behavior. It is the learning that drives a change in your thinking and behavior. The type of experience makes a difference.

A report by McKinsey stated that only a small percentage of senior executives participate in innovation or entrepreneurial projects in their organization. As a result, they often rely on past experience to guide them. They are relying on the brain connections that already exist. Not creating new, innovative or entrepreneurial ones.

So, it is not surprising when one seasoned Intrapreneur told me "*that the executives in her organization could not see what she said.*" Their brains were not wired like hers because she had experiences that they could not relate to. They found it difficult to connect the dots the way she had. This disconnect turned into a learning experience for all of them.

There is scientific proof that learning, and the experience associated with learning (thought and action) are responsible in part for Intrapreneurs being hardwired differently. They have made a conscious choice to learn and in doing so they are changing the chemistry in their brains. They have rewired their brains. Rewired their actions. They have learned how to be an Intrapreneur.

The more Intrapreneurial experiences Intrapreneurs have the more networks and connections they make in their brain. They see patterns and connections that others might not.

No wonder that many of the women intrapreneurs meeting that day said that their organizations often called their ideas crazy. They weren't crazy they just seemed crazy. The difference is how you see the world.

It may depend on if you are hardwired as an intrapreneur or not.

Finding Your True North as Intrapreneurs

We have been programmed from an early age to be this way, do it that way, use experience to guide us, rely on the word of others, prove every point, avoid conflict, embrace conformity and not veer too far off course. Now we are looking at a new way of being that is in conflict with these guiding principles.

It is as if everything has been turned upside down and inside out. The old rules no longer apply in a rapidly changing and complex world. Everything we've known to be true is in question.

Failure was once to be avoided. Now you need to fail to succeed. Experience was important but now past experience can get in the way. We relied on data, logic and reason to guide us, now we are learning to trust our gut and intuition. Organizational hierarchy was important to maintain order and discipline, now seventy percent of the work we do in organizations doesn't need hierarchy. We led with our heads and now we must lead with our hearts, with empathy, understanding and social responsibility.

The old rules no longer apply. They are outdated, no longer as effective, less engaging and less inviting to a new generation of workers. Yet despite these changes we tend to lean on what we know versus what we don't know.

Most people fear the unknown, while the greatest fear should be the known. It is that invisible line between what is and what could be. It is that leap forward into the darkness, into the field of possibilities. It is the empty space where new ideas emerge and take shape. It is the dividing line between the past and the future. It is what makes the difference between standing still versus moving forward.

Needless to say, a large number of workers prefer to stay within the confines of what they know. They use past experience and knowledge to guide them in their thinking, decision making and actions. They prefer to wait until things become clear before proceeding or moving forward. They resist complexity and try to simplify things quickly, narrowing their choices in the process. They avoid risk and minimize failure, preferring to play it safe. They stay within the boundaries of acceptable behavior, unwilling to bend rules. They prefer to live in a more stable and predictable environment.

There are others that prefer to explore the unknown, see what is possible. They are willing to challenge and question conventional wisdom. They resist diving into the data too early; they want to see the whole picture first. They rely on their own gut and intuition to inform their decision making and actions. They experiment and test their assumptions. They are not afraid to fail; they learn from both their successes and failures. They embrace complexity and linger in it; they prefer to look at all the options before narrowing their choices. They are energized and thrive in an environment full of ambiguity and the unknown.

Interestingly we need both types of individuals in organizations today. The first group provides a solid foundation for managing and leading in the core business. The second group is needed to generate new and sustainable growth. It is this second group where we find Intrapreneurs.

The more I work with intrapreneurs and social intrapreneurs the more evident it is that these individuals are in alignment with who they are at the core, not what the organization wants them to be. By being alignment with their true self they are more engaged, productive and innovative. They think, act and make decisions differently. They have different motivations and aspirations. They operate from their head and their heart. They are driven by something bigger than themselves.

In his book True North, Bill George describes True North this way, *"it's the internal compass that guides you successfully through life. It is your orienting point – your fixed point in a spinning world – that helps you stay on track. ...It's based on what is most important to you, your cherished values, your passions and motivations and the sources of satisfaction in your life."*

The key to finding your true north is self-awareness. Intrapreneurs are always asking themselves is there something else they don't know that they should. They take responsibility for their own growth and development. They not only want to know; they need to know. They are peeling away the layers of past experience and conditioning to see who they really are at the core. Reaching deep inside them self to understand what motivates and influences them, what drives them, their strengths, weaknesses and areas needing more development.

"True north is a phrase that is often used to define a person who has clarity and direction in his or her life."

Intrapreneurs bring their A game to every situation. They look at every opportunity as a way to learn, grow, and change. The more they learn, they more they come to know themselves. By exploring the unknown they see what is possible. Find new and innovative ways to solve complex problems; create new approaches to challenging issues. They look at every situation from all sides; making sure that the solution is a win, win for everyone involved. Their energy and passion are contagious. They inspire and motivate others to follow their lead. They are pushing themselves and their organizations into the future.

There has never been a group of people more committed to bettering themselves for their organizations and the world around them. They do not sit back and wait for the organization to offer them an opportunity, the proactively seek out opportunities to do it for themselves. They know that the world is changing and that they need to change with it. The more they know about themselves the better they will be able to deal with those changes.

It was Abraham Maslow who once said "*"What is necessary to change a person is to change his awareness of himself."* Intrapreneurs are doing just that. They are looking inside themselves for guidance and direction. They are finding their true north.

What about you? Have you found your true north?

Chapter 7: Future

- Professional Corporate Entrepreneur
- Why Intrapreneurs Are the Future
- Intrapreneurs – The Road Less Traveled
- The Fork in the Road Intrapreneurs Face
- 12 Ways Intrapreneurs Build Entrepreneurial Muscle
- Why Intrapreneurs Love their Job
- Make Intrapreneurship a Priority in Your Organization
- Future Prospect for Intrapreneurship

Professional Corporate Entrepreneur

Isn't it time we recognized corporate entrepreneurs (Intrapreneurs) as a new profession? If yes, then why aren't organizations proactively acknowledging this role?

If you search the most popular career websites, you find that none of them post jobs for corporate entrepreneurs or Intrapreneurs. If you look at corporate websites, you find the same thing.

Talk to executive search firms and they use other labels to describe these individuals.

Sure, some organizations may use different terms to identify these people but titles like business development don't do justice to these individuals. Call them what they are – *Corporate Entrepreneurs, Intrapreneurs, Social Intrapreneurs, Entrepreneurial Leaders.* Recruit them for what they do and openly acknowledge the contribution they are making to the organization.

One corporate entrepreneur said she had to define her own job spec because the human resource department didn't know how to define what she did. The reality is that she didn't fit the profile of the traditional employee, manager or leader. Corporate entrepreneurs don't fit, *that's the point.*

According to the article Competence in the 21st Century, "*most organizations with over three hundred employees use some form of competency assessments.*" The problem is that these competency models do not adequately reflect what it takes to be an internal entrepreneur. Job specific competencies are needed to identify and develop internal entrepreneurs.

A few progressive organizations are developing new competency models for their leaders that include some of the competencies that corporate entrepreneurs possess. That is a start, but it does not go far enough. Organizations must distinguish between those competencies that make sense for the core business and those that are needed to build new businesses. *They are different.*

Corporate entrepreneurs possess a unique combination of competencies that set them apart.

Organizations have been doing a great job of identifying high potentials for the core business, now they must do the same with corporate entrepreneurs for their new businesses. It is often the depth of a competency that distinguishes and entrepreneurial leader from a traditional leader. *It is a fine line.*

Corporate entrepreneurs exhibit greater depth in the top competencies needed for this role.

It is because of this that most corporate entrepreneurs take ownership for their own growth. They know what they need to do to grow and be successful. They take the initiative to understand their own strengths and weaknesses. *They are willing to look at themselves in the mirror.*

Corporate entrepreneurs want to know what behaviors and competencies are important for their success.

They find it difficult to get good feedback especially from traditional leaders who can't relate to what they do. They seek advice, counsel and mentors outside of their organizations. They find courage and strength from other corporate entrepreneurs who understand their plight. *They face the same issues.*

Corporate entrepreneurs are banding together in networks and communities to support one another.

There are no career paths for these individuals in most organizations. They often feel as if they are on their own. They do not wait for the organization to hand them an opportunity, they actively look for new and challenging situations. *They will look inside or outside their organization.*

Corporate entrepreneurs are restless and need to be consistently challenged to stay engaged.

For these reasons it is exciting to see competency models becoming the benchmark for best practices in talent management. They not only support the overall goals for an organization they enable workers to align their skills to needs of the workplace and the marketplace.

According to the Human Resource Systems Group, "*Competencies are effective because the go beyond the basic requirements of a job to identify the behaviors that top performers demonstrate. …Competencies describe the how a highly effective worker will achieve success.*" Specific job profiles are key.

Nowhere is this more important than where it comes to corporate entrepreneurs. The growing demand for experienced and competent corporate entrepreneurs is on the rise. Organizations that do not proactively identify and recruit these individuals will be at a disadvantage. The 21st century workforce is changing, and corporate entrepreneurs are leading the way. *They are transforming the way we work.*

Collectively corporate entrepreneurs must stand up, speak up and lead the way. Ultimately it will be up to them to establish the role of *Professional Corporate Entrepreneur.*

It will only be through their efforts that organizations see the value of the professional corporate entrepreneur and their impact on the 21st century economy.

Why Intrapreneurs Are the Future

In a recently published book titled Beyond the Champion: Institutionalizing Innovation Through People the authors spent four years researching disruptive innovation in large organizations. What they found is good news and bad news for Intrapreneurs and for those organizations struggling to develop disruptive innovations.

They found "*that the single biggest challenge that companies faced as they worked to institutionalize a strategic innovation capability: that of developing and managing innovation-related talent. It's back to people.*"

Although the research found that many organizations have focused their strategic innovation efforts on process, culture, structure or financial approaches they are not enough. They go on to say that, "*innovation talent is rare*" that "*selection, development and retention approaches for innovation personnel were overlooked, undervalued, and/or misunderstood.*"

The book highlights the fact that "*Companies have not taken a strategic approach to develop innovation capability*" in their organizations or in their people. Most organizations have perfected their ability to develop and launch core and adjacent innovations. Their next move is to do the same with strategic and disruptive innovation.

It is clear that innovation and growth are the key driving forces behind the adoption of Intrapreneurship. That's the good news. The bad news is that you can't achieve either without the right talent – intrapreneurs.

These same sentiments are being echoed everywhere.

In his article Memo to CEO: The Time for Intrapreneurship is Now Gifford Pinchot said that, *"The intrapreneur is an essential ingredient in innovation." "That it's not the right processes that make an organization innovative."* Pinchot states that *"Significant innovation only happens when a committed team of intrapreneurs drives the innovation through all the barriers, failures, mistakes and seizing of emerging opportunities that mark the intrapreneurial journey."*

In the article, Out with the CEO and in with Intrapreneurship, Gina Fairley shares a comment made by Alison Wright, Assistant Director of Engagement and Development at the National Gallery of Australia who was quoted as saying, *"Innovation doesn't come from this big nefarious cultures; it comes from people – it comes from dreamers that do."*

In the document, Unleash Your Intrapreneurial Power, WhatAVenture states that *"It is impossible to achieve significant innovation results without an organizations internal support of intrapreneurs, internal innovation champions – the intrapreneurs."* The document also states that *"People are the most important and challenging building block."*

In his article The Five Leading Trends in Intrapreneurship, Richard dos Santos, states that, *"The future belongs to intrapreneurs. They have the one resource in the coming age of complexity – the willingness to act."* It is for this reason that the key is understanding and unlocking the potential of intrapreneurs by developing the competencies required to meet the challenges ahead.

Unfortunately, most organizations do not provide an opportunity for employees to stretch their entrepreneurial muscle. But that is changing. According to Paul Kurchina in his article Intrapreneurship: From Out-of-the-Box Thinking to Strategic Opportunity, talked about how, *"In the last 5 years, CEOs have started to realize that these once regarded nonconformists (lone wolf, maverick, and rebel) may own the strength necessary to strategically accelerate innovation and growth."*

Intrapreneurs are the future because they intuitively understand what it takes to adapt to a rapidly changing environment. They have turned the traditional organization upside-down and inside-out to show that innovation and growth are grounded in the new reality – complexity, uncertainty, and the unknown. They do not fear the unknown, they embrace it, they do not try to manage complexity they leverage it, they don't wait for clarity they take action to demonstrate what it takes.

Intrapreneurs strive to make work meaningful for themselves and their organizations. In doing, so they are moving their organizations forward into uncharted territory. They recognize that speed is critical for success, so they act quickly, decisively with enough information to make an informed decision. They effectively manage risk by experimenting. They drive change by being the change they hope to achieve. They motivate, inspire and lead others to explore and exploit opportunities in the market. They have a pulse on the market and customer needs. They understand the value of technology in changing business models.

Intrapreneurs are the future because they understand what needs to be done. They only need an opportunity to stretch their entrepreneurial muscle. They are not willing to wait around and see what happens. They are willing to step up and lead. They know what they want to do, how they want to do, and why they want to do it that way. It isn't about ego or glory it's about making a difference. They are the pioneers, the change agents that are creating the future as they go. There are no roadmaps or guidebooks for them to follow. They are leading the way forward.

In the article Can Corporate America Teach us How to Manage Entrepreneurs? Phillip Rowley said, "*With disruption coursing through every industry, we've realized that the key to success – and our survival – likely lies in our ability to innovate and change.*"

Perhaps the answer that has been right in front of us but dismissed up until now are people – the intrapreneurs that are no longer a hidden talent but a loud voice in our ever-changing world.

Intrapreneurs are the disruptors that are changing the way we look at work, business, and society at large.

Intrapreneurs – The Road Less Traveled

Most people know Robert Frost's poem, The Road Not Taken, yet few realize the significance of his words or its true meaning. In the final stanza the poem says, "*Two roads diverged in a wood, and I took the one less traveled by, and that has made all the difference.*" We tend to interpret the poem to mean that choosing the path less traveled will make a difference.

Not so. According to Christina Sterbenz, "*People wrongfully interpret this as evidence of the payoff for freethinking and not following the crowd, when it actually comments about people finding meaning in arbitrary decisions.*" It's about finding meaning in whatever path you choose.

David Haglund interprets it to be about choice. "*At the heart, this poem is about choice: how one decision can change a person's entire life.*" The poem describes two paths that are equally traveled and appealing but which head in different directions. It is only upon reflection that Frost describes the road as being less traveled and then describes it as a defining moment of life.

Frost's biographer Lawrence Thompson looks at it from this angle, "'*The critical regret' analysis supports the interpretation that this poem is about the human tendency to look back and attribute blame to minor events in one's life, or to attribute more meaning to things than they may deserve.*" In this case Frost expresses gratitude for the road chosen. The regret, not being able to choose both roads and see where the other path would have led.

All these interpretations shed a new light on the meaning behind the poem. They also serve to better illuminate the intrapreneur's journey – the path they take, the choices they make, and the difference it creates. Perhaps not in the way we originally thought.

Free thinking and not following the crowd are key attributes of intrapreneurs. It is in doing them that Intrapreneurs create meaning. Finding something is by chance. Creating something is deliberate.

Choosing to be an intrapreneur is a choice. Inherent in this decision is the belief that it will change their life in a positive, more rewarding way. It is an attitude, a way of thinking and acting.

Regret is not something that intrapreneurs reflect on. It is the journey itself that is the reward. In learning, growing, making a difference and adding value. They don't regret something they did, they try and make it better. They only regret it if they don't try.

Despite the actual interpretation of The Road Not Taken, I often use Frost's poem to describe intrapreneurs. They do take the road less traveled by choice.

The fork in the road is a symbol of the critical junctures we all face in deciding what direction to go when a situation presents itself. Do you take the easy road, the known road, the less risky road, the more challenging road, the more meaningful road or do you let your circumstances take you where they may?

Your answer to these questions may be the key to unlocking your own intrapreneurial journey.

Easy Road: Intrapreneurs do not do what they do because it is easy but because it is hard. They know that the traditional path is not working and that there must be another way. There are no roadmaps for them to follow. They are creating a new way forward. They will do whatever it takes. They are charting a new course. They take the hard road.

Known Road: Intrapreneurs by nature are curious and they are willing to explore the unknown – they see it as a field of possibilities. Experience is important but experience itself can get in the way. It can shift the focus in the wrong direction. Intrapreneurs believe that the only way to find a solution is to look at all their options. They prefer to work with a blank canvas. They take the unknown road.

Less Risky Road: Intrapreneurs take calculated risks by weighing the upside and downside of a decision before making it. They understand the inherent risk in doing something that has never been done before. They evaluate their decisions based on what they are willing to risk at what cost. They want to maximize value while managing risk. They are effective risk managers. They take the road with the most manageable risk.

More Challenging Road: Intrapreneurs love to be challenged. They are like mountain climbers. Once you climb a mountain you want to climb a higher more difficult one next time. The bigger the better. It is the excitement of the challenge that keeps them motivated. They want to work in an environment where they can continually learn. They need to be challenged to stay engaged. They take the most challenging road.

Meaningful Road: Intrapreneurs focus on work that has meaning to themselves, their organizations and society at large. They are energized by doing something that delivers financial and social value. They are focused on the greater good. Not what's in it for them but what does it mean for others. They look for opportunities where they can make a difference. They want to make a contribution. They take the most meaningful road.

Let Circumstances Take You: Intrapreneurs take charge of their own development. They are not willing to wait until the organization offers them an opportunity. They proactively seek out opportunities where they can stretch and grow. They are reluctant to wait to see how things unfold. They will make course corrections when the path forward is not clear. They are patient to a point. They find their own path forward. They don't let circumstances take them where they may.

If these statements ring true for you perhaps you are already an intrapreneur. Intrapreneurs take the road less traveled because it is what they need to do to be highly effective and productive. They wouldn't have it any other way.

In taking the road less traveled Intrapreneurs are not only exploring new opportunities for their organizations they are exploring the breadth and depth of their own capabilities. It is about free thinking and not following the crowd. It is also about choosing to live with your choice and having no regrets no matter what happens.

What about you, are you taking the road less traveled or are you playing it safe?

Fork in the Road Intrapreneurs Face

In the article, Intrapreneurs – The Road Less Traveled, the focus was on why intrapreneurs take the road less traveled and what that means. Intrapreneurs also face another fork in the road on their journey – especially if they want to be a serial intrapreneur.

What is a serial intrapreneur? If you search for the term you only come up with a handful of entries. Most of them point you to articles on Serial Entrepreneurs with an 'E'. Even Wikipedia didn't have a section on serial intrapreneurs, but they had one on, you guessed it – Serial Entrepreneurs.

Digging deeper there were only two definitions of serial intrapreneur that I could find. One by JP Nichols, host of the Serial Intrapreneur podcast, that read *"A serial Intrapreneur is about the leaders who battle the status quo inside their own companies to innovate and drive change."* The other by Quora, *"A serial intrapreneur is someone who innovates inside their jobs and company in any way they are able to: finding new working methods, software that better fit their goals, ways to stay motivated/inspire co-workers, seeking efficiency even in the smallest things"*.

There must be more definitions out there for serial intrapreneur but after searching for a while it was time to move on. It seems that we still have a long way to go until the term Serial Intrapreneur becomes part of our lexicon.

A serial intrapreneur is an intrapreneur that continues to innovate, time after time, project after project, no matter what they are working on or where they are working on it or what their role is at the time.

They consistently and continually operate in the same way. You give them a problem and they solve it. You ask them to identify an opportunity and they find one. You ask them to create value and they identify ways to do it. You ask them to drive change and they lead the way. You ask them to take a leap and they calculate the risk before jumping. You ask them to do the impossible and they will give it their best. They are willing to do whatever you are willing to throw at them. They just want to make sure that you do.

A lot of intrapreneurs don't have the luxury of being asked by their organizations to take on challenge after challenge. If that is the case intrapreneurs must choose to find their own challenges inside their existing organization or in a new one.

According to Ian Lavis, author of Rise of the Intrapreneur, "*The concept is simple: your organization empowers employees to take the initiative and solve problems. They become entrepreneurs from within.*" Or they leave to become intrapreneurs somewhere else.

This is the ultimate fork in the road for most intrapreneurs. How many times have we heard, "Should I stay, or should I go?" The answer is always the same. If you have exhausted everything you can possibly learn there, pushed the limits of every organizational boundary, explored every possible opportunity, questioned authority one too many times, or if you are no longer challenged or just board, it may be time to go.

In her article, Creating Change from The Inside-Out, Laura Whitman states, "*Intrapreneurs refuse to sit idly by while the world happens around them. They are interested in disrupting things.*"

You can't be a serial intrapreneur unless you continually innovate, and it is not always possible to do that in one organization. That said there are serial intrapreneurs in very large, bureaucratic companies that approach the situation by recreating themselves and the work that they do. One serial intrapreneur in particular has spent over fifteen years in a Fortune 50 company navigating her way around organizational roadblocks by finding new opportunities for the company to explore. Then she takes charge of developing those opportunities, turning them over and moving on. The constant need and desire to be challenged and grow provides new and greater opportunities for her to stay energized and engaged.

No longer is she constrained by process and practices that stifle growth and innovation. She has become the spark that lights the fire for each new business. The freedom and flexibility enabled her to expand her reach into new areas and to build a portfolio of startups within an existing organization. For now, she has one of the best jobs in the company. Over time she may find the work less challenging, less exciting but for now it makes total sense. She has the benefits of a large organization and the independence to be entrepreneurial. Like all intrapreneurs the day may come when she decides to leave but by then she will have created substantial value for the organization and herself.

This particular situation is less prevalent today because organizations do not fully recognize the value and contribution of serial intrapreneurs. It is often only when the intrapreneur is gone that the loss will become more evident.

One concept that has emerged from this is called, "*The Intrapreneurs Illness. Described as the widening gap between an institutions platitude and the realities of innovating within organizations*," according to Hans Balmaekers. "*Many innovation gurus refer to this contradiction as the new reality of organizational life. Causing frustration, disillusionment, wanderlust*." No wonder we see so much consternation among intrapreneurs.

The other option or fork in the road for serial intrapreneurs is to hop in and out of organizations to find challenges. Once they've accomplished their project they move on to the next opportunity, most likely in a new company. This was the path of another serial intrapreneur. He was lucky to have started his career in a Fortune 100 company, but he soon realized that his company only invested in a few new innovation efforts each year. His ability to find creative solutions to some of the companies most pressing problems helped him build the confidence and competence he needed to excel. But despite his successful track record he found that he was not being challenged and he was hungry for something more exciting.

So, he found an opportunity in a totally different industry that he knew nothing about. The opportunity enabled him to develop new and different capabilities. Once that project was completed, he moved on to another project in the company. When that project was successfully completed, he moved on to a new project in another company. Keep in mind that each of these projects kept him busy for 2-3 years at time but when they were completed and with no other opportunities in sight he'd move on. He worked in and out of both large and small companies which provided a unique perspective and helped him develop a diverse set of capabilities.

Needless to say, this serial intrapreneur was also building a portfolio of successful projects along the way. He created value for each of the companies he worked for and eventually was able to create his own opportunities in other companies.

The companies that hired him were hiring him for his skills not for any one project. They seized the opportunity to leverage a set of skills and competencies that they did not currently have in their company. This serial intrapreneur was the catalyst that enabled these companies to become more entrepreneurial. They followed his lead and let him show them the way. Today, he is a successful management consultant helping large organizations implement intrapreneurship.

If you envision yourself as a serial intrapreneur you will eventually face this fork in the road. Do you stay or do you go? That is a decision only you alone can make. It's not about having a career it's about creating a future as a serial intrapreneur and these are the two paths you are likely to take. Both are great opportunities, each with their own challenges but they lead you to the same place. Developing your capabilities as an intrapreneur.

You may not have a choice like our first serial intrapreneur to stay engaged and thrive in one company for as long as she has by moving around from project to project, business to business. Most serial intrapreneurs are probably more like our second serial intrapreneur. Destined to move around from company to company which isn't a bad thing.

In his article Integrating Entrepreneurship with Professional Leadership, Barry Dym says *"The entrepreneurial journey is never straight or easy."*

Perhaps these are some of the reasons we don't know much about serial intrapreneurs. They are either hidden inside these large organizations or hopping around from company to company. In his article, How Corporate Intrapreneurship Can Help Entrepreneurs, Vikram Upadhyaya, states "*It's not about creating intrapreneurs, it's about finding and recognizing them.*" Rest assure that they are out there and will continue to be out there.

We just need to find them and have them tell us their stories until we fully understand and appreciate the value and impact that serial intrapreneurs are having in companies, across industries and around the world.

12 Ways Intrapreneurs Build Entrepreneurial Muscle

All the buzz about Intrapreneurship has put a spotlight on identifying and developing intrapreneurs.

Workshops, incubators and accelerators are being used to engage employees in entrepreneurial pursuits. There is a proliferation of conferences and educational programs focused on developing intrapreneurs. Recruiters are looking for entrepreneurial talent for their clients. These are all positive signs.

But what about you....

What are you doing to build and develop your own entrepreneurial capabilities?

Here are a few ways that intrapreneurs are building the entrepreneurial competencies they will need to compete in a world that sees intrapreneurs as a key determinant of future growth.

Know Themselves at the Core

Intrapreneurs are consistently developing their entrepreneurial capabilities. They chose assignments that enhance and further develop capabilities that enable them to work effectively as an entrepreneur inside an established organization. They know that self-awareness is a key attribute of successful leaders, especially entrepreneurial leaders. They are willing to take an in depth look at their own competencies and find ways to leverage their strengths and work on areas that need development.

Develop a Creative Instinct

The ability to be creative is something that intrapreneurs do naturally. They are willing to question and challenge everything around them. Just because an organization has done things one way for ever doesn't mean it makes sense today. Intrapreneurs are always asking why or why not. They take a holistic view of a situation to ensure that they see things from every angle. Just think about the rise of Uber, Airbnb, driverless cars and so on. It wasn't that the old way wasn't working. It was that there was a new, better, more efficient, or more cost-effective way. Being creative is a state of mind.

Explore Untapped Opportunities

Intrapreneurs look at every problem as an opportunity. They not only want to solve it; they want to improve it as well. They know that problems are often a sign that things are out of alignment. The context may have changed; a new strategy, a new way of doing things, the introduction of new technology, a competitive threat, change in leadership or unmet need. All these factors create problems and open new opportunities. Perhaps you've seen the commercial for UntuckIt where an entrepreneur decided to create a new men's shirt that can be worn untucked and look good at the same time just because he couldn't find one. Intrapreneurs not only see problems they find solutions.

Embrace Complexity

Today we are faced with more complexity and uncertainty than ever before. So, it is natural to want to simplify things quickly to make it easier to deal with this complexity. But intrapreneurs don't think that way. They want to linger in complexity longer. They want to look at all the options in front of them even if it is messy and overwhelming. They know that if you simplify things too quickly you may eliminate a path that may wind up being the best way forward. Intrapreneurs are willing to evaluate things more diligently before narrowing things to a few simple options. They want to be sure they select the right path forward.

Expand Their Potential

Most intrapreneurs know they can do more, be more and contribute more to their organizations. Yet many of them find themselves stuck in roles that neither challenge nor engage them at work. They know they have more potential that is not being utilized. So, they develop that potential by raising their hand to do work that others may find too risky, too difficult, or more likely to fail at. Intrapreneurs want to learn and grow and by working outside their comfort zone they can expand their own potential. In doing this intrapreneurs increase their value to themselves and the organization.

Nurture Their Inner Compass

Advances in analytics have helped organizations refine their focus, drive decisions and predict markets. But data alone does not always accurately define the playing field or identify undefined or unmet needs. Intrapreneurs rely on their knowledge and experience to guide them. They spend years exploring paths that are dead ends, experimenting with ideas, and making mistakes. Collectively these experiences build and enhance their intuition. It is a capability and ability they develop over time. Intrapreneurs know when to use data and when to rely on intuition. They develop their own internal GPS.

Test Their Assumptions

Although there are plenty of ideas floating around organizations many are not worthy of pursuit. An idea cannot stand alone. It is the context that matters and sheds light on its viability. That's why intrapreneurs versed in the 'business model canvas' will spend the time flushing out the context and test their assumptions by using this template as roadmap. Not only do they see the strengths and weaknesses of an idea through this process, they are able to get feedback and insight by sharing it with others. Intrapreneurs will explore an idea until it no longer makes sense.

Leverage Limited Resources

A recent study by PwC stated that most CEOs are planning on increasing their investments in new growth businesses which is good news. The annual budgeting process has been an effective way to secure funding and resources for ongoing operations but less so when it comes to new businesses. There never seems to be enough resources to go around. Intrapreneurs know they will need more than they are allocated but they are willing to work with what they have not what they think they need. They will beg, borrow and coop resources. Intrapreneurs will do whatever it takes with whatever they have to get things done.

Manage Risk

Despite what most people think Intrapreneurs are not risk takers. They take calculated risks. They weigh the upside and downside of a situation before deciding. They know in advance what to expect. Some intrapreneurs look at affordable loss to evaluate risk. With affordable loss you determine what are you are willing to lose in order to take a particular course of action. No matter which of these approaches they take to manage risk it is clear that Intrapreneurs understand the value of managing risk. The more effective they become at managing risk the more responsibility they get and the more challenging projects they are given. No one feels totally comfortable taking risks but there are ways to better manage risk. Intrapreneurs have found effective ways to take, manage and control risk.

Execute with Precision

Most new projects never wind up where they originally planned to be because as the project evolves so does the information you learn in the process. The target continues to shift as you gain new insights. There are course corrections, twists and turns in your thinking, roadblocks that get in the way. That's why intrapreneurs focus on the process and not the end goal. They test and experiment along the way. Each experiment brings them closer to refining the end goal. One that is more closely aligned with the real need in the market. Intrapreneurs use experimentation to help them execute with precision.

Create Value

The goal of intrapreneurial projects is to create value in terms of revenue, growth or social impact. But what is often overlooked is to understand if the project delivered the business benefits intended – to both customers and the organization. This is because most organizations do not define the business benefits, they as an organization, hope to achieve from these projects. Things like the value of leveraging a new technology, implementing a new development process, creating a more entrepreneurial work environment, developing entrepreneurial leaders etc. Intrapreneurs know that intrapreneurial projects provide as much benefit to the organization as they do to their customers.

Accelerate Learning

Intrapreneurs have a thirst for knowledge and are eager to try new things. They know that intrapreneurship is not an intellectual exercise. It comes from experience – the kind of experiences that challenge what they know and don't know. It is these experiences that ultimately build the competencies and capabilities that intrapreneurs need. No classroom can make them entrepreneurs. They need to get out there and do it. Intrapreneurs accelerate learning by building a portfolio of experiences that demonstrate that they know what to do, how to do it and how to succeed.

We've only scratched the surface of all the ways that intrapreneurs develop their entrepreneurial muscle. Perhaps you know of many more that have worked for you.

So, send us your thoughts.

Why Intrapreneurs Love Their Job

It was while building a new venture for a Fortune 100 company that one of my peers told me that I had the best job in the company. Better than the CEO or anyone else he could think of. His comments stopped me in my track's, but it made sense. Work was fun, exciting and I was having a blast. It was also challenging, frustrating and nerve racking.

It made me think about why the role of Intrapreneur is one that individuals love. That one comment from a peer started me on a journey to explore these questions. Who are these individuals? How are they different? Why do they love their job?

More importantly I wanted to find those individuals that had excelled as Intrapreneurs. Individuals that had stepped up to the role despite all the organizational obstacles that got in their way. Individuals who loved what they did, believed in what they were doing, broke through barriers, challenged the status quo and still achieved great things even without the blessing of their organizations.

It took a while to find them and sort through all the noise that surrounded Intrapreneurs. They were an enigma at the time, a hidden talent, misunderstood misfits that were disruptors in their respective organizations. They didn't know why they did what they did or even how they did what they did. It was time to unravel that mystery together. They wanted answers as much as we did.

Finding a level playing field was the first challenge. Descriptions of intrapreneurs was all over the map in the business and academic world and differed significantly from what the Intrapreneurs themselves thought. Even today there is no consensus on a common definition of what makes a good intrapreneur. There isn't a clear distinction between intrapreneurs and entrepreneurs. This led to confusion about who these individuals were.

The use of traditional predictive tools like personality, social styles, life stages, values hierarchy etc. was not detailed enough to identify or distinguish Intrapreneurs from others. It wasn't just about the way they do things it was their willingness or propensity to do it – their behaviors and competencies. So, after looking at many predictive tools we decided to focus on finding the behaviors and competencies that made intrapreneurs successful.

Then we wanted to find out if being competent in a specific set of behaviors and competences made a difference in their attitude toward work. Our goal was to determine the link between competencies, results and love of work.

We found that successful intrapreneurs thrived in environments where they could leverage a core set of competencies that enabled them to be effective in their role. A competency being a combination of skills, attitudes, knowledge, experience and behaviors that make one competent. It was the breadth and depth of those competencies that distinguished them from others. The more competent they were the more successful they were in the role and the happier they were in doing their job.

Intrapreneurs express themselves in the way they work. It's how they think and act that sets them apart from their peers. It is only when they can express themselves openly, honestly and with conviction that they are able to achieve the impossible. They need the right set of competencies, the space, time and commitment from the organization, and the freedom to manage themselves.

These are six reasons why Intrapreneurs love their job. They are also the six competencies they need to succeed.

1. Enjoy the freedom to be independent – They are independent thinkers.

2. Love to explore the unknown – They like navigating uncertainty.
3. Thrive on being challenged – They are engaged and thriving.
4. Embrace and revel in change – They drive change.
5. Like to stretch and reach their potential – They are effective leaders.
6. Seek to bring things to closure – They are high on execution.

If these are the key things that make Intrapreneurs love their job, why aren't more organizations providing employees with the opportunity to express themselves in this way. Why aren't they developing the competencies that are needed for intrapreneurs to succeed?

When was the last time you heard someone say they loved their job? I suspect the answer is rarely or never. You might be right. We've all heard the statistics that over seventy percent of employees are disengaged at work.

Intrapreneurs are highly engaged at work in organizations that acknowledge and support Intrapreneurs. They are more productive and innovative then their peers. They create higher value and financial results. Intrapreneurs are also disenchanted in organizations that do not provide an opportunity for them to develop their capabilities as an Intrapreneur. They are often the squeaky wheel, the naysayer, the person most likely to question a decision.

These two descriptors – engaged and disenchanted – are the first two places to look to find your own intrapreneurs. One is happy at work, the other is not.

It seems that work today is still predicated on the past not the future. That's why we developed the Intrapreneur Scorecard to help individuals and organizations identify and develop the new competencies that are needed for Intrapreneurs to thrive and succeed.

We felt it was time that companies proactively identify intrapreneurs so that they can thrive and make a bigger and more valuable contribution to themselves and their organizations.

Being competent in a role is predicated on defining the competencies that are needed to be successful in that role. Then getting out of the way. Only then can one truly say they love their job.

Make Intrapreneurship a Priority in Your Organization

A proliferation of articles state that the key to intrapreneurship is building an innovative and entrepreneurial culture. Yet we know that nearly 70% of all change initiatives fail.

There is no doubt that intrapreneurship requires a magnitude shift in thinking and action that will not be embraced by most individuals in organizations.

It requires a strong leader to drive that change, to make it stick and integrate it into the fabric of the organization. This takes time, patience, a strong will and determination. Not only on the part of management but on the part of the individuals engaged in the process.

There is no safety net, no turning back, there is only moving forward toward something unknown, uncertain and ambiguous.

So even if Intrapreneurship is a priority in your organization the elements that enable it must be in place to deliver on it. Ask yourself these questions:

- Is your organizations strategy aligned with the resources and metrics needed to drive growth?
- Is your organization developing the intrapreneurial competencies needed for success?
- Are the systems and processes in place to support and sustain intrapreneurship over time?
- Is the culture one that is conducive to intrapreneurship, learning, growth and failure?
- How innovative, pro-active and risk tolerant are the leaders and employees in your company?
- Are the innovation goals and outcomes of the organization clear, practical and achievable?
- Is there support and ongoing commitment from the Board and senior leaders?
- Is there a focus on profit and purpose for the near and long term?

These are the things that provide a window into the level of commitment your organization has for Intrapreneurship. Not all of these must be in place but most of them should be in place for you to have a chance to succeed. If they are not, then they will ultimately become barriers and obstacles to your success.

It is up to you as the Intrapreneur to evaluate the degree to which your organization has embraced intrapreneurship and for you to determine the amount of effort required to shift not only your thinking but the organizations as well.

According to Barry Dym in his article, Integrating Entrepreneurship and Professional Leadership he states that, ""*One of the major reasons that organizational transitions falter is that leaders do not anticipate and account for uncertainty and difficulty that change brings to the entrepreneurial journey.* It is an iterative process of discovery and learning. Your goal may be clear but your path to achieving it is not. Where you intend to wind up and where you wind up are not always the same.

This is compounded by the fact that change is happening at a faster rate. All businesses are being impacted by the accelerated pace of change. The rapid pace of change makes acceleration a critical part of everything we do. Like a runner, it is not enough to be running fast, you must be running faster over time. Organizations need to be moving faster in a world that is increasingly more complex and uncertain. Change will not happen until someone steps up and drives change.

According to Louis Carter, "*Leading change in an organization requires changing one's self first, then the individual team members, the team and then the organization.*"

Intrapreneurship is all about change and transformation. So, if change and transformation are not a strategic focus for your organization then Intrapreneurship is probably not a priority.

If you look at the things that need to be in place for Intrapreneurship to thrive from this list, you will clearly understand the challenge you face as an Intrapreneur. These are organizational issues that must be addressed to support Intrapreneurship. It is up to you to drive the change that is needed. Do what it takes to enable intrapreneurship to happen despite the potential obstacles that get in the way. This is all about changing the organizational infrastructure and culture – organizational transformation.

All this starts by first changing yourself and then those around you. Changing the way, you think, act, make decisions, communicate, negotiate, influence, motivate, inspire and solicit support. You demonstrate it through your work, attitude, energy, drive and engagement. You then enable others to try new things, explore the unknown, take bigger risks, and push themselves beyond their own limiting beliefs. You show empathy and support through listening and understanding. You become a role model for them to follow and emulate. This is the other side of the equation – individual transformation.

Intrapreneurship can only become a priority when there are individuals willing to rise to the challenge and understand that nothing happens until individuals collectively pursue a strategy of change and transformation.

As an intrapreneur it is incumbent upon you to understand that the old rules no longer apply. They are a relic of the past. According to McKinsey's Recovery and Transformation Services Group, "*The most difficult part of transforming performance isn't determining what to do but rather how to do it.*" This is the ultimate challenge and opportunity for Intrapreneurs.

Making Intrapreneurship a priority is up to you and those around you that see a better way, a better future for your organization.

Future Prospect for Intrapreneurship

The question on the minds of many Intrapreneurs around the world is whether the new normal will include Intrapreneurship or push it aside. Will there be room for Intrapreneurs to help create a new future or will economic concerns diminish their role.

It may depend on your perspective – how you see the world and your reaction to it.

Intrapreneurship has survived for decades through various economic cycles. It will in this one. But only if Intrapreneurs seize the moment. There is no better time to be an Intrapreneur.

According to Michael Page, ADAPT Global Recruiting, "Intrapreneurship is the #1 workplace skill for 2020." We do not know if his comment is in response to the current economic climate or despite it. Either way it is a wake up-up call to individuals and organizations that we can no longer rely on the past. We must create a new future, a new normal, a different way of operating, a new way of being.

The pandemic has forced change on all of us. There is no going back. People who may have resisted change were forced to change, had to accept that change and deal with that change. Like it or not. For the first time many people can see what change looks like, feels like, and they can see their own reaction to it. They experienced extreme change. It is through these types of events that we see how well we respond to uncertainty, complexity and the unknown.

Ask yourself how well you have dealt with the current situation? What did you think, what did you do, how did you feel? Did you just let things happen to you or did you take charge and find new ways to cope with the situation? Did you sit back and wait until things became clearer before acting or did you find a new path forward? What are you doing that is different than what you did before? When did you realize that you had to leave behind many things that you have always known to be true?

A key capability of Intrapreneurs is their ability to deal effectively with uncertainty, complexity and the unknown. They do it all the time. It is what drives them, excites them, and motivates them. It is who they are. Change seems to come naturally to Intrapreneurs, but it was not always that way. They learned to cope with change through their own personal and professional experiences. Change is a learned experience. It is only when you became competent in something (like adapting to change) can you embrace it and eventually feel confident in driving change.

The question about the future prospect for Intrapreneurship may rest in what individuals and organizations have learned from this event and how they apply those lessons learned moving forward.

We have already seen organizations move to a virtual workforce, meetings, webinars, seminars, and conferences. A move that has changed the way organizations conduct business but is it sustainable, effective, productive, and profitable. What impact is it having on employees, customers, stakeholders, and supply chains. Does it fill a short-term need or support a longer-term business model? Think about it. Organizations were forced to change they did not proactively change.

We know that systems and processes have had to change to accommodate the new normal but what about people? Will we see a change in their behavior, their reaction to change, their willingness to try new things, take calculated risks, experiment, and find creative ways forward? I suspect that there will be mixed results.

We may not yet know how this situation has impacted workers. We can see the short-term response but may not know the longer-term impact. Individuals are facing many of the same issues as their organizations – is it sustainable, effective, productive, or profitable to work from home. Workers are spending all day in Zoom meetings, conference calls, or staring at computer screens. They too have been forced to change. For the first time they are now able to step back and look at their work, their organizations and themselves. They know they are facing the harsh reality of a new world order and may be questioning their role in it.

It is for all these reasons that Intrapreneurship is a way forward for both individuals and organizations. For organizations it is a new way of operating that provides significant value – higher levels of innovation, productivity, employee engagement and financial returns. For individuals it is a new model of working that keeps workers – engaged, creative, productive, and valued. We know however, that it is not as easy as that.

Intrapreneurship is all about change and change is all about people. Until we see a change in behavior on the part of individuals and organizations Intrapreneurship will only be a future desire not a new business model.

It seems obvious that things need to change but we know that change does not come easy in large established organizations. Organizations will see the situation as something to fix. Intrapreneurs will see it as an opportunity to create. It will be up to Intrapreneurs to drive change, manage change, and enable others to change if we expect to see progress come out of this crisis.

The biggest challenge Intrapreneurs have faced in the past is resistance to change. Will there be more tolerance for change, more openness to try new things or will organizations tighten things down and fall back to doing it the old way. Will organizations focus on economic recovery or talent recovery? Will they factor in what is best for humanity or the bottom line? Will they operate out of fear, anxiety, frustration, and despair or will they see hope, opportunity, optimism, resilience, and potential. I think the answer will be easy to see once things begin to open back up.

The future of Intrapreneurship may rest with the answers to these questions.

Chapter 8: Challenges

- Challenges Facing Intrapreneurs
- Resistance to Change the #1 Challenge
- Struggle for Legitimacy
- 6 Stakeholders Committed to Your Idea
- Roadblocks Intrapreneurs Face Driving Change
- 20 Insights from Successful Intrapreneurs
- Moving Forward, No Turning Back
- The Last Frontier for Intrapreneurs

Challenges Facing Intrapreneurs

One of the greatest challenges facing Intrapreneurs is finding an organization that has the entrepreneurial mindset and infrastructure to support what they do and how they do it.

Organizations think they know what it takes to be entrepreneurial. *In truth they don't.*

Entrepreneurship for many organizations is etched in words, not actions. The intent is there, it is the entrepreneurial leadership and operational support that is missing.

This makes it more difficult for Intrapreneurs to succeed. They must not only deal with the nuances of building a new business, they must also deal with the obstacles that the current operating environment puts in their way.

Intrapreneurs often find themselves trapped in organizations that claim they are entrepreneurial when in fact they are not. Finding an organization that truly embraces entrepreneurship or intrapreneurship is difficult. *Knowing what to look for is critical.*

To help organizations determine how entrepreneurial there are we developed the Entrepreneurial Audit – Self Assessment. *The Self-Assessment* is a 10-question survey that enables you to rate your company on entrepreneurship and see what things may be getting in the way.

Most organizations see themselves as they would like to be not necessarily how they are. When it comes to being entrepreneurial – an organizations perception is often far from reality.

Organizations from over 27 countries have taken the Entrepreneurial Audit – Self-Assessment to find out if their organizations are entrepreneurial or just think they are. The reality is that only 40% of these organizations were entrepreneurial.

The data from the entrepreneurial audit also revealed several constraints that impacted the level of entrepreneurship in an organization.

- Only 35% of organizations encourage entrepreneurial behavior.
- Only 42% give employees extra time to pursue short- and longer-term ideas.

- Only 44% provide the decision-making latitude, freedom and authority to test new ideas.
- Only 44% say their managers are willing to take bold actions to achieve objectives.
- Only 47% clearly define employee roles, set expectations and align performance metrics.

All of these are key ingredients that support entrepreneurial thought and action. According to Wolcott and Lippitz authors of Grow from Within: Mastering Corporate Entrepreneurship and Innovation, "*The most often mentioned elements shaping innovation in companies were the constraints and gaps derived from factors internal to the company.*" These constraints can impact the development of entrepreneurship.

Most interesting was the fact that there was a clear distinction between perception and reality at the strategic, operational and individual level. The perception at the top is that there is a distinct growth strategy with clear objectives that support entrepreneurship. The reality at the operational level is that even with clear objectives, managers are reluctant to take risks and make bold and wide-ranging decisions. At the individual level the reality is that employees are not given the tools and decision-making authority they need to develop and test their ideas.

Perception and reality are at odds when it comes to entrepreneurship. Being entrepreneurial takes more than strategic alignment it requires having the right people, processes and culture to support it.

Finding out how entrepreneurial an organization is can be a good way for Intrapreneurs to understand why they may or may not feel like they fit in their organization. It is also a useful way to evaluate an organization that you are considering joining.

Intrapreneurs are more effective if they are given the tools and infrastructure, they need to enable them to do what they do best, drive new business growth. The more quickly we match Intrapreneurs to organizations that have instituted entrepreneurship, the sooner we will get business growing again.

Is corporate entrepreneurship a perception or a reality in your organization?

Resistance to Change the #1 Challenge

Resistance to change was the number one challenge that intrapreneurs and social intrapreneurs told us was holding them back. Despite the progress many of them were making in their respective organizations. They felt that resistance created the biggest obstacle to their success.

These were some of challenges they mentioned.

- Resistance to new ideas and innovation
- Driving change in a hierarchical organization
- Resistance from senior executives about the changes that need to be made
- People who refuse to accept change
- Resistance, jealousy and misunderstanding
- Steering change with shared responsibility
- Resistance to change from team members
- Getting required changes onto the priority list

Why do we resist change? According to the article Effective Skills of Change Agents, *"Individuals and organizations do not resist change; they resist disturbances to their frame of reference caused by change."*

The reality perceived by each individual is filtered by their own frame of reference – their attitudes, expectations, behaviors, emotions, beliefs, values, habits, past experience, education, social styles and so on. Resistance comes from asking people to change their frame of reference.

- What are you asking them to change?
- How many things are you asking them to change?
- What impact will the change have on them?

Organizations also have a frame of reference. The extent to which you are asking an individual or organization to change their frame of reference is related to the level of resistance to that change. You are asking them to revise their vision of themselves.

Understanding these things is the first step to dealing with resistance to change.

The challenge is the unlearning and relearning that must occur for change to happen. This includes unlearning attitudes, beliefs, and values that are part of the very fabric of the organization. It requires building new attitudes, beliefs and values that support more entrepreneurial thought and action. Change occurs at the individual, team and organizational level – often one person at a time.

Intrapreneurship is all about change. Changing everything!

- Changing the way people think and act
- Changing the way, the organization operates
- Changing the culture

The goal of intrapreneurship is to build the capabilities that enable organizations to respond to change.

More than ever organizations are under pressure to create new business growth. This need requires the ability and readiness to embrace change. It is a dynamic and ongoing process. Embedding change in the organization leads to growth. Resistance impedes that growth.

Change is one of the most underdeveloped skills in organizations. Approximately seventy percent of all new change initiatives fail. It is multi-dimensional and touches every aspect of the organization. It deals with the soft skills and requires an understanding of human systems. It requires a shift in thinking and behavior. It challenges traditional business practices and processes. It changes the balance of power and politics. It requires rethinking how the organization operates and what it stands for.

So, it is not surprising that intrapreneurs encounter so much resistance.

Individuals and organizations must go through the change process. It takes time, commitment and perseverance. Change is both a process and an outcome. The process is designed to facilitate the change and the outcome is the results you hope to achieve from the change.

Faced with a change we all tend to have selective perception – we only see the positive side of the current situation and the weaknesses of the proposed change. It is up to the intrapreneur to get everyone to understand the positive aspects of the change. Managing resistance requires getting individuals and organizations to reframe their view of themselves. Not an easy task!

Change is a powerful force that changes the dynamics of an organization. An organization needs to change if it wants to grow.

Intrapreneurs are leading change in their organizations despite the resistance they encounter.

How are you dealing with resistance to change?

Struggle for Legitimacy

All entrepreneurial efforts inside organizations encounter resistance. It is how you deal with it that can make the difference between success and failure.

Even though the CEO and corporation have sanctioned the new initiative, the rest of the organization may be slow to embrace it. The organization may understand the need for the new initiative intellectually, but often they can't accept it emotionally.

A Fortune 500 information services company was developing a new online service that would leapfrog their products ahead of their competitors. Although the CEO supported the new initiative the rest of the organization dragged its feet. Apparently, the company had tried developing a similar service a year before that had failed. Organizational resistance would be huge. The new service was designed to leverage assets across five divisions. Gaining cooperation across organizational boundaries would be a nightmare. It was clear that the project team would have to go it alone until they could get others on board.

Although the CEO had established legitimacy for the project by sanctioning the funds needed to develop the new service there was a question about how much more he would be willing to invest. It wasn't the investment that worried the President of the division responsible for the project it was the resistance that he encountered from his peers and the rest of the organization. Moving the company into the future would be difficult as jobs, divisions and power structures within the organization were being disrupted.

Despite all the resistance the team continued to move forward in developing a state of art product that was years ahead of their competitors. They engaged the organizations largest clients in the development effort and built a strong pipeline of prospective customers. It was clear that customers were excited about the prospects of this new service. Not only would it be a valuable resource for them, they saw it as opportunity to leverage this new service with their own clients.

At that point the momentum was so strong that the rest of the organization realized that the train had already left the station. Either they get on board or they would be left behind. Slowly they began to cooperate and engage in the development effort. It was only then that they saw how this one service not only moved the company forward it was providing a new platform that the rest of the organization could use to upgrade their services. The team had finally achieved legitimacy for the new service.

By its very nature a new business initiative, product, or service consumes precious resources and introduces changes that threaten the stability of the existing organization. As a result, you may find that you are *swimming upstream* against an entrenched culture that does not welcome the change.

Establishing legitimacy is part of the process and part of the problem. On one hand, you realize that you need the cooperation and support of other parts of the organization to accomplish your objectives. On the other hand, you realize that the rest of the organization may be silently hoping that you fail, so cooperation is slow and painful. The trick is to find ways to deal with the resistance that will inevitably arise when you are trying to establish legitimacy for your project and your people.

The best way to establish legitimacy is to get traction and show momentum. Often the very fact that you are making progress gets others to understand that you are going to do this with or without them. Eventually they begin to realize that the probability of this initiative succeeding is increasing, and their initial resistance may be viewed negatively. In other situations, you will need the political clout of the sponsor or CEO.

Recognize that it is often necessary to find viable alternatives to support your efforts, even if it requires going outside the organization. Always factor this into your planning. This may not be standard practice within your organization, so include it when establishing parameters with sponsors and the CEO.

The team must do its part in establishing legitimacy as well. Give them the tools and support to deal with resistance. Motivate the team to be creative about getting around organizational obstacles. They will need to challenge assumptions, suspend judgment and look for viable alternatives. The team will need to set the stage for collaboration.

Focus on developing competencies that will come in handy, like influence and negotiating skills. Influence will be the key to gaining acceptance of your ideas. Understanding the best way to influence different types of people is something you can learn. Knowing who the key players are that can influence the outcome may be just as important. Negotiating for a firmly held position may be difficult if the organization has not embraced what you are doing. You may find that you are not bargaining from a position of strength. Linking your position to broader organizational goals may help. Having good influencing and negotiating skills will be invaluable.

You will find that legitimacy alone is not enough. Gaining legitimacy is the first step to acceptance and support. Expectations will have to be met to preserve and sustain legitimacy over time.

What obstacles have you encountered when trying to establish legitimacy for your entrepreneurial project?

6 Stakeholders Committed to Your Idea

Intrapreneurs often struggle with getting their ideas firmly grounded in the organization. The initial euphoria of a new product or service can quickly be replaced by a deafening silence.

It is natural for senior management to get excited about the project in the beginning and lose interest over time. The CEO has one perspective, sponsors have their own interest, your team another, the rest of the organization something else. The key is making sure everyone fully understands the idea and stays committed to it.

A great idea gets better if you shape it and enhance it along the way. Often the initial idea is the starting point for an even greater idea. It is normal for the team to shape and mold the product as it evolves. By soliciting feedback from various stakeholders and acting on them, you strengthen commitment to your idea. Feedback and commitment move the idea forward.

Ideas take shape in the context of a vision. Once it takes root in the hearts and minds of others, then it takes on a life of its own. Everyone will have their own interpretation of what you mean, and they will see it from their specific vantage point. Each of these views is important, not only in shaping the idea but in giving you a clear understanding of what people think it is.

As the idea evolves, so will people's interpretation and expectation of what it is designed to do or deliver to the organization. You will want to make sure that everyone sees the same thing.

Belief in an idea is what gives it life. It grounds it. If you believe in something, you have a conviction that it is true, but believing in an idea does not make it true. A firm conviction will be needed to move your idea forward. If you do not believe in it, you will not convince others of its worthiness. Belief in your idea is a key part of making it so. An idea that is grounded in belief has a longer shelf life than one that isn't. It buys you time to see if the idea has merit.

Getting others to believe in your idea is what is ultimately important. The more people who believe in the idea, the more momentum you will build around it. People will provide additional input that will mold and shape the idea into something bigger and better. As they do, their belief and commitment to an idea will grow.

Getting commitment and keeping it is up to you. Here are 6 stakeholders you must convince.

1. **CEO**: CEO commitment to the project only goes so far. Keeping your project alive in the CEO's mind will depend on his or her ability to clearly and consistently understand its longer-term value to the organization. Getting him or her involved in the development of the idea will be helpful but keeping that commitment alive and strong will be up to you.

2. **Sponsor**: Your sponsor will have a vested interest in keeping close tabs on your progress. Their commitment is often a reflection of what it means to them personally or professionally. Understand why this project is important to them. Make sure that you are in alignment with their interests. Their needs and yours are different.

3. **Team**: The commitment of the team is grounded in something deeper. They are committed to the idea. The commitment to the idea brings them together but their own personal and professional aspirations drive them. They are looking for meaning and making a difference. They want to stretch and grow. They see it as an opportunity to do something new and exciting. Their ongoing commitment is dependent on their ability to see the project as a vehicle to help them experience those things.

4. **Organization:** Commitment from the rest of the organization is up for grabs. You will not know until you move forward. On one hand, they will have plenty of ideas about what you should do. On the other, they will be the first to dismiss the idea. Yet they can often be the ones to help you shape it into something that is more suitable for the realities of the organization and the markets it serves. Getting

them to share them with you will be the best way to understand their commitment.

5. **Salesperson:** Get your salespeople involved from the beginning. They are on the front line and understand the customer the best. They are an excellent source of input into the idea. They are also your best critic. They have a finger on the pulse on the customer and can quickly determine if something will fly or not. They will be committed to helping you if it furthers their goals. You biggest hurdle and strongest ally will be sales. Get your support people involved because they can identify a potential issue before it arises.

6. **Customers:** Internal feedback is good, but external feedback is better. Be sure that your customers are part of your feedback loop. As the product evolves, give them an opportunity to shape it as well. Feedback and commitment go hand in hand. Integrating feedback will help shape and mold the idea into something bigger and better than first envisioned. Commitment is developed by including stakeholders in the process.

Belief and commitment are a powerful force that will attract others to your idea. Doubt will do just the opposite. Be sure that all your stakeholders are on board.

In one situation Mark, an experienced intrapreneur, was hired by a Fortune 500 company to build a brand-new business for the organization. He had met with everyone involved in the project including the EVP who was the sponsor before joining. It was clear that there was real excitement and commitment to building this new business. Although the initial investment fell far short of what was needed to build the business Mark realized that as the project evolved so would the investment in it.

On his first week on the job Mark had a chance to meet with the CEO who had stopped by his boss's office. Mark was introduced and proceeded to tell the CEO what he would be doing. The CEO looked at Mark and quietly said, "*If it ever see's the light of day.*" Later that week word came down that only half of the initial investment would be available. Mark hadn't realized that the only stakeholder not on board was the CEO.

It is incumbent upon you to get and keep all stakeholders committed to your idea.

What do you do to ensure that your stakeholders stay committed to an idea?

Roadblocks Intrapreneurs Face Driving Change

The last few years have been a stark reminder that business as usual is not working. The need for change is greater than it has ever been before. The pace of change is accelerating, and we must change or be changed.

According to Talent Magazine, *"For today's leaders the greatest imperative is leading change."*

Two factors driving change in today's business climate are the need to generate new business growth and attracting and retaining the best and brightest talent. When we think about growth, we must remember that we are talking about change. When we talk about talent, intrapreneurs are the engines of that growth. Talent, growth and change are inevitably tied together.

Change should not be something that happens to you, but something you control. You might not be able to control everything, but you can learn to manage change. Yet, change remains one of the most underdeveloped competencies in most organizations. Due in part to the roadblocks that get in the way.

Intrapreneurs are often referred to as agents of change but what exactly does that mean and what does it take to drive change. We will explore what it takes to drive change, why intrapreneurs struggle to drive change and things Intrapreneurs can do to be more effective agents of change.

You don't need to be an executive or CEO to be an agent of change. You need to have the courage to make change happen. It takes entrepreneurial thinking and action to be effective.

Intrapreneurs that are effective change agents exhibit the following:

- A willingness to take on the toughest challenges.
- They look at every situation as an opportunity to grow.
- They accept the consequences for their actions.
- They are flexible, adaptable and open to change.
- They see the world as it could be not as it is.

Intrapreneurs seek out challenges. The bigger, the tougher the challenge the better. They push themselves to do more. They have an innate desire to learn and grow and they are willing to accept the consequences of their actions. They push beyond the limits of their own understanding. Intrapreneurs understand that the business world is rapidly changing so they are willing to be flexible and adaptable.

Once Intrapreneurs experience one of these projects they now believe that anything is possible. They can envision a different way, a different path and so they seek to achieve it. They demonstrate through their behavior what it takes to make change happen.

The most effective path to change is not always quick or easy but it needs to be change that sticks and therein lies the problem. There are several roadblocks that Intrapreneurs face and struggle to overcome. Here are a few of those roadblocks.

Finding Balance

In any intrapreneurial project there are two opposing forces at work that create tension and conflict. The forces trying to maintain the status quo and those trying to change it. The core business and the new business you are building. Organizations have a good handle on what is required in the core business but less so when building a new one. Many of the things done in the core business are just the opposite of what is required to build a new one.

Organizations must cultivate an entrepreneurial mindset while maintaining a balance between the core business and the growth business. There is a need to guide and control entrepreneurial action. The only way to do that is to understand the inherent conflict between these two forces. This is the paradox of intrapreneurship. It is a two-way street.

Intrapreneurs are responsible for balancing these not the organization. They have one foot in both worlds. They live in a world of contrasts. Being loyal on one hand and independent on the other. Collaborative and competitive, poised and passionate, tough minded and empathic, factual and intuitive. This is what makes all the difference. It is this ability to co-exist in both these worlds that sets them apart from others. They have the breadth and depth to understand that it is a balancing act.

Finding the right balance is a critical aspect of driving change. Only then will you find it easier to make change happen.

People, Process or Culture

The current debate in the business and academic world is whether people, process or culture is most important when it comes to driving change. Seventy percent of organizations think process alone will drive intrapreneurship. Most organizations have an innovation process, yet most new innovations fail. A process can provide discipline and structure, but it can't anticipate or navigate obstacles. It isn't until you are in a process that you understand what needs to be tweaked or replaced. It isn't the process but the people behind the process that make those decisions.

Champions, mavericks and intrapreneurs are known for their ability to push their ideas through to implementation. Their raw determination can make the impossible, possible. It is their belief in what they are doing; their commitment to a project, their ability to be independent, deal with ambiguity, navigate obstacles and bring things to closure that makes the difference. They provide the energy, motivation and drive. It is their actions that move the project and the organization forward.

Creating an entrepreneurial culture lays the foundation for changing organizational behavior. Change however takes time, energy and commitment that most organizations don't have. A recent study by BCG found that 75% of all change initiatives fail to achieve their objectives. Change requires a shift in thinking and behavior, a role model to guide the way

All three of these elements, people, process and culture, are important but the common thread that runs through all of them are people. Change happens when people change and when people change cultures change.

Changing process is not sustainable over the long term. Yet we continue to see organizations start with process or structure to try to make change happen. For change to be sustainable you must change how people think and act.

Change will only happen once you've changed behavior at the individual and organizational level.

Earning the Right

A key hurdle that most Intrapreneurs encounter is not having the freedom and flexibility to make change happen. Intrapreneurs must earn the right. Being an intrapreneur is not an intellectual exercise it is all about the experience. The more experience you get as an intrapreneur the more success you can achieve. There is a quote that says, "Success breeds success" and when it comes to Intrapreneurs that is a key that unlocks the door to driving change.

Intrapreneurs must demonstrate success before they are given the freedom to make change happen. The type of success doesn't matter it is the visibility and recognition that one achieves from that success that gives you the freedom you will need. The higher the visibility in the organization the better. It is all about building the clout and political capital you need to drive change.

Even if you are just starting out, you must earn the right. Every intrapreneur must build a portfolio of skills and capabilities that enable them to be successful. It all depends on the work you sign up for and the challenges you take on. Playing it safe is not the way to build the skills that will be needed. What you need is to find an opportunity to develop and demonstrate your intrapreneurial capabilities.

Individuals that are more intrapreneurial will develop their own capabilities through their work. They earn the right and are then given the freedom to drive change.

Communication Gap

Communication is one of the biggest roadblocks to change especially when it comes to dealing with executives. My inference is that for many executive's innovation and intrapreneurship are concepts that are not fully understood. Due in part to the fact that intrapreneurship is something you learn through experience and few executives participate in these types of efforts. Without experience it is often hard to imagine something if you have not been actively involved in it, believed in or were passionate about it. Executives intellectually understand innovation and intrapreneurship but there isn't a head/heart connection.

This makes it difficult for individuals who are not intrapreneurs to see what you say. They may hear what you are saying but not internalize it. That makes it hard to get your points across in a way that they understand. Part of the communication issue is listening to understand not trying to sell or influence them. Until you understand their perspective, they won't try to understand yours. Finding the gaps in understanding is the first step to better communications.

You won't convince everyone but looking at change through their perspective is a good way to begin to get others to see why the change you are advocating is a positive step forward.

Managing the Valley of Despair

Every project goes through its own life cycle. One day the project is going well, the next day it is not. Individuals and teams working on these types of projects find themselves on a roller coaster. At each step individuals feel differently, and they act differently depending on where they are in the cycle. It's all about breaking away from the old systems and embracing the new.

Most intrapreneurial projects go through what I call the Valley of Despair. At the beginning of a project everyone is excited and energized. They reality sets in and things slow down. The excitement is replaced with pressure and stress. The team runs up against roadblocks. They realize that they have signed up to do something that now seems impossible. The pressure is too much for some. Some go back to the core business; others will leave the company. Holding the team together at this point is a challenge. The team will have to regroup and get back on track.

Eventually the team will begin to build back momentum, turn the corner, and climb out of the valley of despair. The team has created a new way of working, new systems and processes to support them. You are asking them to let go of what is familiar, grounded and stable and grab onto something fragile, shaky and unproven. They have made the transition and have broken away from the core business. They are personally and professionally changed by the experience. They will look back at the core business and see it in a new light. They will see what is now possible.

Going through the valley of despair is part of the process. It will test your patience and resolve. There is no turning back, only going forward. That's how change happens.

Dealing with Resistance

Resistance to change is the number one challenge that Intrapreneurs tell us is holding them back. Despite the progress many of them are making in their respective organizations they feel that resistance is the biggest obstacle to their success. It raises the issue of why we resist change.

Each person's reality is filtered by their own frame of reference. – their attitudes, expectations, behaviors, emotions, beliefs, values, habits, experience, education, social styles and so on.

Resistance comes from asking people to change their frame of reference. What are you asking them to change? How many things are you asking them to change? What impact will the change have on them? Organizations also have a frame of reference. The extent to which you are asking an individual or organization to change their frame of reference is related to the level of resistance to that change. You are asking them to revise their vision of themselves.

The challenge is unlearning and relearning new attitudes, beliefs, and values that support more entrepreneurial thought and action. Change occurs at the individual, then the team and eventually the organizational level – often one person at a time.

Overcoming Barriers

Intrapreneurs encounter a host of barriers, some are obvious – many are hidden. You are creating something new, something that may never have been done before. You will run up against things that the organization has not had to deal with before. You are on your own. You will need to do whatever it takes to get from strategy to execution.

Everything in the organization is a potential barrier. You won't know what they are until you encounter them. Along the way you will run into a myriad of things; things that impede your progress like shifting priorities, processes that don't support you like budgeting systems, policies like long approval processes, cultures where things are done a certain way, or people who are more interested in seeing your project fail then succeed.

Like organizational barriers, there are individual barriers as well. Being an intrapreneur is not easy, you will often find yourself swimming upstream against the tide, you will feel alone, doubt yourself, question what you are doing. The individual barriers include a lack of self-awareness of your own strengths and weaknesses, knowing how you collect, evaluate and process information, or having the right types of experiences that make you stop, reflect and shift your views.

These are some of the organizational and individual barriers that can get in your way. Some things will need to be tweaked, changed or replaced. We've identified over ninety organizational barriers so far that can potentially get in your way. What is important is how you deal with them.

Navigating barriers and dealing with them when they occur is how change happens. It's not about what you do, it's about the fact that you do something about it. Nothing happens until something changes.

Execution

Execution is a learned experience. It is a process that is driven by the decisions and actions that are taken to move a project forward. The measure of success for any project is not whether it was delivered on time or on budget but whether it delivered value. Creating value is the key to growth and change is required to achieve that growth.

Execution is not an event but an integral part of the development process. It is a complex set of interrelated variables that must come together perfectly to achieve precision. Precision in execution begins with a clear understand of the end goal and the intended business benefits.

Clarity of vision is one end of the spectrum; execution is at the other. Visions take on a life of their own. As the project evolves the vision will shift and so will the process for getting there. The project itself will change as you integrate new ideas and new learning into it. It isn't a straight line from point A to point B. There are plenty of twists and turns. The target will shift and change many times throughout the project. There must be the flexibility to change course when it is necessary or kill a project when it no longer makes sense.

Most entrepreneurial efforts never actually wind up where they initially intended because they cannot account for all the variables that will get in the way. You can't anticipate everything, but you can deal with contingencies. Setting and resetting expectations will be an ongoing process because the process itself will change and everything around will be in a constant state of flux. So, it is not surprising that three out of five organizations consider themselves weak when it comes to execution.

As in intrapreneur it is incumbent upon you to stay on top of that change, manage it and lead it if you hope to hit the target. The goal is to maximize the value you deliver to clients and the organization.

Flying Blind

Years ago, I took my team to an outbound facility in the woods for a team building exercise. When we got to the high wire beam, I asked the instructor for a blind fold. It seemed that it would be easier, less fearful, to not look down from the fifty-foot height. Someone on the ground would be guiding me verbally. Well, suddenly everyone on my team wanted a blind fold not for the same reasons as me but for having the courage to try it flying blind.

Why is this important and what does it have to do with being an intrapreneur and driving change – a lot. Most of the time intrapreneurs are flying blind without a net.

It is not only that you are flying blind, but you must consciously keep yourself focused forward. Not letting the noise and chaos around you distract you. You are on a mission and you need to move forward. At times alone or as a team. The rest of the organization may not understand what you are doing, how you are doing it or even why you are doing it. You may be asking yourself the same things. You are creating the change as you move through it.

It isn't until you are on the other side that you will see what you have accomplished or what you have achieved or what amount of change was required to get there. That is why being an Intrapreneur is not easy. It is one of the most challenging and rewarding.

Perhaps you don't need to go around the office with a blind fold on, but you may want to keep your eyes closed at times to avoid all noise and chaos around you only to see in your mind what is possible. Change happens when you can take an idea that seems impossible and turn it into what's possible.

These are only a few of the roadblocks that you will encounter along the way. It is only a roadblock if you let it stop you.

Think about what Randy Pausch said in his speech, The Last Lecture, *"The brick walls are there for a reason. The brick walls are not there to keep us out. The brick walls are there to give us a chance to see how badly we want something. Because the brick walls are not there to stop the people who don't want it badly enough. They're there to stop the other people."*

20 Insights from Successful Intrapreneurs

We spoke with senior executives who had built million- and billion-dollar businesses for their organizations. They shared with us some of the insights and lessons learned from those experiences and they spoke about the challenges and obstacles that got in their way.

A number of these executives were new to the role and didn't see themselves as an entrepreneur or entrepreneurial leader inside their organization. But they were....

In fact, many of them were way ahead of their time. They not only paved the way for all the corporate entrepreneurs, intrapreneurs and social innovators that followed, they laid the foundation for understanding intrapreneurship from an insider's perspective.

They spoke with us about the issues that stifled innovation and entrepreneurship inside their organization. As well as the things that enabled them to be successful in their role.

Here are a few of their insights and lessons learned that they shared with us.

Entrepreneurial Leader: "Our CEO was a corporate entrepreneur. He was an innovator willing to take financial risks for longer term gains, even though we took a loss in the short term."

Strategic Goals: "The new CEO championed the project because it helped him achieve his innovation goals. You need a champion who is visionary and entrepreneurial."

Executive Sponsor: "Executives were interested in the project only if there was political gain in it for them. They were not willing to put their professional career on the line if they did not think it would succeed."

Political Capital: "In our organization the CEO was the good cop, the project sponsor the bad cop. The CEO gave us political capital, the sponsor a dose of reality. We needed both to keep things moving."

Fuse to Short: "The pocketbook was too shallow for what we were doing. The company was looking at this project as an expense not an investment."

Operating Model: "The existing operating model was not good for the new initiative, so we had to work around it. The issue was breaking down stovepipes and leveraging existing expertise in new ways, a task that even the most astute find challenging."

Power: "Power and politics began to rear its ugly head and soon became an anchor that slowed us down. The politics surrounding our project were huge. They extended way beyond what was visible on the surface."

Operating Committee: "Decisions were made at the operating committee. We had to present a solid case for the new product. Despite pressure to put money back in operations the CEO would intervene and allocate funds to new projects."

Right Environment: "The right environment for corporate entrepreneurship includes funding, freedom, top management support and a global agenda. The company must have the appetite for this type of project for it to be successful."

Change Agenda: "Our CEO made it clear that the train was leaving the station and that the company was going to change. His commitment and the support of senior management were critical for paving the way to make change happen. It reinforced our mission."

Measurements: "The existing measurements and metrics didn't work for what we were doing. We needed to develop new measurements to track and monitor our progress."

Being Entrepreneurial: "Large companies don't want people to be entrepreneurial. In most companies there is no career future for corporate entrepreneurs."

Independent Agent: "Eventually I got a reputation as an independent agent. Organizations don't know how to deal with independent people."

Resentment: "We were getting all the attention, funding and resources. We were the rising stars; I think we were a threat to the rest of the organization. They were not supportive, so we had to find ways to do it on our own."

Self-Awareness: "These types of initiatives force you to see what you are made of, your strengths and weaknesses. Self-awareness is a critical factor needed for success."

Resistance: "We found that jealousy and resistance got in the way of integrating new business/product/service back into the organization."

Deliverables/Execution: "Everything is harder and takes longer than you expect. We did not factor that into our plans. There was little choice but to work around the clock or be late on our deliverables."

Diversity: "Having a mix of internal and external people on the team shook things up and got us to think outside the box."

Pressure: "The pressure was on us to deliver something that many thought was impossible and many people were waiting for us to fail. They were critical of the effort and were more willing to criticize than help."

Failure: "If you had a prior track record of success you were allowed a margin of error. Otherwise there was no room for failure. Failure was not tolerated."

These are only a few of the insights and lessons learned that the executives shared with us. There insights help us better understand some of the complexity of building intrapreneurship as a core competency inside an established organization. But they also show us the value of active involvement and commitment by the CEO and senior level executives. Threaded throughout these insights are things that CEOs did that supported and enabled intrapreneurship in their organizations.

Innovation and intrapreneurship are inexplicitly entwined. So is leadership. Not traditional leadership but entrepreneurial or transformative leadership. CEOs and senior executives that were actively engaged in innovation and intrapreneurship in their organizations had a deeper and richer appreciation for the challenges of transformative innovation. They were instrumental in helping their organizations achieve their innovation goals and objectives.

In his article, Why Every Company Needs a Chief Entrepreneur, Alexander Osterwalder spells out the growing need to have an entrepreneur at the top of the organization inventing the company's future. As noted in the article, *"The best CEOs are excellent at growing and running a company within a known business model. What they don't do well enough is reinvent and innovate."*

That said, the most successful companies we spoke with had a CEO that could do both.

Leadership support should be encouraged by a clear mandate and through performance management metrics that promote intrapreneurship.

Active involvement in innovation projects is the best way to understand the nuances that support and impede progress.

Leadership of course is only one piece of the puzzle. These executives had to deal with a host of issues and roadblocks. Despite these challenges every one of them told us that they learned an extraordinary amount about themselves and their organizations. It was the experience itself that taught them how to be an intrapreneur. One CEO told us he put the lessons learned from their innovation center into a case study to share with the rest of the organization.

Innovation and intrapreneurship begins and ends at the executive suite. It requires strategic oversight and involvement. If the CEO and board of directors don't fully understand or commit themselves to innovation and intrapreneurship it will not fly.

What about your organization? Is your CEO and senior executives involved, committed or sitting on the sidelines?

Moving Forward, No Turning Back

Entrepreneurial experiences inside existing organizations are revealing. They put everything in a new light. It is a personal and professional experience that will change the way you look at work.

The experience forces you take a hard look at yourself and the organization. It changes you, but it may not change the organization. You find yourself living in a different world. You have transitioned to a new way of working. The old rules no longer apply. Going back to the old model is no longer inviting. You begin to wonder if you still fit. *The experience changes your whole perspective on work.*

Unless you have gone through an entrepreneurial experience inside an existing organization, it is difficult to fully understand the experience. You have gone through a change process that you created. You designed, shaped, and tested it along the way. You built a new operating model, culture, and way of working that is now foreign to the rest of the organization. You have left the old model behind and embraced a new model of working. You have enhanced your skills as a corporate entrepreneur. You now know what is possible.

Unfortunately, the rest of the organization has not had the same opportunity. They are still operating in the old model that keeps the core business going. They are comfortable in that role and prefer to stick with a proven business model. They aren't interested in taking on new risks and challenges. They would prefer to work the traditional route to the top. That is fine with you. Somebody needs to keep the core business afloat. You, on the other hand, see a new way to grow the business. You have no desire to climb the corporate ladder the traditional way.

Because of this, you are now perceived as a threat. You have demonstrated that there are alternative ways to grow the business. You know how to change the paradigm and accelerate growth. This will rock the very foundation of the core business. Political factions are likely to step in and squash any efforts to promote this new way of operating, because it will threaten their world. They will perceive that it gives you an unfair advantage.

In turn, you will look around and wonder where you go from here. Chances are, you have just completed one of the more exciting jobs in your career and you are ready to take on even bigger challenges. There may be none where you are. You may be offered a line position as a promotion, but that doesn't seem to excite you. You have reached a point on the road where you must decide if you are going back or moving forward.

A number of corporate entrepreneurs decide to leave their companies after they have completed an entrepreneurial project. Often, they feel that they have no choice. During their experience they've grown and stretched themselves beyond what they thought was possible. They recognize that unless the core business can offer them another similar opportunity, they know they will grow bored. They will be taking a step backward if they stay. They realize that the experience itself has changed them and that they will want to continue to work on similar, challenging opportunities if they are to remain. Perhaps they will go off and start their own firm.

You may have heard the phrase "you can't go home again." It means that you will never be able to go back and see home for what it was when you first experienced it. This is the same type of experience for the corporate entrepreneur. Once you've had the experience of being on an entrepreneurial project, you will find it difficult to go back to the core business.

Although there is a lot of talk about the talent shortage and the need for organic growth, there are still very few companies that acknowledge corporate entrepreneurs as a critical corporate resource. Corporate entrepreneurs are the engines of the growth, the change agents. But until organizations begin to understand the value of corporate entrepreneurs and entrepreneurial leaders, these people will probably continue to walk out the door.

Corporate entrepreneurs are the future, and the hope is that more organizations will wake up to this reality and actively recruit them.

Are you prepared to deal with the consequences of being a corporate entrepreneur?

The Last Frontier for Intrapreneurs

One of the biggest challenges facing Intrapreneurs is successfully getting their ideas across the finish line with the value that was intended still intact. Not an easy task given all the uncertainty and complexity facing intrapreneurs internally and in this new environment.

The journey from idea to implementation is not easy. It is like navigating an obstacle course. Not knowing what you will encounter until it is staring you in the face. We know from experience that everything in the organization is a potential obstacle. Everything from strategy thru to execution. Some of them are obvious, many of them are hidden.

Our research and work with intrapreneurs have identified over ninety potential barriers that can get in your way. These barriers serve to slow you down, make you question what you are doing, marginalize your innovation efforts and diminish the value you deliver to your clients and the organization.

What you start out doing and what you wind up delivering often fall short of the expectations and goals set at the beginning of the project. The true value is gone and the profitable growth you expected are not realized.

Organizational barriers can and do have a major impact, but they are often not the main reason why new innovations are not successful.

A barrier only impacts your work if it prevents you from delivering on the promise your organization makes to the market or diminishes the value of your offering. Both of those result in less value to your customer and less profitable revenue growth for your organization.

The simple truth is that most new innovations fail because the link between the buyer and the seller (your organization) are out of sync. This is the biggest barrier to success. It is also the last frontier for Intrapreneurs.

Organizations have made tremendous progress in supporting Intrapreneurs by providing the necessary training, experience, and tools to enable them to be successful. There are new processes, roadmaps and techniques that help refine the way innovations are developed. There is more support, encouragement, and commitment to bringing new innovations to market. These are all positive signs.

That said, the problem is that most new innovations are still not successful despite all the resources going to them. *Why?* ...... That is the question we need to answer.

According to Rick McPartlin, CEO of Revenue Science, "*You need a RoadMap to align your business and resources to support a profitable revenue strategy. One where opportunities, organizational capabilities and revenue are in alignment.*" Revenue Science provides the tools to evaluate and assess that alignment.

Many of the existing revenue models are outdated. They are rigid and inflexible, filter out high risk innovations and focus on traditional ROI measures. These models are designed to play it safe. Or at least the organization thinks that is what they are doing. Instead, they may be eliminating high potential, higher value projects.

New revenue models more closely align the market needs to the organizations capabilities to meet those needs. This requires taking a deeper look at the needs of the buyer and aligning them with you as the seller.

This requires an analysis of your value chain and the resources needed to support this alignment. Many organizations use the Value Proposition Canvas, Jobs to be Done or Design Thinking as a blueprint for this alignment. The goal is to find a fit between the product and customer.

These tools are effective when you are trying to map new or established products to relieving existing buyer pain points. Pain points that are often a result of an organization doing the wrong things very well. Mapping buyers to products and products to buyers ensures that you have a match. But may not be as helpful in creating new value that is not currently identified or recognized by the buyer. Buyers purchase products that solve problems that exist today. The value that is created is often short-lived. It is the value they know, not the value they need.

Revenue Science takes it one step further and focuses on the 'Ideal Buyer'. They provide the steps you need to take to identify, qualify, communicate, and transfer the value needed to the buyer. A step-by-step process that helps your organization provide short-term value linked to longer-term value to those same buyers. The tighter the alignment the less risk you take on. The higher the probability that you will address an unmet short-term and long-term need that will generate profitable revenue for your organization and significant value for your customer.

All of this requires a shift in thinking and actions. A refinement process that focuses on the salient factors needed to align the perfect buyer with the organizations capabilities to deliver the highest value possible. Each new opportunity may require a different set of resources and capabilities. Revenue Science provides the insight you need to effectively align your organization to the specific needs of the buyer. Ensuring that the value delivered extends beyond the short-term and addresses the underlying issues that created the pain points in the first place. It is both a diagnostic tool and forecasting tool for both the buyer and seller.

At first, you might think that having a revenue strategy is all about marketing and selling but when you get to that point the damage has already been done. Now you are asking marketing and sales to compensate for any discrepancies between the product/service offering and the value you hoped it would provide to clients. Your salespeople are left closing this gap. It is far easier to start the alignment of the buyer and seller at the front end of the innovation process not the back end. It is a matter of knowing your buyer far better than they know themselves by showing them what new and incremental value is possible. That is what Revenue Science does.

As an intrapreneur you may be asking yourself if this is the missing piece to getting my idea across the finish line. It may very well be. The closer the link between buyer and seller the higher the probability that your innovation will be a success. Having a roadmap that you can follow and everyone else can see and understand helps you deal with the barriers and obstacles that will get in your way. Everyone in organization will be on the same page, understand their role, the resources it will take, the changes that will have to be made and the systems that will be needed to make it happen. Your customers will understand exactly what they are getting and why. The value to both organizations will be apparent.

This is a process that ensures that you deliver innovations with the highest value to clients and your organization.

It is the last frontier for Intrapreneurs.

Chapter 9: Value

- Power of Intrapreneurs That Stick Out in a Crowd
- Intrapreneurs – Bridging the Great Divide
- Intrapreneurs Closing the Gap for Success
- Intrapreneurs Turn the Impossible to Possible
- Intrapreneurs - Small Change, Big Impact
- The Path from Ordinary to Extraordinary
- The Intrapreneurs Journey to Now
- Intrapreneurs: The New Face of Leadership

Power of Intrapreneurs That Stick Out in the Crowd

The reality for Intrapreneurs is that being different is what makes you do what you do. You are willing to try new things, test your assumptions and explore the unknown. You change your thoughts and actions based on what you see, experience or learn. You are willing to shift your stance and take a new approach. It's what makes you stick out in the crowd.

You can call it being a rebel, a non-conformist, a maverick or even a positive deviant but what it means is that you do not resist change, you embrace it. You do not sit back and wait until things become clear before you act, you act and see what you learn from it. You are willing to step outside of what you know to explore what you don't know. These small things make you able to adapt, change and transform who you are. It's all about changing your behavior.

This is what makes you different. According to his article Leaders Focus Too Much on Changing Policies, and Not Enough on Changing Minds, Tony Schwartz asks why transformations are so difficult. "*Among many potential explanations, one that gets the very little attention may be the most fundamental; the invisible fears and insecurities that keep us locked into behaviors even when we know rationally that they don't serve us well.*"

Everything that goes on in an organization is the result of someone's actions – their behavior. How they behave reflects how they think and the level of risk they assign to any decision. It's not about what they say but what they do. Often, we are locked into our own beliefs and assumptions that prevent us from moving in a new direction. It creates resistance, fear, insecurity. That is not the case with Intrapreneurs.

It's not about being unique it's about being open to new possibilities. Intrapreneurs stick out in the crowd because others are not willing to step outside of what they know to explore what they don't know.

Years ago, I visited The Monroe Institute (TMI) after reading an article in Omni Magazine about the organization's exploration into various levels of consciousness. The Monroe Institute (TMI) is a nonprofit education and research organization that is the preeminent leader in human consciousness and expanded states of awareness. As a prelude to the week ahead of us we were all asked to give up our watches and phones. There were no clocks on the walls, no radio, or no TV to keep us connected to the outside world. We were all strangers gathered to explore the unknown under the guidance of Bob Monroe. Among us were executives from Fortune 50 companies, entrepreneurs, photographers, graphic artists, students, and musicians from around the world. A mixed bag for sure.

The experience and learning were profound for all of us and made us aware that there are things beyond our current ability to fully grasp or put into words. That we are more than what we see and that there are always new things to explore. It was Bob Monroe who said that the greatest fear most people have is 'fear of the unknown.' Yet he went on to say that the greatest fear should be 'fear of the known' because it keeps us locked into the present, comfortable, content and complacent.

Little did Bob know that he was describing the majority of organizations that many of us worked for then and now! The inability to change is rooted in each one of us. Not in something out there but something inside of us. It's how we think and how we express our thoughts through our behavior. Not just any behavior but behaviors that enable us to deal with the external world around us in ways that move us forward. Like dealing with complexity, uncertainty and the unknown. Collectively these behaviors form the basis for organizational cultures. They don't change if we don't change.

According to Tony Schwartz, "*What organizations typically overlook is the internal shift – what people think and feel…This is where the resistance tends to arise – cognitively in the form of fixed beliefs, deeply held assumptions and blind spots; and emotionally, in the form of fear and insecurity that change engenders.*" It reflects how we see the world and react to what we see.

Intrapreneurship is about change. Changing everything. The way people think and act, changing the way the organization operates, changing the culture. The goal of intrapreneurship is to build capabilities that enable organizations to respond to change and accelerate new business growth. So, it is not surprising that among the top competencies of successful Intrapreneurs is Navigating Uncertainty and Driving Change.

As we've stated numerous times, Individuals and organizations do not resist change; they resist disturbances to their frame of reference caused by change. These frames of references include, attitudes, expectations, behaviors, emotions, beliefs, values, habits, past experience, education etc. To make change happen there needs to be a major shift in many of these. The reality perceived by each of us is filtered by our own frame of reference. Organizations also have their own frame of reference.

Resistance is futile. We are living in a world that is constantly changing. If we don't adjust to those changes we will be left behind. Managing resistance requires getting individual and organizations to reframe themselves. There is a direct correlation between the extent to which we modify our frame of reference and the amount of change and pain that an individual or organization will undergo. The key to unlocking individual and organizational potential is demonstrating change through your behavior.

That's what intrapreneurs do. They stick out in the crowd because they are consistently exhibiting change in the way they think and the way they work. In doing so they are not only changing themselves they are changing organizations. This is the power of intrapreneurs. They not only drive change; they are opening the door for others to change.

Instinctively and intuitively Intrapreneurs learn the behaviors that enable them to thrive in an ever-changing world. They do it through their experience of being an intrapreneur. In most cases they have done this on their own. Without the aid or assistance of their organization.

Sticking out is not always easy, comfortable or welcomed by Intrapreneurs but like everyone they must look at their own frame of reference and ask themselves what they need to change to move past these feelings.

In doing this they come to understand the power of sticking out in the crowd.

Intrapreneurs – Bridging the Great Divide

In our work we help individuals explore their own entrepreneurial orientation. We provide a window into who they are, what they do and how they do it.

We look at how they approach work – are they more traditional, entrepreneurial or both. We look at their propensity to act in a certain way, in a given situation, at a certain point in time.

It isn't just a matter of thinking and acting like an intrapreneur. Being an intrapreneur is a two-way street. Its understanding the great divide that separates you from the rest of the organization.

It was Jeffry A. Timmons, Distinguished Professor of Entrepreneurship at Babson College that talked about the paradox of entrepreneurship. That it is a two-way street. The paradox is that entrepreneurship inside organizations requires two sets of capabilities – managing the core and leading the new business – at the same time.

Telling yourself that you are an intrapreneur, is only half of the equation. Understanding the other side of the equation is equally important. It is the gap between these two factions that create the greatest barriers and obstacles for intrapreneurs. Identifying and closing those gaps can be the difference between success and failure.

It is the ability to coexist in both these worlds simultaneously that distinguishes the true intrapreneur from the rest. That's why the focus of our work is looking at both sides of this great divide. Only in gaining a clear understanding of both perspectives will you be able to find a way to bridge that divide.

We often hear experts talk about the antibodies that exist in established organizations that prevent Intrapreneur from being successful. Keep in mind that everything in an organization is a potential obstacle. We've identified over ninety barriers and obstacles that can get in your way. These obstacles stifle innovation and growth. Often these obstacles involve doing something one way versus another. But it's not about the obstacles…it's how you deal with them that makes the difference.

Do you walk away when you hit the wall, or do you try to understand how to bridge the divide? You can't begin to build bridges until you put yourself in their shoes. See things through their eyes. Understand their perspective, how they think, act and make decisions. Explore their concerns, understand their resistance and listen to understand what's getting in their way. It isn't about you, it's about them.

The advice that many Intrapreneurs get when they hit the wall and can't move forward, is that it is probably time to leave and move on. In fact, that was the same advice we gave Intrapreneurs who asked us those same questions. It is only in hindsight that we realized that we were wrong. It isn't about deciding to move on, it's about deciding to find a way to close the gap between these two worlds. To do that you must understand the differences between them.

Finding common ground requires being comfortable having one foot in both worlds – the core business and new business you are building. Sounds simple but it is much more complex. That's why it is not easy being an Intrapreneur. It's like having a split personality, each with its own sets of demands. The organization has one view of the situation, you have another. It is up to you as the Intrapreneur not the organization to manage this.

Understanding if you have what it takes to be an intrapreneur is only the first step on your journey to becoming an effective intrapreneur. Understanding the rest of the organization is just as important. So how do you do that. What do you need to know?

First understand yourself and how what you do shapes your perspective.

- How your work environment influences the actions you take.
- How innovation defines the degree of change and resistance you will encounter.
- How metrics influence the decisions you make and the actions you take.
- How specific competencies determine how traditional or intrapreneurial you are.
- How well you understand the gaps in what you do versus what you think you do.
- How well you know yourself and how your actions impact others.

- How confident and competent you are in the eyes of those you manage.
- How your level of commitment to the organization influences what you do.
- How you see and evaluate the external world around you.
- How you gather and process information to create new ideas.
- How you evaluate and analyze data to reach a decision.
- How you determine when you have done enough to move forward with your idea.
- How internal and external factors influence and enable you to take action.

These are the things that help you see yourself more clearly. Help you understand the why behind your thinking and actions. Help you see where you stand. Sometimes you may need to be more entrepreneurial, other times more traditional or maybe a little of both. It's a starting point for understanding the distance you may have to travel to close the gaps between you and the rest of the organization.

Secondly, once you know where you stand you will be able to see how what you do is different from the rest of the organization. Keep in mind that the same dimensions from above can be applied to everyone throughout the organization.

The most simplistic way to look at this is to consider that everything that is done in the core business is just the opposite of what is needed to support a new business. Think of it as a 180-degree difference. It's not just the things others do in the core business but the way they do them. It's about how they operate, short term versus long term, incremental versus disruptive, analytical versus intuitive, traditional versus entrepreneurial, and so on. It isn't as simple as that, but it is a starting point.

Once you understand those differences you can begin to see how large the gap, how difficult the challenge. It will be up to you to determine how far you can push the boundaries of what is acceptable behavior or decide when you need to pull back. You can think of it like a dial, you dial it up to see more change or turn it back to minimize change. Speed it up or slow it down. These are things Intrapreneurs do to keep their projects moving forward.

This is the playing field. The great divide between you and the rest of the organization. It is the clarity you will need to be effective in your role as an intrapreneur.

Intrapreneurs Closing the Gap for Success

We are reaching a tipping point where internal and external forces are transforming companies whether they like it or not. One of the forces at work include Intrapreneurs that are stepping up and speaking out about how things need to change to deal with a rapidly changing world.

Intrapreneurs are not content to sit back and wait for change to happen. They are impatient, frustrated and disappointed with the slow pace of change and lack of progress. They believe that they can make change happen more quickly given the chance. But their success depends on having the skills and competencies needed to bridge the gap between the old way of doing business and the new way. A gap that pits these two worlds against one another.

A common mistake Intrapreneurs make is thinking that if they have the capabilities of an Intrapreneur, that is all they needed to succeed. This is only half of the picture. That's not to say that it isn't important to have the right skills and competencies. It is. What is more important is understanding how your capabilities complement, contrast or conflict with others in the organization.

What many intrapreneurs fail to realize is that the gap between the existing business and creating a new business is greater than you can imagine. It isn't just about systems, processes, policies, practices or structure. It's about mindset, attitudes, expectations, behavior, emotions, beliefs, values, habits, experience and actions. You have a certain frame of reference and so does everyone else. The more you understand your own frame of reference the more you will understand everyone else.

This is the great divide that separates you from others in the organization. It is the disconnect that exists, that separates you from others and can prevent you from achieving your goal. The first step to address this situation is to look at your own frame of reference. Then identify the gaps between you and everyone else.

The more intrapreneurial you are the wider the gap between yourself and everyone else. It is up to you to bridge the distance not the other person. This is a gap that most intrapreneurs struggle with most of their working life. Getting other people to see what you see, grasp what you've learned, believe in what you are doing, relate to your experience, adopt your thinking and accept the premise for your idea. It is one of the most frustrating aspects of being an intrapreneur. Yet it is the essence of what it means to be an intrapreneur.

We often hear Intrapreneurs say that they know they have the competencies required to be an intrapreneur. But do they really. Many of the Intrapreneurs that have taken the Intrapreneur Scorecard acknowledge that it helped them confirm their own belief that they have the competencies to be an intrapreneur. That's only part of what it takes to be an intrapreneur. The other part is understanding everyone else's perspective, their capabilities, and competencies. Then understanding how you will bring them into your way of thinking and acting. Your success will depend on it.

You've developed a set of capabilities and competencies through the experiences you've had. Not everyone has shared in the same experiences. Nor do they see things the same way. Their thinking, decision making, risk taking, and actions will be different than yours. Like you they rely on their own past experiences to guide them. It is what influences their actions.

The gap in capabilities and competencies between individuals and groups is what slows things down and puts the brakes on progress. One thing you can do to deal with this type of disconnect is to take an inventory of your own capabilities, competencies and fit. You can do this by taking any number of assessments that provide greater insight into your capabilities and competencies. Then look at the capabilities and competencies of those individuals you must connect with to be successful.

Often this will help you understand how much effort and energy you will need to expend to close the gap. It's like a sliding scale. Either you must pull back or move them forward. It's a matter of understanding how intrapreneurial you are and how traditional they may be.

Everyone has the potential to be an intrapreneur but not everyone has had an opportunity to experience being an intrapreneur. It is up to you to understand the gap. It is the only way you will understand how to close it.

As an Intrapreneur it is incumbent upon you to invest in your own growth and development. You are the product. You need to build your own portfolio of capabilities. You cannot leave this up to the organization. It is only through experience that you learn what you know, don't know and need to know. And the only way to do that is in the work you choose to do. Choose wisely.

Your experiences turn into skills and competencies that translate into value in a talent-based economy. The more you come to understand yourself, the better able you are to understand others and the distance you must go to close the gap.

The prediction that Intrapreneurs would be 'the most sought-after talent in the 21st century economy' has now become a reality. It is up to you to develop yourself as a brand, market yourself and demonstrate through your experience that you are an intrapreneur whether you are inside or outside of an organization. Your true value will be reflected in both your successes and the lessons you take away from failure.

It isn't always about winning, it's about learning. Learning to close the gap between you and the rest of the organization.

Closing the gap is the key to success.

Intrapreneurs Turn the Impossible to Possible

As we celebrate the 50th Anniversary of the Apollo 11 landing on the moon I am reminded about the value of having a vision. An audacious, challenging and seemingly impossible vision to land a man on the moon.

A vision that inspired a generation of individuals to make it happen and change how we see our world. Literally and figuratively.

There were several factors that contributed to this vision including a commitment to expand our knowledge of the universe, fierce competition to be the first, and a desire to show that anything is possible. It took ingenuity, grit and determination.

It may seem like a walk in the park for many of you too young to remember but to put it in context – you have more computing power in your phone than they had to put a man on the moon.

Everything was new. It all had to be developed, tested and reworked until they got it right. Along the way there were plenty of failures and false starts. There were financial constraints, political issues, and a skeptical public seeing hunger and homelessness as higher priorities.

Sound familiar. It should. As intrapreneurs and social intrapreneurs you face similar issues every day. You see a problem, an opportunity, or injustice that needs to be addressed. You are eager to explore all the options, push the boundaries of what is acceptable behavior, experiment and test your hypothesis, and take responsibility for your actions.

But…it all starts with a vision. An idea that bubbles up, percolates in your mind and becomes an obsession that you can't let go. No matter how fuzzy or unclear it may be at the start you are convinced that it is viable, and you set out to fill in the blanks, find data to support you, money to fund you and people who believe you. Yet it is not as simple as that.

You may think you have what it takes to drive your idea through to implementation, but it is everyone else that you encounter along the way that will need convincing. They may intellectually understand your vision but not see the nuances that turn it into something of value. They may not understand the benefits that can result from your idea. The progress your idea can make in moving an issue forward toward a bigger and better solution. Neither of you will truly understand the impact of an idea until you are past it.

It's more than a vision. It's the value and benefit that derives from your idea.

Think of all the things that came from NASA and the Apollo program. According to Saiskia Otto, here are a few of those things.

1. CAT scanner: this cancer-detecting technology was first used to find imperfections in space components.
2. Computer microchip: modern microchips descend from integrated circuits used in the Apollo Guidance Computer.
3. Cordless tools: power drills and vacuum cleaners use technology designed to drill for moon samples.
4. Ear thermometer: a camera-like lens that detects infrared energy we feel as heat was originally used to monitor the birth of stars.
5. Freeze-dried food: this reduces food weight and increases shelf life without sacrificing nutritional value.
6. Insulation: home insulation uses reflective material that protects spacecraft from radiation.
7. Invisible braces: teeth-straightening is less embarrassing thanks to transparent ceramic brace brackets made from spacecraft materials.
8. Joystick: this computer gaming device was first used on the Apollo Lunar Rover.
9. Memory foam: created for aircraft seats to soften landing, this foam, which returns to its original shape, is found in mattresses and shock absorbing helmets.
10. Satellite television: technology used to fix errors in spacecraft signals helps reduce scrambled pictures and sound in satellite television signals.
11. Scratch resistant lenses: astronaut helmet visor coating makes our spectacles ten times more scratch resistant.
12. Shoe insoles: athletic shoe companies adapted space boot designs to lessen impact by adding spring and ventilation.
13. Smoke detector: Nasa invented the first adjustable smoke detector with sensitivity levels to prevent false alarms.
14. Swimsuit: Nasa used the same principles that reduce drag in space to help create the world's fastest swimsuit for Speedo, rejected by some professionals for giving an unfair advantage.

15. Water filter: domestic versions borrow a technique Nasa pioneered to kill bacteria in water taken into space.

All of these are things that we take for granted today but they were developed in support of a vision, an idea to put a man on the moon. It took imagination and a deep exploration of the unknown. It captured the hearts and minds of a whole generation of people who believed that "no dream was impossible."

Millions of people began to believe that it was possible. That translated into more support, further funding and a stronger commitment. Things needed to keep that vision alive.

Today, it has become increasingly clear that we are facing a myriad of social, environmental and economic problems that can only be addressed by individuals that have a vision, a better way forward. That's why intrapreneurs are needed more than ever. They see a better, brighter future than exists today. They want a world that can support and sustain future generations. They believe that everyone should benefit from advances in technology. That there should be programs to empower the poor and disadvantaged. That we need to find ways to protect our environment… and so much more.

Intrapreneurs not only think that anything is possible they take steps that put their words into action. They test their hypothesis, experiment intelligently and learn from their success and failure. They are resilient, persistent and determined to find a way. They leverage what they've got, not what they think they need. They take responsibility for their actions.

Intrapreneurs are committed to making a difference but they often fail to understand the differences that exist between those that see their vision and those that don't. What do they see, what do they think, what do they believe and what stops them from embracing your vision?

As intrapreneurs and social intrapreneurs your worst enemy can be yourself. You may think you know who you are, what you think and how you act, but according to a research study at Harvard only 15% of individuals are self-aware. That means that you need to understand who you are at the core – not only how you think but what you do.

Only then will you be able to understand the other side – those that don't see your vision, accept your premise or buy into your approach.

It's not about being capable it's about being capable to deal with everyone else that does not see what you see, believe what you believe or see any way to get from here to there. That's why we suggest that you take the time to explore exactly who you are, so you can understand how to move your idea forward.

It's all about closing the gap between what you see and what you want everyone else to see. That's how you turn a vision into reality.

The moon landing was a vision that became a reality when Neil Armstrong stepped on the moon and said those famous words, "*One small step for man, one giant leap for mankind.*"

What's your vision and what steps must you take to achieve it?

Intrapreneurs: Small Change, Big Impact

Individuals in large organizations often feel that it is difficult for any one person to have an impact. Yet, it only takes one person to change the course of things and move the corporation in a new direction. It doesn't have to be a big thing but a small strategic move that reaches a lot of people. Something visible that sends a signal that things have changed. *A small change can have a big impact.*

We tend to forget that most change unfolds naturally. It is not a series of starts and stops. We tend to look at change when it occurs not as it evolves. The cumulative effect of a small series of gradual changes can have a significant impact on the environment and people around it. One person, one change can ripple throughout the organization.

It was Buckminster Fuller, a well-known futurist that used the trim tab as a metaphor for leadership and personal empowerment. Individual initiative was the key – everyone should feel empowered. The trim tab is the small device attached to a rudder on a ship used to control the pitch and keep it level to maximize speed. This little device can control the direction of a large luxury liner or a Boeing 747. Fuller felt that everyone has the capacity to be a trim tab. He believed that even *"small, strategically placed interventions can cause large-scale and profound change."*

As a futurist Fuller had an uncanny ability to spot trends and anticipate potential problems. This enabled him to focus his efforts in areas that would provide the greatest value to society and mankind. Like a trim tab, one must know where they are headed, the obstacles likely to get in the way, and how much pressure to apply to the situation to bring about the change that is needed. A trim tab offers tremendous leverage with a minimum of effort to bring about change.

Fuller believed that anything is possible. He once said that only "*one out of 10,000 people is aware of what is going on around us.*" Those that think beyond what we know to be possible soon realize that there is a lot yet to be discovered. As a result, Fuller looked at the world through a wide-angle lens. Expanding his view of a situation into multiple directions enabled him to thoroughly evaluate the cause and find alternative solutions. A small change in perspective changed the context for finding a new creative solution.

Individuals can make change happen by their very actions. Action – reaction. A change in behavior or a shift in the way you respond to someone. Real change not contrived change. A subtle shift in the way you respond to emails, how quickly you return a phone call or how you address your co-workers in a meeting. All these little changes will make a difference. Your change creates a change in others that moves the conversation, the idea or solution forward. No longer cloaked in old patterns new patterns emerge that stimulate thinking and change behavior.

Looking back, we can see how a one small decision or change makes a difference.

Yet not every idea or decision has the same positive outcome. Take for example the Titanic. That fateful night the decision was made to turn the starboard left to avoid the iceberg. Experts suggest that had the ship stayed on course it is possible that the bow would have been damaged, but the ship would most likely have stayed afloat. A split-second decision and change in direction that cost the lives of 1500 people and doomed the ship once called unsinkable.

Of course, it is easy to look at the world through the real view mirror. What is less obvious is to understand how and why a particular decision was made.

In a minute, the world can change. A small decision can change the course of history. A new idea can make things obsolete in a matter of months, not years. We've seen that happen over the last few years. The world is moving at a much faster pace so every move, every change in direction is more critical. Veering off course can be disruptive.

Intrapreneurs see and interpret the world through their own lens – a unique combination of competencies, their own internal operating system, and the way they think. These three elements help shape the person, their behavior, and their reaction to the world.

Why are these three elements important? Without them we are like a ship without rudder. We are drifting wherever the current takes us. We are basically unconsciously flowing through life without direction, purpose, and focus. Letting others dictate our future. At the end of the journey, we must accept where we land without question, without remorse, without purpose. This is how most individuals operate today unconsciously moving forward, going wherever the flow takes them.

Not intrapreneurs, they take charge and engage in changing their future and that of their organizations. They see change more clearly, more precisely. They feel emotion that guides their internal compass. They look at every situation as an opportunity to make a difference. They aren't just looking to go with the flow but navigate every twist and turn.

Like a trim tab, Intrapreneurs know one small move can change the future. It can set the organization in an entirely new direction.

In large organizations in particular making course corrections does not come easy. Each organization settles into a rhythm and flow that becomes the norm. Everyone falls in line and gets on board with the program. Plans are put in place and marching orders are issued. Even the slightest interruption in the current strategic direction can upset that rhythm.

Maintaining the status quo is what is most important in terms of the core business. But changing the status quo is exactly what Intrapreneurs are programmed to do. Not every change must be big, bold or earth shattering.

One intrapreneur in a large consulting firm saw a pattern in the types of problems that clients brought to them to solve - large information systems problems. Consistently the firm was being asked to work on one of five types of issues. Yet this intrapreneur saw that these five problems were all related and interconnected in a way that nobody else had seen. So, he put together a schematic showing the interconnection of these five issues and how each one impacted the others.

The next time a client came in with one of the five problems he would build a model starting with their issue and proceed to explain and educate the client on how their problem was connected and dependent on the other four. Then when it came to a discussion about price the Intrapreneur would tell the client what it would cost to solve their one problem. Inevitably the client would ask about the cost for solving all five – now understanding the interconnection.

Not only did this generate millions of dollars in additional revenue for the consulting firm it solved a major systems problem for the client and saved them money in the long run. All this Intrapreneur did was see a pattern, look at it from a systems perspective and find a way to educate the client about the value of solving the whole problem, not just one part of the problem. Small change, large impact.

As Intrapreneurs we do not always have to push for large scale change, some small changes can make a big difference.

Co-authored with Sydney Rice

The Path from Ordinary to Extraordinary

Intrapreneurs are ordinary individuals that do extraordinary things. Many of the individuals that have become successful intrapreneurs never set out to be one. They never thought of themselves as an intrapreneur until they became aware of the term itself – intrapreneur. It wasn't until they were on the path that they began to understand the true meaning of what it meant to be an intrapreneur. These are some of the insights they shared from their journey.

For most of these individuals becoming an intrapreneur was not a revolution but an evolution. It was not one event but a series of circumstances that they were involved with in their companies. It was not what they did but what they learned from the experience. It was not what they achieved but what value they created. These experiences laid the groundwork for them becoming an intrapreneur. It helped them develop the entrepreneurial insight and muscle that would be needed for their success.

It is a journey not a destination.

You don't just wake up one day and look in the mirror and see that you've turned into an Intrapreneur. It's about unraveling the core of who you are as an individual. Your core beliefs and values. Your motivations and aspirations. Your strengths and weaknesses. It's about finding your hidden self. The person you really are and the person you can become. It's about reaching your untapped potential. Stretching yourself way outside your comfort zone to explore the breadth and depth of your own capabilities.

It is a journey of self-exploration.

Learning to become an intrapreneur starts with a clean sheet of paper. It is being open to seeing what is possible from what seems impossible. It is about exploring the unknown and challenging that which is known. It's about having a vision that others can't see yet. It's about having conviction, commitment and confidence in the face of adversity. It's relying on intuition when you don't have all the data. It's having a strong belief in yourself, your ideas and your mission. It is a way of looking at the world. Connecting the dots in a new way for the greater good.

It is an intellectual journey.

Intrapreneurs know that being an intrapreneur is not just an intellectual exercise. It is grounded in experience. The actions one takes to move an idea or solution forward despite obstacles and roadblocks that get in the way. It's about challenging long held beliefs. Creating new systems and processes along the way. It is the ability to navigate internal and external landmines that stall and slow down progress. It is not about taking big risks but taking calculated risks. It's not about failing but failing to act. It's about creating the future not letting it evolve.

It is an action-oriented journey

The energy that motivates and drives intrapreneurs is purpose and passion. A goal much greater than yourself that solves a problem, creates value or addresses an unmet need. Driven by the desire and belief that what you do will have an impact and make a difference. To maintain your emotional composure when confronted with resistance. To be empathic and listen to the voices around you. To show courage in the face of threats and failure to execute as planned. To be willing to stop and start over when it no longer makes sense. To keep going when you are convinced that it will work.

It is a journey of the head and the heart.

The path from ordinary to extraordinary does not happen in a vacuum. It occurs when Intrapreneurs join forces with others to move a project forward. Building a diverse team. Negotiating for limited resources. Co-opting others to support you in your efforts. Collaborating with internal and external partners to provide advice and valuable resources. Cultivating support from senior level executives who can provide coverage when things get crazy. Communicating effectively with key stakeholders to hold their interest and keep them happy. Integrating customers and clients into the development process. Being all things to all people. Taking a 360 view of your world.

It is a journey you cannot take alone.

Despite the growing interest in intrapreneurship, Intrapreneurs still struggle to gain traction in large organizations. For most it is a certain level of frustration with the organizations inability to fully embrace what it means to be intrapreneurial. The people, the processes and the culture that are needed to support and enable intrapreneurship. Intrapreneurs find themselves alone, lost, without a sounding board. Intrapreneurs get that support from others like themselves outside the organization through networking, at conferences and in community groups focused on Intrapreneurship. It isn't that it can't be done without this support, it is far easier to learn from others who are in the same boat.

It is a journey where you need community support.

Along the way Intrapreneurs begin to realize that they must take responsibility for their own growth and development. They select opportunities that will stretch and challenge them. Opportunities that others may find too difficult or career limiting. Experiences that push them beyond the limits of what they currently know. It is through these experiences that they learn what they know and don't know, what is important and what isn't. Often, they are engaged in things that the organization has never done before. They must make a new path forward. They see themselves for who they are, what they can achieve and what they have left to learn.

It's a journey of self-reflection.

Every intrapreneurs' journey has its own twists and turns. Its ups and downs. Its detours and distractions. Its success and disappointments. The path from ordinary to extraordinary is not an easy one but a rewarding one. These are just a few of the things that intrapreneurs have done on the path to becoming extraordinary. It is not rocket science. As Peter Drucker said, "*It is not magic; it is not mysterious; it has nothing to do with genes. It is a discipline, and, like any discipline, it can be learned. It is a way of thinking and acting.*"

Not everyone has an aspiration to be an intrapreneur but those that do must realize that you can't decide one day to be an intrapreneur. Being an intrapreneur comes from experience – intrapreneurial experiences. It is a journey that starts with a single step.

A step that takes you on the path from being ordinary to being an extraordinary intrapreneur.

The Intrapreneurs Journey to Now

We are excited to report that it has been a very good year for intrapreneurs.

We see more and more individuals taking on the role of Intrapreneur and leading the way in their organizations. They know that it isn't always easy, but they are on a mission to change the status quo in and outside of their organization. Their voices are being heard by some of the largest organizations in the world.

Intrapreneurs are putting pressure on organizations to explore Intrapreneurship and challenging them to understand what they need to do to attract and retain intrapreneurial talent. They are making organizations see that talent is their most valuable asset. That profit over purpose can only take them so far. That the organization of the future is beginning to look very different from the past.

A colleague of mine once said that a tiny shift can have a big impact and that is what we see happening now. It's not to say that we are at a tipping point yet but very close. My hope for next year is that we tip the scales and recognize Intrapreneurs for who they are and what they do. That we acknowledge their contribution to the organization, their ability to drive change and their unique leadership capabilities.

Intrapreneurship is helping transform our businesses and the way we work. It is also helping us understand our responsibility to society and the environment. Intrapreneurs are the driving force behind this movement.

Intrapreneurs are turning business upside-down and inside-out by leveraging technology, AI and data in a way that it has never been used before. They see things through a different lens and relate to the world in a more compassionate way. They see the value in bringing people together into communities with a mission, a goal, and a desire to build a better world.

We are grateful for their commitment to this cause.

Over the last decade we have followed thousands of Intrapreneurs on their journey. We recognize that they have come a long way but still have a way to go. One of the ways we look at Intrapreneurs is in how they approach their work. Are they more traditional or intrapreneurial? Here are a few things we've learned about Intrapreneurs:

1. Intrapreneurs are slightly more traditional than intrapreneurial in their approach to thinking. Although intrapreneurs are independent thinkers most of them rely on proven processes for collecting and processing information. They continue to use reason, logic and argument to make decisions versus relying on their own experience and knowledge to guide them. They want evidence to support their arguments and they make judgments based on well supported reason.

2. Intrapreneurs are both traditional and intrapreneurial when it comes to navigating uncertainty. They rely on their intuition to guide them and use creativity to define the future. They are willing to move forward without having all the data. Yet they are reluctant to start projects without having all the resources they think they need to achieve their goals. They are not willing to pursue opportunities without being sure they can win.

3. Intrapreneurs are equally traditional and intrapreneurial when it comes to being engaged and thriving. Half of them prefer the freedom to experiment while the other half want clarity about what is expected of them. They are split between those that want recognition for good performance and those that want recognition for trying even if they fail. Intrapreneurs are highly motivated by a challenge but look to management to sanction their actions before taking them on.

4. Intrapreneurs are intrapreneurial when it comes to driving change. A strong majority of them understand that making change happens requires changing behavior not process. They know that structure alone will not drive change, that most change is incremental and that you must be patient. More importantly they know that demonstrating change through their actions is the key to enabling change in the organization.

5. Intrapreneurs exhibit strong intrapreneurial leadership. They tend to manage risk through action not analysis. They are effective at leveraging limited resources to achieve goals. Understand customers as people not just data. They are good at motivating others and keeping stakeholders informed as things evolve. They tend to place small bets quickly rather than big bets slowly.

6. Intrapreneurs are mostly intrapreneurial when it comes to execution. They view execution as a process not a goal. They take measured and controlled steps forward. They explore variability and contingencies to move forward. They don't try to eliminate mistakes but learn from them. They understand that execution is an iterative process and never follows a straight line.

What this tells us is that Intrapreneurs have found a way to balance the demands of the core business at the same time that they are building a new one. They continue to rely on more traditional business practices when it comes to processing, analyzing and evaluating information and more traditional in their decision making. But they are more intrapreneurial in the steps or actions they are taking to move their organization forward. They are doing more experimentation and are more willing to try new things even if they fail. They are more effective in getting others to change and follow their lead.

Digging deeper we see that Intrapreneurs consistently rate themselves higher in these six areas than their actual score. This is not a bad thing because being highly confident in your abilities is a key factor for success.

It does however indicate that there is a gap between their perception of their abilities and their actual actions.

Not surprising the largest gaps in perception were when it comes to independent thinking, navigating uncertainty and engaged and thriving. Intrapreneurs rated themselves significantly higher in these areas. They rated themselves high in the three other areas driving change, leadership effectiveness and execution but not as much.

Intrapreneurs must not only think but act intrapreneurial.

What we are seeing is that the balance between thinking and action has shifted over time. In the past Intrapreneurs had been more intrapreneurial when it comes to thinking and more traditional when it comes to action. Now we see a reversal where Intrapreneurs are more traditional in their thinking and more intrapreneurial in their action. It is not surprising that we have seen this shift.

This shift signals two things:

> First, Intrapreneurs have learned that changing existing business practices in the core business can be a frustrating and futile exercise. They realize that they must find a way to deal with inflexible and rigid business practices that limit their ability to act intrapreneurial. Instead of resisting them, they are embracing them and leveraging them in new ways to satisfy the demand of the core business as they are building a new one. They have found a way to balance the core business with the new. A key indicator of a true intrapreneurial leader.

> Secondly: Intrapreneurs have gained more confidence and competence in their ability to make change happen. They have a deeper understanding and appreciation for the obstacles and roadblocks that can derail their efforts. They are finding creative ways around them. They are more willing to experiment and test their ideas before staking a major claim on an idea. Intrapreneurs have also found that there is no reward in standing still they must move outside of what they know through action. A sign Intrapreneurs are willing to take on more personal and professional risk to succeed.

We think these are all good signs that Intrapreneurs are not only evolving they are maturing in their understanding of the role and what it takes to be successful.

Intrapreneurs: The New Face of Leadership

Intrapreneurs are the new face of leadership. They are willing to step up, speak out and make a difference.

They are demonstrating confidence, commitment and courage in the face of adversity. They are open, transparent and committed to moving their organizations forward.

They are showing us what is possible. Not in their words but in their actions.

Intrapreneurs are helping us re-think what works means to us as individuals and redefining the role of business. They are demonstrating through their actions what it takes to more innovative, productive, and engaged. They are transforming organizations to be more entrepreneurial and more relevant in a rapidly changing world.

In doing so they are ensuring a future for their organizations and the customers that they serve. They are also paving a path for the next generation of workers. Workers that are ambitious, restless and searching for meaning. Workers that see work not as a place but as a community of like-minded individuals that want to make a difference. Workers that that are not motivated by money but motivated by purpose and value.

It is these workers that in a recent study said they felt current business approaches were too traditional, that there was a need to create a new work environment and redefine leadership. That is exactly what intrapreneurs are doing.

Intrapreneurs are creating that environment. Not by what they say but what they do. They are leading the way. But what does the new face of leadership look like. How do we know when we see it?

Here are 11 things that these leaders do:

1. Question decisions made at the top.
2. Challenge traditional business practices.
3. Break down silos and organizational barriers.
4. Deal effectively with complexity and uncertainty.
5. Leverage limited resources more effectively.
6. Tear down old systems and building new ones.
7. Co-create innovations with customers and partners.
8. Motivate and engage others in work that is challenging.
9. Build a flexible, adaptable and entrepreneurial culture
10. Generate business value for customers and the bottom line.
11. Learn from both their successes and their failures.

Intrapreneurs have always been pioneers, builders and change agents driving innovations. Now they are doing the same thing for organizations. They are forging a new path to success, building a new operating model and transforming cultures to align with the new business reality.

So why is that most intrapreneurial leaders don't feel like the fit. If they fit, they wouldn't be intrapreneurs. They are challenging the very foundation of the organization, rocking the boat, taking it in a new and different direction. They are turning the organization upside down and inside out. It is unsettling, disruptive and frightening. Not knowing where they are taking the organization or how they will get there makes people uncomfortable.

It is the gap between traditional leaders and intrapreneurs – the known and unknown. It is the difference between playing it safe or taking a risk, relying on past experience or experimentation, needing detailed information to decide or leveraging what you know, minimizing risks or maximizing value, asking for what you need or leveraging what you've got. They see what is possible. It's a mindset, a way of operating that is foreign to many of us.

Intrapreneurial leaders are wired differently. They look at everything as a two-way street. It is not my way or your way. It's what makes sense for the situation, at that moment in time. Instead of choosing one way over the other, they will find a new and different way that combines the best of both. They are integrative thinkers.

For intrapreneurial leaders it's not just about how they think but how they act that distinguishes them from traditional leaders. They learn by testing their ideas, experimenting and trying new approaches. They manage risk through action; place small bets quickly, embrace complexity, and leverage contingencies. They work with what they've got not what they need. They are action oriented.

Intrapreneurial leaders make decisions differently. They resist diving into the data too early in the process. They seek to understand complexity, not simplify things too quickly. They will make decisions without sufficient data; take calculated risks, shift gears or change direction when new information becomes available. They do all this while managing the tension between short term demands and long-term strategy. They are decisive

Intrapreneurial leaders are authentic, resilient, emotionally intelligent and self-aware. They take responsibility for their own growth and development. They don't wait for opportunities to be given to them; they actively seek them out. They are stepping up, speaking out and moving forward. They are not only modeling change, they are driving change and creating an entrepreneurial culture along the way.

These are only a few of the reasons how intrapreneurs are changing the face of leadership.

They are pushing the boundaries of what an organization is and what it can become.

Chapter 10: Leadership

- Growing Need for Intrapreneurial Leaders
- Key Distinction – Traditional versus Intrapreneurial Leaders
- Entrepreneurial Leaders – Chief Business Architect
- Creating an Environment for Change
- Entrepreneurial Leaders: Trust and Risk Intertwined
- Entrepreneurial Leaders: Alone on an Island
- Leading through the Valley of Despair
- Time for Intrapreneurs to Step Up and Lead
- Innovation Edge - Intrapreneurial Leaders
- Is the Crisis Turning CEOs into Intrapreneurs

Growing Need for Intrapreneurial Leaders

In most organizations new business growth is a critical imperative. Yet, most CEOs don't feel like they have the capabilities inside their organization to achieve their growth agenda. They are probably right. Despite the desire for growth thru innovation – it remains both a challenge and opportunity. There is a gap between an organizations need to innovate and their ability to effectively execute.

The reason for the interest in Intrapreneurship is because organizations recognize that they need to close this gap. Innovation alone is not enough – they need to create the entrepreneurial mindset and infrastructure to build and sustain innovation over time. Organizations have been good at creating ideas but not as good at implementing them. There is a lack of understanding about the innovation process. A lack of understanding about how intrapreneurship enables and supports innovation.

A key part of the problem is that everyone is in favor of innovation, but nobody much likes change. The largest factor to an organization's success is its ability to drive and manage change, which is all about people. Many organizations have underestimated the impact and value of their people in achieving their growth agenda. For many organizations' innovation is all about process. In the most progressive organizations innovation is about people. It is people that create the entrepreneurial culture needed to support and sustain innovation.

The result is a shortage of entrepreneurial role models at the top of most organizations that is stifling innovation and growth. The skills and capabilities that are needed in the core business are not the ones required to build new growth businesses. There is a growing need for organizations to think and act differently. In his article, Why Culture is The Heart of Organizational Innovation, Chris Cancialosi says that, "*Many business leaders don't recognize their own unconscious beliefs and behaviors that stifle the psychological safety needed for their organization to embrace innovation.*" Leadership readiness varies considerably across organizations.

The answer for many organizations is to take high performers in the core business and turn them into intrapreneurial leaders. But that may be a mistake. Research shows that a different mindset is required. Leaders in the core business are more linear, fact based in their thinking and decision making. They rely on data more. Manage risk through analysis. Are more likely to miss opportunities. Tend to place big bets slowly. They have different motivations and aspirations. They are most effective in an environment that is more stable and predictable.

There is also an experience trap. Leaders reflexively rely on the skills and strategies that worked for them in the past, after all it was their previous successes that propelled them to this new opportunity. This is a mistake. Most senior executives do not lead or manage these innovation efforts. Only one third have managed or led them on an ad-hoc basis. Few have led a project through from concept to implementation. They intellectually understand what it takes but they have not experienced what it takes. They don't know what they don't know.

Leadership effectiveness is more difficult today because of the uncertainty, ambiguity and the unknown that leaders face every day. Intrapreneurial leaders must deal with all the complexity of starting something new. Envision all the possible outcomes that could occur. Build a commitment toward a common goal. Seek and secure agreement among stakeholders. Deal with their own personal barriers and those of members of their team. Tear down old systems and build new ones. Erect new structures that are fluid and changeable. Find creative ways to leverage limited resources and build bridges across organizational boundaries.

It is all about transformation. Changing everything that is needed to support the new growth business. That requires knowing where the organization is flexible and where it is not. Making unpopular decisions and going against the grain. According to McKinsey they found that "*Executives focus too much on individual initiatives rather than on how the business must change.*" It is not just about how the business must change it is about how leaders must change as well.

As a result, organizations are actively building intrapreneurial capabilities to address these issues. Many believe that what is missing are the soft skills. The most innovative organizations are setting up intrapreneurial leadership development programs that integrate the soft skills and hard skills in their programs. They recognize that identifying and developing specific behaviors are the key to unlocking intrapreneurial potential. That learning by doing is how they build new, more relevant and more effective experiences that guide individuals through the innovation process.

Together these experiences embody what is needed to develop the intrapreneurial leadership skills that are needed for the 21st century economy.

Being an effective intrapreneurial leader requires a head and heart connection that is only gained through the experience itself. It is a shift in mindset and behavior. It requires leaders that are entrepreneurial thinkers and possess a core set of action-oriented competencies.

Making gut wrenching decisions that challenge your beliefs in what you have always known to be true. Putting your words into action by stepping outside the boundaries of what has been acceptable behavior and business practices. Testing the limits of your own knowledge and capabilities. Walking the tight rope between success and failure. Leading others into the unknown.

These are only some of the qualities that intrapreneurial leaders will need to be effective in that role.

If organizations want to increase the speed in which they respond to change and achieve business growth they must develop intrapreneurial leaders by changing their thinking and their behavior.

Key Distinction - Traditional versus Intrapreneurial Leaders

What distinguishes a traditional leader from an intrapreneurial leader? That is a question that many large organizations are exploring.

The pressure to understand this difference is put into perspective in the article Taking Charge - Entrepreneurs in Pursuit of Innovation, "*One of the biggest contrasts between corporate leaders and those who excel as entrepreneurs is an attitude of exploration and risk-taking that isn't always the first course of action for traditional corporate leaders.*" A disconnect that can result in the exodus of some of the most entrepreneurial (intrapreneurial) leaders to pursue their own ventures.

Part of the issue is that only a small percent of executives in large organizations are intrapreneurs or intrapreneurial. As a result, there has been limited research in understanding the real differences between these two types of leaders.

Our research has shown that there are key differences in the way traditional and intrapreneurial leaders approach situations, think, take action, make decisions, motivate, inspire and lead people. We found that traditional leaders are good at what they do but intrapreneurial leaders are good at being both – a traditional leader and an intrapreneurial leader. *This is a key distinction.*

Intrapreneurial leaders live in a world of contrast. They must operate in the core business at the same time they are building a new one. They must know where the organization is flexible, how far they can push and the extent to which they can bend the rules. They understand that it is a balancing act.

- Being loyal on one hand and independent on the other
- Collaborative and competitive
- Poised and passionate
- Tough minded and empathic
- Factual and intuitive
- More....

It is this ability to co-exist in both these worlds that sets the intrapreneurial leader apart from others.

Beyond this you can dive deeper and look at the competencies and behaviors that distinguish traditional leaders from intrapreneurial leaders. Take for instance the top competencies that make intrapreneurial leaders successful: independent thinking, navigating uncertainty, engaged and thriving, driving change, leadership effectiveness and execution.

Traditional leaders possess these competencies but not at the depth that intrapreneurial leaders exhibit them. It is the depth of the competency that separates these two types of leaders.

The reality is that organizations need both types of leaders to build and sustain their business.

The question is what kind of leader are you?

Are you more of a traditional leader or more of an intrapreneurial leader?

Entrepreneurial Leaders: Chief Business Architect

Entrepreneurial leaders design and build new growth businesses. These leaders are less likely to have a political agenda. They have an organizational agenda that speaks to the need for the organization to move to a new operating model.

Entrepreneurial leaders know that the old model can get in the way and they are willing to take unpopular positions. They understand the need for change, and they are eager to lead that change. Tearing down old systems and rebuilding new ones is part of the job. They are business architects who design and build the entrepreneurial mindset and infrastructure for growth.

These leaders assert a certain amount of independence but are also loyal to the core business. Their loyalty is divided between the organization and their project. They need a certain degree of independence and autonomy to break through barriers and set up new systems. Over time, their loyalties will shift to the project as new systems are created to support a more entrepreneurial environment. They are often forced to make tough decisions that will test their loyalty to the company. It will come down to doing what is right, versus what is politically correct.

Entrepreneurial leaders understand the strategic significance of their project to the company's overall goals. They can envision the financial, political, and cultural impact these changes will have on the organization. They know the boundaries of the organization and recognize where they are flexible and where they are not. The project will test the limits of those boundaries. It will be necessary to push those boundaries beyond what is currently thought possible — and accept responsibility for the results.

Entrepreneurial leaders set the tone for the entire project by establishing an operating framework to support their efforts. They create organizational structures that are fluid and changeable. They create new systems and processes to support the end goals. They set new standards for productivity and performance. They reward risk-taking and initiative. They build a new entrepreneurial culture.

As the entrepreneurial leader, you will be designing and building a new infrastructure to support corporate entrepreneurship as you move forward. It is something that evolves over time. The goal will be to leverage the existing systems, policies, and practices of the core business, but that is often easier said than done. You will need to determine which systems, policies, and practices work and which ones don't. There is no research that describes the best type of operating environment for corporate entrepreneurship.

Your goal will be to transform the way your organization works to more effectively grow the business. You will need to ensure that the right people and processes are in place to accelerate business growth, minimize risks, and increase success rates. You will need to help your organization build the following capabilities.

- Develop the leadership skills needed to operate differently
- Create cross functional collaboration to support new ideas
- Instill program management discipline into operating practices
- Define the operating framework required for success
- Provide the tools, techniques and practices needed to be more effective
- Build execution competencies to increase buy-in and successful implementation

As an entrepreneurial leader these are just a few of the things that you will need to do to build the entrepreneurial mindset and infrastructure in your organization.

Entrepreneurial leaders are business architects that design, build and execute. They are true entrepreneurs in that sense. Although entrepreneurial leaders exhibit a high degree of independence, they are still very loyal employees. They are more entrepreneurial in their behavior. Their affiliation is more aligned with the project than the company. They are committed to their own personal values and those of the team, but they recognize that what they are doing is for the core business.

Entrepreneurial leaders create the mindset and develop the entrepreneurial infrastructure for success. They create the change that is required to transform the organization.

How do you create the entrepreneurial mindset and infrastructure for success?

Creating an Environment for Change

As an entrepreneurial leader, you soon come to understand why culture is often the biggest obstacle to creating an entrepreneurial venture inside an existing business. Culture is the social fabric of an organization, its personality, its values, norms, behaviors, rituals and beliefs. Like a human personality, it has evolved over time and is not easily changed.

Creating an entrepreneurial culture is hard work and it will be met with resistance by those most heavily invested in protecting the status quo. Change will be slow and painful. You will wonder if it is even possible to do what you have set out to do. It will test the very essence of who you are. You will be creating a new culture as you go.

Culture is a powerful force that shapes our individual and collective behavior. It influences everything we do and puts limits on our thinking and behavior. It sets the tone for how we work and how we relate to others in the organization. It is a reflection of our identity, our status and power. Changing these things is difficult and scary. But change them you must.

Creating an environment for change begins with setting the stage for change. It starts with a CEO who has a propensity for change. It requires a business sponsor committed to the project and willing to stick with it despite political obstacles. It will take an entrepreneurial leader who thrives in an environment of change. It will mean building a high-performance team that can stick with it.

Embed change in the process by building a team that is a mix of individuals from inside and outside the organization. If you are not lucky enough to hire from the outside, work with outside consultants who can help you develop the necessary behaviors and team dynamics. Develop values that encourage and support entrepreneurial behavior. Establish new norms and rituals with the team. It is often the "unlearning" part of change that is the most difficult.

Be prepared to deal with ambiguity, uncertainty, and failure. If your organization is not willing or able to effectively manage these, then *you* will have to. Living with ambiguity is part of the process. Dealing with uncertainty is a daily event, and failure is always a possibility. These are core characteristics of an entrepreneurial culture and will become part of the culture you create. Learning to manage them is what will be important. Capture the lessons you learn and share them with the group. They help shape and mold future decisions.

Value and acknowledge entrepreneurship as a core competency. Provide the training and development necessary to embed these competencies into daily work practices. Establish execution as a core competency and develop execution skills as the project progresses.

Over time, the vestiges of the old culture will quietly slip away, and a new culture will emerge. It is not an event but a process that is created through the collective efforts of the group. It is all about changing behaviors. It is a bonding experience that occurs because of a common vision and belief in achieving the end result. It is subtle and quiet, but it is extremely powerful.

The collective efforts of the group will shape and create a new culture. The team will begin to slowly move away from the core business and establish its own identity. The team will assert their independence and establish eminent domain. This will be threatening to the rest of the organization, which will interpret the behavior as a shift in power. Senior management will sit on the sidelines and observe this process as if it were some kind of scientific experiment. They may even question what they have created.

Change is an emotional experience and creating a new culture is a daunting task. Often this new culture is as temporary as the project that spawns it. If not, it must coexist with the core business and be an enabler for other entrepreneurial initiatives.

Does your organization have a change agenda for innovation?

Entrepreneurial Leaders: Trust & Risk Intertwined

As you transform your organization to be more entrepreneurial, you will find that trust and risk are woven throughout the process.

Trust between the leader and team lays the foundation for risk taking. Trust between the leader and the rest of the organization provides the framework for collaboration. Trust between the leader and senior management helps accelerate the transformation. Ultimately it is the trust in the leader that is the key to success.

As an entrepreneurial leader, you will have to navigate through uncharted waters and make unpopular decisions to keep things moving. There will be tradeoffs on the best way to use resources and allocate limited funds. You will have to take hard stands on issues that may be unpopular with the team and the organization.

Many organizational transformations are met with a certain level of skepticism in the beginning. People prefer to wait until they see progress before they are willing to lend their support. They are often more comfortable putting their trust in doing things the old way.

As the leader, it will be incumbent upon you to build trust. You may find that you must build that trust one person at a time. Having the ability to develop effective working relationships with those around you is a key component of building trust. It is all about relationship building and collaboration. As others begin to understand and see the value in what you are doing, then their trust in you will grow.

Building trust with senior management will be crucial in moving things forward and getting the support you need when unpopular decisions must be made. Trust is a double-edged sword that cuts both ways. Senior management will not always be comfortable with your decisions, but they will demonstrate their trust by delegating risk when it is required. The question is whether they will be willing to accept the results of those decisions when they don't go according to plan. There will be plenty of opportunities for you to test your trust in one another.

As your trust grows, so does your confidence in taking bigger, bolder risks. So, it is imperative that you have the self-confidence and conviction upfront to see things through until the end. You will need to be proactive, organized, disciplined, and decisive. It will be important that you are politically savvy and operate from an internal locus of control. You will need influence and good communication skills. These are the characteristics that will help you build the trust you need. Building trust will help you convince some of your skeptics, but not all of them.

As the leader you will never get the full trust of those around you. The team will present a united front to the rest of the organization but may question you behind closed doors. There will be times when you ask the team to make commitments that are above and beyond the normal call of duty. You will need to motivate and encourage them to stretch outside their comfort zone.

In turn, you will want the team to develop trust in them self. Over time you will be able to determine their level of trust through their work when they stop delegating the risky decisions to you. More importantly, you will know that they have developed a level of trust in themselves to take on greater risk. As you build a stronger relationship with your team, you will come to realize that trust and risk are intertwined.

Even though your peers may lend their support, they are not always totally supportive. It is not until they are willing to put some skin in the game that you can measure their trust. There are competitive forces at work here that transcend trust. Everyone is competing for limited funding and resources. So, it is not surprising that perhaps the greatest resistance you will encounter will be from your peers. You should not expect them to trust you.

It may be easier to understand the level of trust you've built with senior management. You will see it more clearly when there is a high-risk decision to be made or a major departure from normal operating procedures. Although they may have promised their support and encouragement in the beginning, it is not until you reach a pivotal point in the project that you understand their risk profile. Only then will you understand the level of trust they place in you.

Trust in leadership is becoming increasingly important as organizations deal with the rapid pace of change. Finding a leader people trust is only a small part of the challenge. Finding a leader that is willing to proactively take risks may be more difficult. Finding an organization that is willing to put their trust in allowing you to do whatever it takes without negative consequences for your actions is rare.

An entrepreneurial leader must demonstrate through their actions that trust and risk are part of the process, part of the learning, and part of the success that is required to move an idea, a project or an organization forward. The real risk is not taking risks. Trust on the other hand must be earned.

Developing entrepreneurial leaders who embody trust and risk will be one of your organization's greatest achievements as you build its capability to achieve business growth. Leaders will not only be judged on how well they executed, but how effectively they led.

The fact that trust and risk are intertwined creates an opportunity for you, your team and the organization to become more entrepreneurial.

Entrepreneurial Leaders – Alone on an Island

Can you imagine being stranded on a desert island with hundreds of boats sailing by and nobody seeming to notice you? Well, if you have ever been an entrepreneurial leader, you know what it's like dealing with isolation. It is the loneliest part of the job.

It isn't as if you are alone in the organization, it's that you find yourself sailing alone, often against the tide. You are trying to do new things, you are charting a new course, and you are making waves. Dealing with isolation and resistance is one of the loneliest parts of the job.

Not everyone understands or accepts what you are doing. It's as if you are sitting on the other side of the continent. You are the one charting a new course, laying a new foundation, experimenting, creating new methods and processes. You are creating a new world. Yet you know you must co-exist with the core business, so you balance the tradeoffs of what policies, procedures, systems, and measures fit and which don't. You have no guide to show you the way. You are often on your own.

Part of the isolation comes from not having a resource who fully understands what you are experiencing. Unless someone has been an entrepreneurial leader, they can only imagine what it is like. Since you are often blazing a new path, you are the one who sees the situation most clearly, and it will often be difficult for others to see things the same way. You may be able to bounce ideas around with others, but the clarity with which you see it can only be shared by someone else who's experienced it.

Another part of the isolation is the resentment and resistance you get from your peers and others in the organization. New initiatives are in the spotlight, with much attention and focus given to promoting the new and maintaining the old. There will always be a faction in the existing organization that is hoping you will fail. It is easier for them to sit on the sidelines and watch until they get a better handle on whether you will succeed or fail. It often comes down to a fear of change. If the project succeeds, then things will change, and they will need to change.

The resistance you face can slow things down. Understanding why you are getting resistance can help you deal with it more effectively. People resist for a number of reasons including a loss of control, uncertainty, surprises, past resentment, perceived or real threats and fears. This resistance is often expressed in their words and actions. "Give me more details" or "this is impractical" or "I'm not surprised, we have tried this before."

Keep in mind that the resistance is rational to the resistor but may not seem logical to you as the observer. Dealing with resistance when you encounter it may be easier than letting the situation go unresolved.

In many cases you are transitioning to a new organizational model that is uncertain. Many people will be reluctant to accept the new model until it has proven itself. There is a certain level of risk in embracing the new. This is especially true if the organization is experimenting with many new business opportunities. One entrepreneurial leader talked about the fact that their organization started so many new initiatives and finished so few that the organization viewed every new initiative as the "initiative of the quarter." The rest of the organization was not willing to support or embrace any new ones until they were solidly entrenched in the organization.

Isolation and resistance are the toughest part of the job. It is discouraging and it makes life tougher for the leader and the team, but it develops the skills and competencies that are needed to chart a new course.

At some point the island will become very attractive to others and the rest of the organization will be watching you on that island. They will be taking your lead. It's all part of the job and it is all part of the learning.

Leading through the Valley of Despair

Every entrepreneurial initiative eventually hits a wall called the "valley of despair." This is a point when the project gets bogged down, people are totally stressed, a negative attitude permeates the team, and progress slows to a crawl. Team members will get discouraged, spend time complaining, give up, and some will even quit.

When you get to this point you will know it. Understanding what it is, planning for it, and dealing with it appropriately will get you through, but it isn't easy, it isn't always fast, and it will take all the energy and emotion that you have left as a leader to manage through it. Each project will hit a wall that will dramatically change the team.

The challenge is recognizing that most projects reach a point where they face their own "valley of despair." Preparing the team for this and helping them through it will be challenging. They need to understand that it is a normal part of the process. They are transitioning to a new operating model and leaving the old model behind. There is anxiety in moving from something that is grounded and secure to something more fragile. Each person will react differently, but if they anticipate it, they can deal more effectively with it.

In turn, it's important that you prepare your sponsor and the CEO for this event. It will not only enable them to assist you through this process, but it also provides you with a sounding board. Like you, they must realize that the pressure and stress have been building to a point where the team can't take much more. The team will be tired, short-tempered, and rude to one another. They will find fault with things that they totally accepted before. The stress and pressure are natural byproducts of such an effort.

The valley of despair is not an event but a process that builds up. A team will naturally be energetic and enthusiastic at the beginning. Once they get deeply entrenched in the project, they often lose sight of why they are doing it in the first place. They ask themselves if the stress and pressure are worth it. They begin to question the viability of what they are doing. Fear begins to run rampant throughout the team that they will not make it.

Like dominoes, one person's fears play on another's until everyone is involved. The team slides further and deeper into the valley of despair.

At this point some people decide they've had enough and ask to go back into the core business. Others will decide it is time to leave. Either way, it has an impact on the team and organization. As the entrepreneurial leader, you will be trying to hold things together and find alternative solutions to fill the gaps. You begin to go through the same process as the team. You will need the support and encouragement of the CEO and sponsor to keep you energized. You may start having your own doubts.

As the team slides into the valley of despair, they will reach a transition point. This is when the team needs you the most. It is physically and emotionally draining. The team needs to stop and catch their breath. Pushing harder will only make things worse. They need to regroup and recalibrate where they are. They must put new plans in place to pick up the slack, find alternative resources to fill the gaps. This can be reenergizing and start to build back some of the confidence they have lost.

The team will then begin to build back momentum, turn the corner, and climb out of the valley of the despair. They have made the transition and have broken away from the core business. They are still scared and a little shaky, but they get back on track. These individuals will be changed forever because they made it through and reached the other side. They have created a new way of working and they have left the old systems behind. They can look back and see the core business for what it is and what they know it can become.

Each team member is personally and professionally changed by this event. They now see what is possible. There is no turning back.

You may never really understand what triggered the slide toward the valley of despair. It could be organizational pressure, time pressure, or self-imposed pressure. In most cases the team realizes that much is riding on the project and there is a growing feeling that they may not make it. It is as if you are stuck in quicksand or moving in slow motion.

Going through the valley of despair is part of the process. It will test the patience and resolve of the entrepreneurial leader.

Have you ever experienced the "valley of despair"? Let us know.

Time for Intrapreneurs to Step-up and Lead

A report by the Association of Executive Search and Leadership Consultants (AESC) showed that there is a high degree of anxiety among senior executives about their ability to keep up with a business climate of increasing uncertainty and rapid change. These executives are keenly aware of the disruption caused by the shift to a digital economy and increasing demands from their customers.

These factors combined with the changing demographics is putting pressure on organizations to identify and develop their next generation of leaders. Many of these executives recognize that leaders are the new competitive advantage. But do these executives truly understand what it takes to lead in the new business economy.

They themselves admit that they don't understand the new digital environment and are far removed from customers.

Despite being more traditional these executives do understand what is required to fill this role. Among the top five attributes cited in the report are leading change, being entrepreneurial, emotional intelligence, critical thinking and being innovative. Not surprisingly these attributes address the top factors that these executives are worried about the most, business continuity, revenue growth and succession planning.

There couldn't be a bigger neon sign than this report to say it is time for Intrapreneurs to step-up to lead. Intrapreneurs can no longer sit back and wait for an opportunity to present itself. They must rise to the occasion. It is not about being given the lead but taking the lead.

Although many executives can describe what they are looking for in the next generation of leaders, they are not always as clear on what they want them to do. Dealing with uncertainty, complexity and a rapidly changing business environment is key but directing these individuals toward strategic objectives that contribute to the longer-term viability of the company is just as important.

Still many executives are unwilling or unable to venture outside their own comfort zone. Financial uncertainty and increasing complexity make's most executives risk adverse. They may set goals that they know are achievable. Direct resources toward initiatives they feel are more likely to succeed. Fund initiatives that have a short-term payback. It is for these reasons that intrapreneurs must step-up to the challenge and not only identify potential opportunities but develop a roadmap for moving forward toward those objectives.

The challenge for Intrapreneurs is knowing how far they can push the boundaries of the organization. Learning where the organization is flexible and where it is not. Determining the level of risk that will be acceptable. Leveraging resources that they don't own. Making decisions that they don't have the authority to make. Stepping on toes and breaking rules. Challenging long held beliefs. Pushing others outside their comfort zone. Aligning themselves with customers first, then the organization. Taking responsibility and accountability when things go wrong. Being willing to risk it all for the company despite good intentions. And so on….

These are things that Intrapreneurs must consider when they step-up to lead. Management won't always be happy or condone what you're doing but they will admire your courage, commitment and persistence in trying. It is through your example that management will learn what it takes to be an intrapreneur, to be innovative and drive change. They don't always know what they don't know until they see it, experience it or deal with it in real time. Even then, it may only be in hindsight that they see the situation can be seen more clearly.

Intrapreneurs must demonstrate through their actions that they are ready to lead. Not in what they say but in what they do. Being an intrapreneur is more than a mindset, it is a set of behaviors and actions.

Ask yourself the following questions:

1. Do you openly question and challenge authority?
2. Do you tolerate ambiguity and uncertainty or embrace it?
3. Do you trust your ability to make judgements even if they contradict others?
4. Do you rely on what you know or are you eager to explore the unknown?
5. Do you try to simplify things too quickly or linger in complexity?
6. Do you let organizational barriers and obstacles stop you from moving forward?
7. Do you evaluate decisions through the lens of past experience?
8. Do you wait until you have all the data before making a decision?
9. Do you manage risk through analysis or through action?
10. Do you try to minimize failure or maximize results?

These are only a few of the questions that you need to ask yourself before you step-up and take the lead. There is no right or wrong answer. These questions help you understand your intrapreneurial orientation. Are you more of a traditional or intrapreneurial leader when it comes to how you approach work? The true intrapreneurial leader is a little of both.

As an intrapreneurial leader you must be able to manage the core business while you are creating a new one. That means consciously living in both these worlds simultaneously. Managing the past and leading into the future.

It is time for you to step-up and lead. Let the experience take you where it may because it is the only way to develop, refine and perfect your capability as an Intrapreneurial leader. If you don't step-up now somebody else will. The lack of intrapreneurial leadership at the top of most organizations is putting the longer-term survival of those organizations in jeopardy.

Keep in mind that there can be consequences to your actions. Even if you received encouragement from management in the beginning or along the way. The expectation is that things will work out for best. In reality, they may not. You must be prepared to deal with the consequences. It's up to you.

In the end, no matter what the outcome, you will have gained valuable experience that you can build on or take with you into your next intrapreneurial pursuit.

Innovation Edge – Intrapreneurial Leaders

In most organizations growth through innovation is a top priority. So is talent. Yet, few organizations adequately look at the link between innovation growth and talent.

According to McKinsey, "*The number one predictor of innovation success is leadership.*" It is a special kind of leadership – intrapreneurial leadership. Research shows that there is a strong correlation between intrapreneurial leadership and higher levels of innovation growth.

The key to enhanced performance and innovation success is aligning the right leaders with your innovation goals. It is crucial to find, support and develop these innovators the best way possible. But do you know who they are?

Future leaders are often molded in the image of the existing leaders who run the core business. That is a mistake.

The skills and capabilities that propelled most executives to the top of organizations in the past are not the ones required to build new innovations. These executives are often blinded by their own experience. They rely on proven approaches that worked well in the core business but may not in a new business. They make decisions based on reason and argument not creative thought. They trust data more than intuition. They focus on minimizing risk versus maximizing value. They will sacrifice the long-term potential for short term gain. They prefer to wait until things become clearer before acting.

Perhaps this is part of the reason that revenue and innovation growth in organizations has slowed. Organizations marginalize their innovation efforts by playing it safe with individuals who represent the past, not the future.

In the article, How to Innovate When You're Not the Big Boss, John Beeson said "*Given the unrelenting pace of change surrounding organizations in virtually every industry, companies are looking for executives who know how to innovate and introduce change, not simply caretakers who can manage the status quo.*"

Often the types of individuals needed to lead innovation projects are not even considered for the position. These individuals represent a small minority of independent thinkers who do not fit the corporate mold. They see the world differently and they think and act differently. They don't let existing systems and processes get in their way. They find new and creative ways to get things done. They are energized and engaged in learning and driving change. They will leverage whatever resources they have available to them. They are focused on execution – creating value and generating revenue growth.

Keep in mind that there are no roadmaps or guidebooks for intrapreneurial leaders to follow. They must create a new path, new processes, and new ways of working. They will encounter obstacles that the organization has not encountered before. Face seemingly impossible hurdles and resistance to change. They will need to be strategic and tactical at the same time. Influence and negotiate effectively for ideas and concepts that many will find hard to comprehend. They will have to make decisions without sufficient data. Take calculated risks based on affordable loss. Break rules and step on toes to get things done.

These individuals must have the interpersonal competencies needed to deal effectively with the turmoil and chaos that exists in innovation ventures. It is not just a matter of being adaptable or accountable but being collaborative, tolerant, and passionate. Listening for understanding, communicating effectively, and being empathic to the needs of those around them. They need to have a realistic and honest assessment of their own strengths and weaknesses. They must have a high tolerance for stress. It is not about positional power but personal power that enables intrapreneurial leaders to break new ground.

A key challenge for entrepreneurial leaders is that they don't feel like they speak the same language as many of the other leaders in their organizations. They are probably right. Not everyone can see what they say. Bosses and peers may not have a frame of reference or experience base to relate to. It is up to the leader to paint a clear picture of where they are headed and the process to get there so that everyone sees and understands the same vision.

Of course, that vision will change as the innovation moves forward so it is incumbent upon the leader to keep everyone up to date. Setting expectations that innovation is not a straight line but a series of twists and turns. It's about embracing the unexpected, leveraging contingences and changing course when it no longer makes sense.

We found in our research that intrapreneurial leaders that are successful in leading innovation projects have three different types of competencies that enable them to be effective.

- Intrapreneurial Competencies
- Business Competencies
- Interpersonal Competencies.

The intrapreneurial competencies help leaders step outside of their traditional role and operate as an independent entity or startup within an established organization. The business competencies are capabilities that are more traditional and are leveraged in both the core business and in an innovation project. The interpersonal competencies are unique to the individual and reflect their outlook and how they respond to the challenges they encounter.

According to research only 4 to 5 percent of individuals in large organizations are intrapreneurs or intrapreneurial. The true intrapreneurial leader is rare. That is why the most innovative organizations are proactively identifying and developing their intrapreneurial leaders.

Innovation has become a critical imperative for many organizations and a survival strategy for others. The difference between success and failure may rest with the leaders you choose to lead these efforts.

Intrapreneurial leaders give your organization an *innovation edge.*

Is the Crisis Turning CEOs into Intrapreneurs

The impact of the current crisis has put extraordinary pressure on CEOs and executives to react quickly, deal with uncertainty, experiment with new ideas, reallocate resources, accelerate decision making and drive change needed to deal effectively with this new environment.

It has challenged them to adapt to a new way of operating that is foreign to most executives. They have had to change their mindset and their actions to align with a new reality - dealing with the unknown. It has also given them time for reflection, time to assess their own leadership style, and time to enhance their communication skills. It has driven them to become more open, transparent, and humane.

CEOs recognize that existing strategic plans may no longer make sense. That the current operating environment may be getting in their way – creating barriers to higher levels of productivity. That organizational policies and procedures designed to streamline processes may be too rigid and inflexible – stifling innovation and growth. That leadership practices that worked in the past may be ineffective moving forward. That there is a shift taking place that will change the direction and culture of the organization.

More importantly CEOs have a deeper appreciation for all stakeholders especially workers that have become energized, more creative and inspired by the need for change. CEOs see how the crisis has motivated employees to work harder, smarter, and engage themselves in their work. They see the value and contribution that workers are making to keep the organization vibrant and moving forward in the face of adversity.

The crisis has forced change on all of us but nowhere is it more evident than with the CEO and senior executives. We are talking about leaders that have built their careers exploiting the core business. Now they must explore building a new one – one that leverages the best of the past and incorporates the potential found in new technology, socially conscious workers, and demands from stakeholders to build a better, more just world. Like a startup, CEOs must reimagine a future that blends the best of both worlds – the old and the new.

According to McKinsey in the article The CEO Moment: Leadership in a New Era, "*The changes have been birthed by necessity, but they have great potential beyond the crisis. .... It has unfrozen many aspects of the CEO role, making possible re-fusing of new and existing elements that could define the CEO role of the future.*"

All of this begs the question whether the crisis is turning CEOs into Intrapreneurs?

The crisis has set the stage for CEOs and senior executives to experience what it takes to be an intrapreneur or Intrapreneurial leader. As we know, being an intrapreneur is not an intellectual exercise - it is developed through experience. The crisis has placed that type of experience directly in the hands of CEOs. They can respond to it as a traditional leader or an intrapreneurial one.

The best way to think about this is to look at what it takes to be an Intrapreneurial Leader and evaluate the way's CEOs are responding to the crisis. We can use our checklist of Intrapreneurial competencies, characteristics, and success factors to help us answer the question. Looking first at competencies.

- As the crisis unfolds, we see CEOs networking with other CEOs to solicit ideas, input, and advice on how to best deal with the situation. They see value and solace in working with peers. They are less comfortable relying on their own observations and experience to guide them. Just the opposite of what intrapreneurs do as independent thinkers. CEOs are however, seeking new knowledge, questioning the status quo, willing to try new things and open to exploring the unknown which are all key aspects of independent thinking – the top competency of intrapreneurs.
- CEOs recognize that speed is critical in this uncertain time. Finding new ways to accelerate their response to market changes has become an imperative. They cannot afford to wait until things become clearer or more certain. According to The Need for Speed in Post Covid-19 Era, "*It requires executives to rework many of the long-standing constructs within their organizations.*" As a result, CEOS are open to blazing new trails by looking for opportunities to stretch themselves and their organizations. They are willing to take risks, navigate uncertainty, and change systems and structures to move their organizations forward into the future - like Intrapreneurs do.
- Every CEO is being pressured to establish new goals and reimagine a new future. To do this they must not only be committed they must be actively involved. This requires a concerted effort on their part to be totally engaged while motivating and inspiring the rest of the organization. They need to be self-motivated to do whatever it takes, deal with barriers that get in their way, have a high tolerance for stress and achieve closure. CEOs appear to be energized by the challenge in front of them. Being engaged and thriving leads to higher levels of productivity and financial performance – a key competency of Intrapreneurs.
- The unprecedented challenge facing CEOs is magnified by the pace and nature of change. It is forcing CEOs and leaders throughout the organization to lead change. Not just changing structures, policies, or practices. It requires a shift in mindset, beliefs, and

behaviors. Behaviors that need to be learned, experienced, and modeled that show what is expected, what will be tolerated, and the value these changes can bring. McKinsey found that "*More than half of leaders surveyed are considering or planning large scale changes.*" Many CEOs are now driving change in their organizations – something that Intrapreneurs do well.

- To be an effective leader during a time of uncertainty leaders must shift their focus, their posture, and their communications. They must deal with all the complexity of starting something new, build a commitment toward a common goal, break down self-imposed barriers and those of their team, erect structures that are fluid and changeable and find creative ways to leverage limited resources. CEOs are doing just that. They are reallocating resources, communicating more effectively, becoming more transparent, listening more, and building trust. Things Intrapreneurs do to build a more adaptable, flexible, and responsive environment for growth.
- CEOs have stated that speed is paramount, but that execution is the ultimate test in defining success in this new environment. According to Art Petty, Leadership and Management Expert, "*The challenge for senior leaders is to create the environment and systems to enable emergent and adaptive strategies and flexible execution, all fueled by rapid learning.*" That requires having a clear understanding of the end goal, knowing how the target may shift, changing course when it is necessary, or killing a project when it no longer makes sense. This requires being decisive, balance acceleration with control, explore variability and contingencies and effectively communicate – things CEOs are doing and intrapreneurs have always done well.

The crisis has put a spotlight on leaders and their response to the situation. It has given them time to look at themselves, their leadership style and assess their own performance. Leaders that are successful exhibit the following characteristics.

- The crisis has given CEOs more time for self-reflection which has enabled them to step back and evaluate their leadership style and look at what is required moving forward. Understanding one's strengths, weaknesses, thoughts, beliefs, motivations, and emotions is the first step in becoming more self-aware. CEOs are showing their willingness and ability to be mindful, take time for self-reflection, and to look at their own beliefs and values. There is a strong correlation between self-awareness and leadership effectiveness - a key characteristic of intrapreneurs.

- Executive presence is the ability to connect and engage with others in a manner that is authentic, intentional, resilient, balanced, and trustworthy. It is how you perceive yourself and how others see and respond to you. According to Shruti Dhupia, in his article, How COVID-19 is Redefining Leadership, "*In these challenging times, leaders seem more intrinsically motivated to be visible and have a heightened sense of responsibility and ownership.*" This has created a stronger connection and higher levels of motivation for employees. A strong presence helps leaders drive innovation, change and transformation successfully – like intrapreneurs.
- Understanding your brain dominance (left brain analytical or right brain creative) has an impact on communication and leadership effectiveness. The current crisis has highlighted the growing need for more whole brain thinking. "*Unfortunately, most of today's C-suite leaders say their right brain is the weakest – that includes intuition, empathy, self-awareness and vigilance to the external environment,*" according to Accenture Research. Their research showed that "*Adopting a more whole brain leadership style has resulted in a positive bottom line, higher revenue growth and profitability.*" Intrapreneurs are more likely to be right brain or whole brain thinkers.
- A measurement that organizations use to gauge their commitment of employees is level of engagement. Not surprisingly we see that CEOs are highly engaged. They recognize the value of keeping themselves, the organization and its various stakeholders engaged during this crisis. Leaders and teams with higher levels of

engagement, produce substantially better financial and operating outcomes, treat customers better and attract new ones, and see higher levels of innovation and productivity. In this case, CEOs are the ones that have been instrumental in setting the tone for greater collaboration among stakeholders and creating higher levels of engagement among them – the same things Intrapreneurs do.

The pandemic has forced executives to move outside their own comfort zone to think and act differently. It is how they see and react to the external world. Thinking and acting differently are key leadership success factors for Intrapreneurs and CEOs. It is not whether they are competent to do something, but how they approach a situation. There are four key success factors – intrapreneurial mindset, thinking process, decision making and taking-action.

- A challenge facing CEOs is changing their mindset to be open to new possibilities. "*CEOs are recognizing that the barriers to boldness and speed are less about technical limits and more about such things as mindsets toward what is possible, what people are willing to do, the degree to which implicit and explicit policies that slow things down can be challenged, and bureaucratic chains of command,*" according to How Covid Has Forced CEOs to Change the Way They Lead. CEOs are taking stock of what is now possible. There is a focus on people, rethinking their portfolios, taking a longer-term view, experimentation, and willingness to take bold moves. These are things that distinguish a fixed mindset from an intrapreneurial mindset.
- As CEOs rethink their strategy and business models they are focused on iterative and scenario planning. The crisis is challenging everything they have known to be true. It is changing their thinking process and how they gather and evaluate information. In the article, How to Think Differently About Leading and Managing, "*Much of the work of thinking differently feels counterintuitive. The ideas fly in the face of the patterns and approaches we've grown conditioned to in our lives,*" The crisis is forcing leaders to rely

more on intuition, see patterns and relationships to form new concepts, analyze and synthesize large amounts of data, evaluate ideas through experimentation, and create new innovative solutions - the way intrapreneurs do.

- Decision making has taken on increased importance during this crisis. Speed in decision making has become a priority. Decisions that may determine the future direction of the organization. According to The CEO Moment: Leadership for a New Era, "*CEOs are being called upon to make decisions they have never been trained for. Tough decisions with profound human consequences.*" They must be willing to make decisions without having all the data, take calculated risks, be flexible and adaptable while balancing short-and-long term demands. In the article, Developing Speed for the Post-COVID-18 Era, "*CEOs…are using technology, sharpening their focus on customers, and improving communications to expedited decision making and collaboration,*" – things intrapreneurs do.
- The pandemic is being called the 'burning platform' that has ignited change and prompted action among CEOs around the world. In the article, Innovation in a Time of Crisis, Larry Clark states that the pandemic is "*Creating a bias toward action. Unfreezing organizations and generating real demand for action.*" This requires being creative, leveraging contingencies, embracing surprises, and controlling uncertainty by acting. Intrapreneurs understand the value of taking- action without having all the answers – something CEOs are doing now to adapt to this new environment.

The changes brought on by this crisis has prompted CEOs, leaders, and workers to be more creative, decisive and action oriented. Illustrating the value of being more intrapreneurial in a world that has been changed forever.

Is the Crisis Turning CEOs into Intrapreneurs? – *It is starting to look like it.*

Chapter 11: Talent

- Resurgence of Intrapreneurs
- Why Intrapreneurs Remain Elusive
- Intrapreneurs and the New War for Talent
- Intrapreneurs as Free Agents and Freelancers
- Intrapreneurs – Product or Service
- Intrapreneurs Path to Conscious Leadership
- 10 Reasons Why Intrapreneurs Need a Success Profile
- 6 Reasons to Hire Intrapreneurs Now

Resurgence of Intrapreneurs

Although interest in Intrapreneurs seems to rise and fall with the economy the current interest is being fueled by a growing recognition that growth through innovation is a critical imperative for most organizations.

The term Intrapreneur was first used in 1978 in an article written by Gifford Pinchot and later in his book *Intrapreneuring for Action.*

The book highlights how Intrapreneurs are the key to effectively implementing innovation. Pinchot defined the term Intrapreneur as, "*A person within a large corporation who takes direct responsibility for turning an idea into a profitable finished product through assertive risk-taking and innovation.*"

Today Intrapreneurs are also known as corporate entrepreneurs, mavericks, change agents, positive deviants, growth leaders, change wizards or as I like to call them internal entrepreneurs. No matter what you call them, these individuals are entrepreneurs – inside themselves and their organizations.

The importance of internal entrepreneurs is being reinforced with an increase in blog posts, articles, and books on the topic. Articles like 10 Tips for Intrapreneurs, Exit Managers Enter – Intrapreneurs, Google and Its New Management Method: Intrapreneurs, etc. Plus, the interest in social Intrapreneurs is breathing new life into this concept.

Despite Pinchot's definition and the growing interest in Intrapreneurs there still remains a lack of understanding about who these individuals are, why they are different, or why it is important. Internal entrepreneurs will tell you that their organizations don't understand them or appreciate them for what they do or how they do it. They are frustrated with their organizations inability to effectively capitalize on their skills and capabilities.

Ten years ago, if you searched on Google for the term Intrapreneur, corporate entrepreneur or internal entrepreneur you were lucky if you came back with a page and a half of links. Today if you search on those same terms you come back with millions of hits. If you think this is good news, think again. The proliferation of information has only served to confuse not clarify who these individuals are.

The book *Acceleration – Changing the Speed of Growth* provides an in depth look at the top competencies that distinguish internal entrepreneurs and entrepreneurial leaders from others. It is a good starting point for understanding who these individuals are, why they are different and why it is important.

Finding and developing internal entrepreneurs has become a top priority for organizations that want to achieve new growth through innovation. They know that if they don't find these individuals, some other organization will.

Why Intrapreneurs Remain Elusive

Innovation and growth are the critical factors behind the interest in Intrapreneurship. That's the good news. The bad news is that you can't have either without the right talent. Finding the right talent to achieve innovation and growth is what is proving to be elusive.

This is a challenge for organizations and an opportunity for intrapreneurs. As an organization, if you don't know what you are looking for then how will you know when you find it?

You can't solve today's problems with the same people who created them. You need to look beyond the obvious. So, it is not surprising that there is a shortage of talent needed to deal with increasing complexity, uncertainty and the unknown. That is what is driving the interest in intrapreneurs

Organizations focused on intrapreneurship are realizing that talent is their competitive advantage. That in the next decade most of them will be facing a new War on Talent. According to The New Wave: Next Generation of Executive Talent – AESC report, "*There is a premium for top talent and not enough immediate successors at the helm ready to take over as the Baby Boomers retire. This has created anxiety among CEOs and senior executives that recognize that a new type of leader is needed to deal with 'global uncertainty.*" An Intrapreneurial Leader.

All of this is happening at a time when the largest demographic millennials want to work in an entrepreneurial role – in or outside of the traditional organization. Being an intrapreneur is the new aspiration of millions of workers around the world. Technological advances are one of the forces impacting work but despite these advances in technology most of the capabilities needed for strategic innovation cannot be replicated by a machine. It is all about people.

Part of the reasons why organizations are not effectively leveraging their intrapreneurs relates to what Kara Kavensky talks about in her article, Intrapreneurship: A Driving Force with Companies, "*Intrapreneurs have a rare mix of corporate experience and existing business connections alongside risk taking and trial mentality of entrepreneurs.*" Yet most organizations don't know who these individuals are or the best way to find them.

So, what is it about Intrapreneurs that seem to be so elusive? Like you I've seen tons of articles outlining what is required to be an effective Intrapreneur. It is an endless list of attributes that are mostly based on anecdotal data which continues to swirl around these individuals - intrapreneurs. The problem is that very little of the reported lists are grounded in research - research with Intrapreneurs that have been successful in this role. According to Human Resource Development, "*The research to date has produced an inconsistent body of research with limited empirical evidence.*"

If you tried to live up to all the hype you read about of what it takes to be an intrapreneur - you'd be superman or superwomen. This is what you are being led to believe. It's not true.

The truth is that entrepreneurs and intrapreneurs are different. Traditional leaders are different than intrapreneurial leader. Disruptive innovations require different skills and capabilities than core or adjacent innovations. These differences are what distinguish the true intrapreneur from others. In a recent study, the Thought Leadership Institute found that, "*The goals of operational excellence and breakthrough innovation are different enough to require distinctions in assessing talent for both roles. But on average less than one third do.*"

Part of the issue for organizations is creating an environment where individuals can experience what it takes to be an intrapreneur. Experience is the key to unlocking the mystery of what it means and what it takes to be an intrapreneur. Understanding what you don't know is just as important as what you know. The other part is understanding what competencies intrapreneurs need to succeed. Putting your competencies to the test helps you see if you have what it takes. It is the only way you will know what competencies you need to enhance and develop.

A competency is a set of knowledge, skills and behaviors, attitudes and characteristics that distinguish one person from another. But more importantly it refers to a set of behaviors that an individual must possess to perform a specific job. The job of intrapreneur.

A key factor in the shortage of intrapreneurial leaders at the top of most organizations is a result of this lack of understanding of what competencies are needed to succeed and creating an environment where individuals can have an intrapreneurial learning experience. Thinking you are an intrapreneur is not the same as being an intrapreneur.

Organizations that define a common or generic set of competencies for everyone in the organization are missing the boat. High performance companies develop success profiles for specific job functions within their organizations that are tied to targeted outcomes. To develop intrapreneurs there needs to be a concerted effort to identify and develop competencies aligned with the goals and outcomes of the organization to be more innovative and entrepreneurial.

In his article Competencies: Alternative Frameworks for Competitive Advantage, Robert Cardy states that "*The importance of competencies to organizations cannot be overstated; in fact, they can be the key to competitive advantage. They allow the concept of strategic intent to be operationalized.*" Resulting in higher levels of performance.

Our research has identified a set of core competencies Intrapreneurs need to be effective and successful in their organizations. Over the last ten years we have tracked successful intrapreneurs and determined that beyond all the hype intrapreneurs need to build and strengthen a core set of competencies to succeed in this role. It's a success profile for Intrapreneurs. An independent analysis of our data revealed that intrapreneurs are in fact 'a distinct group of professionals'. They outperformed more traditional professionals by a wide margin.

Intrapreneurs possess a unique combination of competencies but most people have these competencies. It is not one or two unique competencies; it is a unique combination of competencies. It is the breadth and depth of those competencies that distinguish the true intrapreneurs. These competencies are capabilities that can be learned. It is a mindset, a set of competencies and behaviors that are learned along the way.

Competencies are developed through experience. Understanding what type of experience is critical for development of these competencies. If your experience is grounded in the core business then great, you will probably learn some new things. If the experience involves a new product, service or venture that you've never done before you will learn more about yourself, the organization, and what it means and what it takes to be an intrapreneur.

Think about a time when you experienced something for the first time. What impact did it have? How did it make you feel? What did you learn? Did it change your beliefs? It is through experience that we see the world in a new light. We let go of long held beliefs and open ourselves to new possibilities. It forces us outside our comfort zone and opens ourselves up to being surprised at seeing what we don't know – especially about being an intrapreneur.

Although the concept of competencies is not universally understood and has been the province of the HR or OD departments within organizations. Research has found that competencies are a better predictor of capability than a functional competency. "*High performance competencies are associated with individuals that perform their job at a superior level,*" according to Dr. Tony Cockerill, London Business School. It is for this reason that understanding what competencies are required in the role of intrapreneur is critical.

The reason why intrapreneurs remain elusive for many organizations is that they have not focused on developing the core competencies needed for intrapreneurs to be successful in that role. As a result, we see more and more individuals taking matters into their own hands and developing their own intrapreneurial competencies through the work they do and the projects they elect to take on. It is having the right set of competencies and experiences that enable intrapreneurs to succeed.

Despite the glaring need for intrapreneurs and intrapreneurial leaders, the intrapreneur continues to be elusive? Yet what we've found is that there is no longer a reason for that to be true.

Intrapreneurs and the New War for Talent

According to KPMGs report on CEOs "95% of CEOs see organic growth as the key to drive corporate growth and profitability."

All of this is happening despite the geopolitical uncertainty and instability in the US and around the world. The pressure is coming from the technological advances that are transforming businesses and industries, the lack of investments in the past in developing new products and services, shareholder pressure for increased revenue and unrest among workers.

These factors are forcing organizations to rethink their business models and the people who work for them. According to McKinsey," *In tumultuous times, a company's talent is its most valuable and reliable asset.*" Thus, we are finally hearing the term 'Talent Driven Companies.'

In the new book Talent Wins, the McKinsey authors state that "*In our combined 90 years of advising CEOs and their boards, we have never come across a moment like this, when virtually every CEO we work with is asking the same daunting questions: Are my company's talent practices still relevant? How can we recruit, deploy, and develop people to deliver greater value to customers – and do so better than the competition?*"

The current optimism among CEOs is putting pressure on organizations to strengthen their pool of talent. Not just any talent, the right talent. Individuals that can generate new business growth.

Yet despite the fact that talent is now becoming a strategic priority, workers are looking outside these organizations for work that they are passionate about, that has meaning, creates value and aligns with their own personal and professional ideals. These are goals and aspiration we see among all types of workers, especially intrapreneurs.

Intrapreneurs are reinventing work as we know it. They are not willing to accept the status quo.

These Intrapreneurs are restless and are becoming freelancers, free agents and independent consultants. No longer are organizations competing against other organizations for talent, they are competing against the talent itself. The growing need for Intrapreneurs and the rise in freelancers is redefining the war for talent.

The Pew Research Center found that, "*Freelancers accounted for $1.4 trillion in economic activity last year. Entrepreneurship gives people freedom over their work, which also improves well-being. One study of 11,000 graduates from the Wharton School of Business found that those running their own businesses were happier than graduates in other jobs – no matter how much money they made.*"

The new war for talent pits organizations against the best and brightest talent. Intrapreneurs in particular are in high demand. They are exerting their independence at a time when organizations need them the most. They are looking for work they want, projects they are interested in doing, and organizations that enable and support them in these efforts.

Although the spotlight is now on talent, many organizations may find themselves playing catch up. It's nice to say you are a talent driven company, it's much more difficult to actually be one. The ability to attract, develop and retain the best and brightest may just have gotten a lot harder. There is a shortage of entrepreneurial talent in most large organizations. The intrapreneurs who are already in them are often discouraged, disenchanted, and disengaged.

Part of this is a result of neglect in developing entrepreneurial talent needed to deal with a more complex and uncertain business environment. Although this is changing. Part of it is a reluctance to make the necessary changes required to create an entrepreneurial environment. Part of it is a shift in the demographics of the work force and the emergence of technologically savvy workers wired to think and act differently. Part of it is not understanding who intrapreneurs are and how they operate. Part of it is a shortage of entrepreneurial leadership at the top of organizations.

Two key dynamics are making the war for talent more challenging.

Experience for one. We have a growing pool of intrapreneurs who have over the last decade been building their own entrepreneurial capabilities despite the obstacles that have gotten in their way. They have been proactive in selecting projects that challenge them and accelerate their learning curve. They have been building a portfolio of skills and capabilities they can take anywhere. They know what they are capable of doing and are more discerning in the projects they take on. They know what they need from an organization to be effective and successful. They are taking the initiative to learn from others like themselves through networking, conferences and workshops. They are deciding what organizations they want to work with, not the other way around.

Freelance movement is second. The growing trend toward freelance work provides an alternative to the daily grind of a traditional nine to five job. It provides the independence that many workers crave and the flexibility to control their own destiny. They are better able to balance their personal and professional life. They can work on projects that they are interested in pursuing. They find satisfaction in knowing they are making a difference and having an impact. Many prefer self-employment to being an employee doing work that does not take advantage of their skills. Experienced intrapreneurs in particular are comfortable with the trade-offs of being on their own. They have essentially been on their own, often without the full support of their organizations.

Much of this is a reflection of the growing dissatisfaction among workers seen in the high number of disengaged employees. A lack of understanding of what motivates and engages today's workers, especially intrapreneurs. Plus, there is a shortage of workers to fill key positions. As a result, organizations are being pressured to hire more and more freelancers and consultants. Many freelancers already partner with Fortune 1000 companies on a project basis, including intrapreneurs that are now out on their own.

All of this is happening while organizations say they want to be a Talent

Driven company. It's great to hear that more organizations want to be talent driven but do they really know what that means and what it will take. If the goal is to leverage talent to achieve organic growth, then knowing what talent is needed is key. Entrepreneurial talent and leadership are what is needed.

The challenge will be bridging the gap between the needs and desires of these workers and the organizations that now need them. Until that is resolved....

The new war for talent has put talent, especially intrapreneurs in the driver's seat.

Intrapreneurs as 'Free Agents and Freelancers'

According to the Career Advisory Board, "*One in two American workers is projected to be self employed by 2020.*" The recent study highlighted the fact that professionals today are choosing self-employment in order to control the type of work they want to pursue. Many are abandoning the traditional career path and choosing to work part time. They see contract work as a viable alternative.

These dynamics are changing work as we know it and creating new issues for organizations.

Organizations are being forced to embrace this new paradigm given the gap in supply and demand for critical talent. They are creating new business models based on a combination of full-time, part-time and freelance workers. These hybrid business models enable organizations to design work around the individual and leverage talent across the organization. In the next five years half of the workforce will be comprised of external talent.

In his article The New Free Agent Nation, Max Mihelich makes it clear that, "*The notion of the free agent worker has not only changed the way people think about work. It has altered the employer-employee social contract.*" Millennials in particular want to take control of their own futures and work where they are most productive. Generation X workers are independent, entrepreneurial and more committed to their profession than their company. Baby boomers not ready to retire prefer to work part time in positions that are aligned with their own interests and passions.

All of this is happening at time when there is shortage of high performing individuals.

Talent managers are under pressure to meet the demand for professionals who can help their organizations grow and deal with a rapidly changing competitive landscape. They are actively identifying freelance workers who can fill specialized positions. Individuals that that are interested in innovation activities that drive business value. Individuals that have the competencies needed to achieve success. Individuals that think and act like entrepreneurs. Among them are intrapreneurs.

Intrapreneurs are one of the most sought-after professionals in the 21st century economy.

The demand for intrapreneurs however outstrips the current supply. According to numerous studies only a small fraction of executives and professionals are entrepreneurs or entrepreneurial. We know there are more. In many organizations efforts to adequately identify, engage and develop intrapreneurs has been slow and ineffective. Part of the issue is that these organizations have not had a clear definition of what it takes to be a successful intrapreneur. Many intrapreneurs go unnoticed or overlooked because they don't fit the typical profile of a high potential.

A high potential in the core business is not necessarily a high potential when it comes to building a new business. It is for this reason that we see many intrapreneurs deciding to go out on their own and join the ranks of the self-employed, freelancer, contract worker movement. They understand being different is what sets them apart but also makes them more effective in the role. These differences often stand in stark contrast to the rest of the organization. Not fitting in is the very reason why many intrapreneurs feel alienated and disconnected from the rest of the organization.

It is also why intrapreneurs take ownership for their own growth and development. They are not willing to wait for the organization to hand them an opportunity. They proactively seek out opportunities where they can stretch, grow, and learn new ways of working. They want to understand their own strengths and weaknesses. They look at every opportunity as a way to test themselves. They are not content to just learn a skill; they seek to perfect it and turn it into a competency. If an organization does not provide them an opportunity to do these things, they will either do it themselves or look for another company that will.

It is for these reasons that intrapreneurs may be the most valuable pool of free agent candidates an organization can hire. The question for organizations is how you identify, develop and engage intrapreneurs. The current shortage of intrapreneurs makes that more difficult. Competitive forces will only drive demand for intrapreneurs higher and higher. It will not only be a question of finding them, it will be a question of providing an environment that keeps them engaged over the longer term.

For intrapreneurs it is a matter of demonstrating that you have what it takes to be an intrapreneur no matter whether you are inside or outside an organization. Being an intrapreneur is not an intellectual exercise. You need to experience being an intrapreneur to build the competencies that are required to be effective in that role. Think of every opportunity as a way to learn, grow and challenge what you know.

If you buy into the premise that we will all be free agents in the future, then preparing for it now is critical. Explore your strengths and weaknesses. Understand what motivates and inspires you. Create a personal brand, develop presence and demonstrate credibility. Raise your hand to work on the toughest challenges and biggest problems. Build a portfolio of intrapreneurial experiences that show that you have what it takes. Take a hard look at yourself. Self-awareness is the key to your success.

As a free agent you stand alone. You are the product. It's up to you to take the lead and pave your own path forward. The more experience you gain, the more success you have, the more valuable you will become to the companies that are embracing this hybrid business model. Individuals that do it well will grow and prosper. Those that don't will resign themselves to work as we did in the past.

Intrapreneurs are uniquely positioned to take advantage of this growing trend. The current shortage of intrapreneurs provides an opportunity for existing and aspiring intrapreneurs to take ownership for their own destiny. It's up to you. The future belongs to you.

Intrapreneurs: Product or Service

If we look at Intrapreneurs and the value they bring to organizations, they are more than just an organizational asset. So, ask yourself – Are they more like a product or service? It may sound crazy to think of Intrapreneurs this way but is it?

In many ways Intrapreneurs are a product of their environment, experience and their learning. They are either fortunate to work in an entrepreneurial culture that helps them build their entrepreneurial muscle or they independently seek out opportunities where they build them on their own. Like many organizations that produce things, organizations develop and produce intrapreneurs or they do not. Even if organizations do not look at Intrapreneurs that way they are a product.

Intrapreneurs are also a service because they provide capabilities so desperately needed in organizations today; creativity, innovation, change etc. Like a consultant or coach Intrapreneurs model the behavior and change that is needed to enable organizations to be more entrepreneurial. As a common practice organizations hire consultants to advise them and help them achieve their goals. This is a capability intrapreneurs perform as part of their role. They provide a service even if organizations only think of it as work.

So perhaps Intrapreneurs are a little of both.

Over the last several years we've seen a shift taking place in business where organizations are tailoring jobs to individuals not the other way around. According to Chauncey Lennon JPMorgan's Workforce Initiatives, *"The workforce of the past was organized around the company. The workforce of the future is organized around the worker."* That makes intrapreneurs a product that has value and is in demand.

There are several factors at play here that are driving this trend.

In today's work environment, results are driven by a smaller set of high performing individuals. Organizations want people who generate innovative ideas and create new products. They need people to drive and lead change, turn problems into opportunities and effectively deal with complexity and ambiguity. They know that if they do not the find the right people it may hurt their bottom line.

Organizations are under pressure to generate new growth from within. They have spent the last decade investing in products and services that were mature or at the end of their life cycle. Many organizations are being hurt by start-ups that are operating in the fast lane and leaving them in the dust. New growth must come from new services and offerings created by internal intrapreneurs.

Most knowledge work can be done electronically and remotely. Work is being organized around networks and communities not organizational structures and hierarchy. Technology has freed workers from their desk, their offices and their organizations. It is easy for workers to set up, launch and build their own business. That's why we see a growing number of employees leaving their organizations. Technology is driving this change and organizations are having to respond to this change.

Workers are in now in the driver's seat. It may not seem like that, but it is true.

The true intrapreneur is creating their own opportunity, their own career path, their own way of working. The research shows that one of the key reasons for being successful in today's business environment is due to understanding, embracing and living by an entrepreneurial mindset in the organization. It's a matter of thinking and acting like an entrepreneur. That's why intrapreneurs are needed more than ever.

It is also because Intrapreneurs are aware of the opportunities that are out there. They know that the next Uber, Airbnb are out there waiting to be discovered. It is just a matter of finding the opportunity and building a business around it. In today's environment they have the tools, resources and ability to make it happen.

According to Tom Friedman, *"Employers will no longer pay you for what you know, but only for what you do with what you know. This is the great divide between success and failure in the 21st century economy."* From this perspective it looks like Intrapreneurs provide a service.

Either way you think about it, in order to prepare yourself for the new reality at work you need to think about how you package, promote and sell yourself.

Here are a few things you can be doing now.

- Build a personal brand: Who are you, what do you stand for, what experiences and capabilities do you bring to an opportunity and what tools and techniques do you use?
- Self-awareness: Know yourself, your strengths, weaknesses, what makes you different and how you stand out from your peers.
- Competencies: Assess whether you have the intrapreneurial competencies to be successful and then take the initiative to develop those capabilities that need further work.
- Demonstrate Potential: Demonstrate that you have what it takes to be an intrapreneur by putting your thoughts and words into actions and getting results.
- Experience: Build a portfolio of intrapreneurial experiences that show that you understand what it takes to be an intrapreneur in a variety of situations.
- Increase Visibility: Increase your visibility thru social media, blog postings, speaking engagements, presentations so that you find your voice.
- Networking: Start networking with other intrapreneurs, build your own community and stay on top of intrapreneurship by attending workshops, conferences and seminars.

The more you do these things the better prepared you will be for taking advantage of this opportunity.

It doesn't really matter if you think of Intrapreneurs as a product or service. What is most important is having the ability to package and promote yourself as if you were.

Intrapreneurs Path to Conscious Leadership

Intrapreneurs are destined to change our outlook on leadership and what it means to be true to oneself and society. To leverage what is right, just, and fair in the face of adversity.

They have already made strides in changing our interpretation of what business is and should be. Now it is time for them to step up to demonstrate their commitment and conviction to implementing conscious leadership. To show us the path forward.

It is not just about having an entrepreneurial mindset but putting that thinking into to action that is the ultimate test.

It was over 10 years ago that one of the first conferences on conscious leadership was held at Bentley College near Boston. The Conscious Leadership and Marketing conference was filled with well-known business leaders, consultants, futurists, academics, independent business owners and even a shaman. There were nuggets of wisdom in every speech that related to being a conscious leader but not everything seemed to fit.

Like many of the participants I found myself at a conference with a topic I knew little about. Relating to the topic meant drawing on my own mental models to see connections, draw conclusions and find a way to understand. Being present meant putting aside my own beliefs and being open to what is possible.

After spending two days at the conference, I wondered if Intrapreneurs were conscious leaders or on the path to becoming conscious leaders. At the time the answer eluded me. It seemed appropriate to revisit that question considering today's business environment.

Here are a few of the key takeaways from the conference. They highlighted a shift in mindset and operating principles needed for conscious leadership.

- *Transformational leadership* - leading with head, heart, and soul.
- *Fearless pursuit of purpose* – purpose first then strategy.

- *Leading with your values* – take a set of values and make them real.
- *Meaning is the anchor* – leaders with purpose transform organizations.
- *Trust and confidence are the same* – trust is a key part of reputation.
- *Integrating the masculine and feminine* – highest level of adult development
- *Manifesting who you are* - self-awareness and self-expression.
- *Culture eats strategy for breakfast* - soft is the new hard.
- *Reframing how we do business* – making short term tradeoffs for the long term.
- *Redefining return* – doing good and doing well.

Now ten years later I can see that conscious leadership is not a revolution but an evolution. It reflects where we have been and where we need to go. It is a rejection of all that is bad about business and an acceptance of all that is good about humanity. It goes beyond *Corporate Social Responsibility or Social Innovation* to embody the power of human expression, self-determination and doing things for the greater good. Being all, we can be as individuals and as organizations.

Many of the things on this list are what motivate and drive intrapreneurs. Not everything they do is for the greater good, but the intent is there. As Michael Gelb a pioneer in innovative leadership said, "*Things are the way they are because we designed them to be that way.*" He went on to say that the only way to change the landscape is to redesign it.

Intrapreneurs have been trying to do just that within the constraints of a system where profit was *king*. What could they do if they worked in a system where *people, planet and profit* reined?

The concept of conscious leadership continues to evolve. So, what does it mean to be a conscious leader today in the face of complexity and uncertainty?

Here are a few definitions of Conscious Leadership.

"*The conscious leader is one who brings a higher level of awareness into their own self and the world around them. They have a deeper connection into their own internal states which allows them to see what's really going on within and outside themselves in a given moment.*" Kevin Rafferty, The Conscious Leaders Coach.

"*Conscious leaders speak with integrity, lead with authenticity and hold themselves accountable. They listen with the intent to understand and not just to respond, and they do it by being in tune with themselves and the world around them.*" Jennifer Cohen, Forbes

"*A Conscious Leader builds trust and earns credibility. They are Grounded in Self-Awareness and exudes the Gratitude that drives their vision. A Conscious Leader is purposeful and focused on solutions that sustain positive momentum.*" Syntesis Global, Executive Coaching

"*Conscious leaders are skilled in self-awareness and self-management, especially of their emotions. Great leadership is connected with the deepest parts of ourselves and is about character, courage and conviction.*" The LeaderSharp Collective, Leadership Development and Business Advisory Professionals

"*Conscious Leadership comes from within and is a highly personal stand for being responsible for how we show up, experience and contribute to the world. As a conscious leader, you are drawn by a compelling vision and intentional about what kind of future you want to bring into existence.*" Conscious Leadership Evolution

"*Conscious leadership: This is the idea that conscious leaders understand and embrace the higher purpose of business and focus on creating value for and harmonizing the interests of the business stakeholders. Driven primarily by service to the firm's purpose, rather than by power or money, conscious leaders "inspire, foster transformation, and bring out the best in those around them.*" The Arthur W. Page Center

The common theme that runs through all these descriptions is self-awareness. It seems that the path to conscious leadership is paved through self-awareness. The ability to know oneself – your strengths, weaknesses, thoughts and feelings, beliefs and values, behavior patterns and the capacity for self-reflection. According to researchers, self-awareness is a key determinant of leadership success. A person that is self-aware is better able to manage themselves and others more effectively.

Being conscious requires being authentic, responsible, and accountable for the greater good. It means being conscious about the world around us both internally and externally. Understanding that there is a higher purpose to business than just profit and acting accordingly. That is the essence of what being a conscious leader is all about. It is the path forward.

My guess is that intrapreneurs are already well on the path to conscious leadership. *What do you think?*

10 Reasons Why Intrapreneurs Need a 'Success Profile'

The world of work is rapidly changing and being an entrepreneur in or outside of an organization is what it is all about.

The research shows that one of the key reasons for being successful in today's marketplace is due to understanding, embracing and living by an entrepreneurial mindset. That's why the most sought-after professionals for the new economy are intrapreneurs, corporate entrepreneurs, social intrapreneurs, and social innovators.

In a talent-based economy, results are driven by a small set of high performing individuals. People who create new products and innovative ideas. Organizations are under pressure to generate new business growth and that growth must come from new services and offerings. If organizations do not find the right people, they know it will hurt their bottom line.

Technology is changing how we work and where we work. Most knowledge work can be done electronically and remotely. Work is also being organized around networks and communities not organizational structures and hierarchy. Plus, many professionals are abandoning the traditional career path. They want to have more control over the work assignments they pursue. These dynamics are shifting the focus from full time employment to freelance and independent contract work.

By 2020 it is estimated that 50% of the work force will be free agents, independent workers or freelancers. This creates a problem for organizations and an opportunity for you.

In response to this organizations are tailoring jobs to individuals – not the other way around. The future of work looks very different.

Workers must now think of themselves as a 'product'. You need to think about how you package, promote and sell yourself. You will need to build a personal brand. What do you stand for, what are the tools you bring to an opportunity? How well do you know yourself? What are your strengths and areas that need development? Do you have the entrepreneurial competencies that are needed to be a successful corporate entrepreneur/intrapreneur? What experiences have you had that demonstrate that you have what it takes to an intrapreneur? What are you doing to increase your visibility through social media, blog postings? These are only a few of the things you will need to do.

Many professionals think they are entrepreneurial when in fact they are not. Research has shown that only 4-5% of individuals in organizations are entrepreneurs or entrepreneurial. We know there are more. It is just a matter of accurately identifying them, developing them and giving them the freedom to do what they do best – generate growth and create value for clients and the organization.

Most companies have a core set of competencies they look for in their employees but intrapreneurs are different. Therefore, most competency models do not address the core of who intrapreneurs are. In fact, many organizations promote high potentials that have been successful in the core business but often fail when they are put in charge of a new business venture. A different set of competencies and capabilities are required.

Organizations are looking for successful business leaders that can lead the company into the future.

Tools and assessments that profess to help you identify intrapreneurs only skim the surface of what it important and what is critical for these individuals to be successful. Some use personality assessments like the Big Five that are high level but don't identify the nuances of intrapreneurs. That is why we have spent the last ten years identifying and developing what we call 'success profiles' that clearly articulate what it takes to be successful in these roles – for corporate entrepreneurs (intrapreneurs) and social intrapreneurs. Think of it as a roadmap. Our work is grounded in research and working with successful corporate entrepreneurs (intrapreneurs), social intrapreneurs and entrepreneurial leaders. The most successful intrapreneurs are too impatient to wait for the organization to recognize, acknowledge and reward intrapreneurial behavior.

Intrapreneurs don't just want to find out if they have what it takes to be a successful intrapreneur, they want to find out what they need to work on to get better.

Here are ten reasons why you should see for yourself if you have what it takes.

1. Validate your competence as an intrapreneur
2. Distinguish yourself as an experienced and capable intrapreneur
3. Be one of the most sought-after professionals for 21st century
4. Define your own career path in or out of an organization
5. Unlock the key attribute of successful leaders, self-awareness
6. Take ownership for your own growth and development
7. Leverage your strengths and develop areas needing work
8. Differentiate yourself among your peers and in the marketplace
9. Enjoy the personal and professional rewards of being engaged at work
10. Be able to measure your progress over time and with more experience.

Corporate entrepreneurship is a mindset, a set of competencies, a way of thinking and acting. It's how you look at things and what actions you take as a result of that thinking.

Everyone has the potential to be an entrepreneur but not everyone wants to be one. Entrepreneurs must not only 'think and reason' about opportunities they must 'act' on them. Success comes from putting your thoughts into actions. Action comes from having confidence and the competence to succeed.

But if you don't know if you have what it takes, neither will your employer or the organizations that would hire you as an employee, freelancer or contractor. The number one characteristic of leaders is self-awareness. The more you know about yourself the better prepared you will be to take on the challenges of work in the 21st century economy. That's what success profiles do. They define the competencies you will need to succeed in a particular role.

Workers are in the driver's seat. But...only if you step up and take responsibility for controlling your own destiny either as an entrepreneur or intrapreneur.

6 Reasons to Hire Intrapreneurs Now

While speaking to a group of sixty mid-level managers last week one question that was asked was whether large companies are selectively looking to hire Intrapreneurs and Corporate Entrepreneurs.

Unfortunately, too few organizations are actively recruiting individuals who have the entrepreneurial capabilities that are needed to re-energize their business. *That is a mistake!*

The fact is that growth in many large companies has stalled even though they are sitting on piles of cash.

Individuals who have the skills and capabilities to lead new growth initiatives are left sitting on their hands. They are eager to move their companies forward, but they are being held back. *That is a waste of talent!*

Hiring entrepreneurs inside a large organization is still a foreign concept. Many organizations say they want these types of individuals, but their actions say something else. They are using hiring criteria that gives them more of what they have not what they need. *It keeps them stuck in the past.*

There are six reasons why you should hire Intrapreneurs now:

1. Internal entrepreneurs are independent thinkers. They make sense of the world based on their own observations and experience. They are willing to try new things. They don't let past experience get in their way or cloud their judgement. *They see possibilities where others don't.*

2. Internal entrepreneurs are good at navigating uncertainty, complexity and ambiguity. They don't sit back and wait for things to become clear. *They control uncertainty by acting.*

3. Internal entrepreneurs are totally engaged and energized by a challenge. They bigger the challenge the better. It is like climbing a mountain. Once you've climbed a mountain you want to climb a higher more difficult one next time. *They take on the toughest jobs.*

4. Internal entrepreneurs are good at driving change. They are willing to take on risks to change their comfort zone. They not only lead change but become the change they hope to achieve. They model change so others are comfortable changing too. *They make change happen.*

5. Internal entrepreneurs are highly effective leaders. They find creative ways to leverage limited resources. They know where the organization is flexible and where it is not. They can break down barriers and create new systems to support them. *They lead through complexity.*

6. Internal entrepreneurs are good at execution. They have the discipline to stay focused and bring things to closure. They know how to take a complex set of interrelated variables and put them together to achieve results. *They close the gap between strategy and execution.*

The skills and capabilities that were needed in the past are not the skills needed moving forward. The reality is that we all need to be entrepreneurs now whether we are in a large organization or on our own.

Its time organizations got serious about hiring leaders who have the entrepreneurial talent to *shake things up* and *get things moving*

Conclusion: Turned Inside-Out

The Age of Enlightenment in the 18th century was a time when there were tremendous advances in all branches of human knowledge especially those related to scientific rationality.

Individuals involved in the enlightenment were known as *Free Thinkers.* They were committed to critical inquiry emphasizing logic and reason. *"Anything that could not be proven by science was regarded as unworthy of acceptance."*

Reason, logic and argument made sense in a world that was stable and predictable, but we have entered a period of rapid acceleration and uncertainty.

Everything we've known experienced and understood is being turned inside-out.

- It has become increasingly difficult to predict new market opportunities. We can no longer base our decisions on precise data, forecasts or past experiences. *We need to trust our intuition.*
- Business is faced with unprecedented levels of ambiguity and uncertainty. We cannot wait until things become more certain. *We must control uncertainty by acting.*
- Globalization has created increasing levels of complexity. Trying to simplify things too quickly narrow the opportunities. *We need to explore complexity.*
- Demand in existing markets has slowed. Finding new market opportunities is difficult and imprecise. *We must now create markets.*
- Resources are scarce so new projects are often put on the back burner. Growth will have to come from the resources we do have. *We need to be resourceful.*
- Risk is inherent in everything we do. If we aren't taking risks, then we aren't learning and moving forward. *We must take calculated risks.*
- Experimenting is part of the creative process. It is important to

test our ideas before we commit to a direction. *We need to experiment smartly.*

- Failing is a sign of courage. We must accept the fact that we will fail. Failure now seems to be a prerequisite for success. *We must fail fast.*
- Standard methods of analysis are not as effective. We can no longer calculate an expected return for everything we do. Instead we must decide on how much we are willing to lose. *We need determine an affordable loss.*

The *Free Thinkers* of today are Intrapreneurs, Corporate Entrepreneurs and Entrepreneurial Leaders who are showing us that anything is possible in business.

These individuals are creating a future in a way that is very different from what we have come to know. They are showing all of us how to deal effectively in a world that is being *turned inside-out.*

Appendix: Exploring the Entrepreneurial Orientation of Intrapreneurs

According to research Entrepreneurial Orientation (EO) is the cornerstone of innovation success for organizations.

EO is defined as the degree of risk-taking, innovativeness, and proactiveness in a company.

Organizations that have successfully developed entrepreneurial orientation have realized a positive impact on growth, predicting innovation and business performance.

So, it is not surprising that most organizations today are striving to develop their own Entrepreneurial Orientation. They are committing time and resources to the development of cultures that embody these three main capabilities.

Few companies or researchers, however, have looked at extending entrepreneurial orientation to individuals. According to the Journal of Business Research, there are "limited number of papers investigating an individual perspective on EO."

Historical Perspective

Researchers in the 1960's and 1970's started investigating the characteristics of individuals that gravitated to entrepreneurship. Terms like, "need for achievement, a locus of control, self-efficacy, risk-taking propensity, family influence, educational influence, work experience etc." were used to identify entrepreneurial behavior. But beyond this, there was little evidence that these characteristics, traits or behaviors had validity.

Then researchers started to look at "psychological variables" like cognitive abilities, knowledge, skills, personality tendencies, applied social skills, interests, and preferences." They gravitated toward the Big-Five-Factor Model of Personality of Extraversion, Emotional Stability, Agreeableness, Conscientiousness and Openness to Experience. This approach dominated the literature for years but did not adequately explain the entrepreneurial orientation at the individual level. In fact, research showed that the

Five-Factor Model of Personality was too high level to accurately predict entrepreneurial orientation.

At one-point researchers started asking questions about the interplay between a firm's Entrepreneurial Orientation and the Entrepreneurial Orientation of the individual. Realizing that in both cases neither the organization nor the individual had all the requisite capabilities of risk-taking, innovativeness, and proactiveness. They realized that they needed to drill deeper below the broad definitions of the Big Five-Factor Model to "specific facets of personality" or behaviors like assertiveness, influence, and self-efficacy. They found that these behaviors contributed to both leadership and organizational performance. The research did not, however, predict or identify the propensity to be an intrapreneur inside of an established organization.

Much of the research in the past had been on external entrepreneurs and entrepreneurs in small, medium enterprises (SMEs). Thus, translating this research to intrapreneurs inside established organizations was mostly antidotal and not grounded in empirical research. Attributes of external entrepreneurs were randomly applied to internal intrapreneurs. There was no validity to equate external entrepreneurs to internal entrepreneurs (intrapreneurs).

Moving Forward

Over the next few decades' researchers continued to study the three key dimensions of Entrepreneurial Orientation – risk-taking, innovativeness, and pro-activity within firms and the individual characteristics of entrepreneurs. The main conclusion was that very few firms will have all three dimensions of EO and to supplement that deficiency they would have to look at individual characteristics to fill those gaps.

Again, much of this work was focused on the Big Five-Factor Personality that was already deemed too high level to be a reliable indicator. So, researchers selected one dimension of the big five-factor, Extraversion where entrepreneurs scored higher and identified "assertiveness" as a key factor. The second factor was "self-efficacy". They defined assertiveness as "the ability to influence others" and self-efficacy as "how well one can execute courses of action to deal with prospective situations." Both were theoretically linked to both leadership and business performance.

According to the Journal of Business Research 2017, the key question researchers were looking at was, "Can a firm's innovation and growth be explained by integrating firm-level characteristics and individual psychological variables." The conclusion was that these two personality variables (assertiveness and self-efficacy) can often overcome deficiencies in EO at the organizational level. That when innovativeness and pro-activity are present but risk-taking is absent or when proactivity and risk-taking are absent then the individual characteristics can help fill the gap to achieve firm performance.

The key take away from this is that EO requires the integration of individual and organizational characteristics to achieve entrepreneurial success - people and culture. It was clear that EO for organizations was grounded in risk-taking, innovativeness, and pro-activity and that the absence of any of them, could be supplemented by individuals. As far as EO for individuals that was still an open question. Relying on two variables (assertiveness and self-efficacy) was not enough to explain EO at the individual level.

During this time work continued trying to define the individual characteristics of entrepreneurs. According to an article titled Personal Characteristics of Entrepreneurs, researchers found that "the most important personal qualities for an entrepreneur were: courage, self-reliance, responsibility, determination, perseverance, proactive approach, creativity, and scholarship in a particular area of business." They found entrepreneurs to be "independent, creative, autonomous, risk takers, individually oriented, rely on themselves and make decisions under conditions of uncertainty."

Since then, the list has only continued to expand. There is no common definition for what it takes to be an entrepreneur, no agreement between the academic and business world. More disturbing is that this list has been randomly applied to intrapreneurs without a thorough investigation into what it takes to be an intrapreneur versus an entrepreneur.

Growing Interest in Intrapreneurs

As intrapreneurship has evolved so has the interest in applying EO to organizations engaged in intrapreneurship! Not surprisingly the same three components of EO, risk-taking, innovativeness, and pro-activity make sense for a group, team or venture inside an established organization. What is still missing however is understanding the entrepreneurial orientation of individuals.

According to research titled Intrapreneurial Behavior: An Empirical Investigation of Personality Traits, the authors noted that less attention has been given to the individual level of entrepreneurial behavior. Their initial hypothesis was that "Personality is considered a major determinant of entrepreneurial success." To address these researchers again turned to the Big-Five Factor Personality to explore the "relationship between personality traits and intrapreneurial behavior."

Although this research was useful in identifying key personality factors and their influence on intrapreneurial behavior. It highlighted only a few characteristics that were directly related to EO. They found that "extroversion, emotional stability and openness to experience" were positively related to intrapreneurial behavior and risk-taking. That emotional stability and openness to experience were to some extent related to innovativeness.

The research showed that these three personality factors (extroversion, emotional stability, and openness to experience) can help organizations identify individuals with intrapreneurial behavior but are not necessarily determents of success. The findings did not show a direct link to firm performance. But it gave us some additional items to add to the ever-growing list of individual characteristics of intrapreneurs that have already been identified.

Here is a partial list of what we've compiled from academic research, business journals and intrapreneurs themselves about the characteristics of intrapreneurs:

Abstract Thinker	Agreeableness	Authentic	Collaborative	Conceptualizes	Responsible
Creative	Demanding	Effective Leader	Energy	Experimenter	Proactive
Future Scanners	Independent	Instructiveness	Intuitive	Logical	Creative
Motivated	Observer	Patience	Problem Solver	Relationship	Perserverance
Restless	Self-Confident	Strategic & Analytical	Team Builder	Tolerance for Stress	Independent
Accountable	Ambiguity	Big Picture Oriented	Commitment	Conflict Manager	Effectual
Critical Thinking	Detail Oriented	Detemined	Engaged	Extraversion	Decisive
Goal Oriented	Independent Thinker	Integrity	Inventive	Loners	Autonomous
Mystery Seekers	Open	Planning	Process Management	Reliability	Delegation
Results Oriented	Self-Reflective	Strategic Thinker	Team Oriented	Unsociable	Imaginative
Achiever	Analytical	Challenger	Compelling Communicatior	Conscientious	Non-conformist
Curious	Determined	Emotional Composure	Enthusiastic	Self-Efficacy	Self Reliance
Growth Oriented	Influencer	Intellectual	Leadership	Facilitator	Dogged
Negotiating	Opportunity Oriented	Risk Taker	Questioning	Long Term	Inspirational
Risk Taker	Simplify Complexity	Leadership	Tenacious Challenger	Reserved	Passionate
Action Oriented	Approachability	Change Agent	Competitive	Visionary	Strategic
Customer Focused	Developing Others	Emotional Intelligence	Entrepreneurial	Coping Skills	Empathy
Hardworking	Initiative	Intensity	Leading Change	Flexible	Introverted
Networking	Optimistic	Agreeableness	Quiet	Manage Uncertainty	Priority Setting
Risk Taker	Sociable	Systematic	Theoretical	Resilience	Task Completion
Adaptive	Assertiveness	Closure	Composure	Vitality	Execution
Decisive	Disciplined	Emotionally Stable	Exciters	Courage	Listener
Honest	Innovative	Internally Motivated	Learner	Focuser	Realistic
Neuroticism	Optimizing Diversity	Presentation Skills	Rational	Market Oriented	Time Management
Ruthless	Storyteller	Takes Action	Thriving	Resolute	Practical
Agile	Associating	Coach	Concentration	Political Savvy	Self-Reliant

Can you tell me which of these are the most important? Is this helpful or more confusing? It has been impossible to know what you are looking for.

Entrepreneurial Orientation of Intrapreneurs

We decided there was a better way to get at this question. Go to the source – successful intrapreneurs. Identify individuals inside organizations that have been successful at building new business ventures inside organizations. Work with them to find out exactly what they do, how they do it and what characteristics, competencies and behaviors contributed to their success.

At first, we thought it would be easy to go into large organizations and ask the executives if we could talk to their internal entrepreneurs. They told us they didn't have any. That made us realize that findings these individuals would be more difficult and take more time. We eventually did and we found internal entrepreneurs who had built million- and billion-dollar businesses for their organizations.

We worked with them to identify the characteristics, competencies, and traits that helped them succeed. They were eager to help because they told us that their organizations did not understand them, what they did or how they did it and they wanted them to know. It was a matter of self-preservation for many.

Our research revealed several key things. First, there was no concise language to describe intrapreneurs, so we had to develop some. We looked at all the characteristics, attributes and traits that were discussed in the academic literature and business world. We found that there was some overlap but in general there were wide gaps in the language used to describe intrapreneurs. It was clear that the current descriptors were insufficient.

Secondly, we needed a tool to help us conduct our research. We looked at all the predictive tools that were available at the time: Personality Styles like Myers Briggs and the Big Five-Factor, Values-Hierarchy, Social Styles, Life Stages, Hermann Brain Dominance, Neuro-linguistics, Behavior Patterns like DISC and Success Profiles that evaluate both competencies and behaviors.

We decided to settle on Success Profiles because competencies and behaviors focus on what individuals "will do" – their propensity to act. A competency is a set of behaviors that are combined to define a certain level of expertise. "For over 20 years, competencies have served as a universal language to effectively measure and individual's ability to succeed in a particular job and fit within an organizations culture, regardless of industry" according to The Devine Group a competency and behavioral assessment vendor.

Thirdly, in order to do our research, we had to first build a Success Profile for the specific role of intrapreneur, something that had never been done before! We worked with our intrapreneurs and The Devine Group to build a profile that showed the key competencies and behaviors that Intrapreneurs inside established companies needed to be successful. We tested it in the market, refined it and then eventually used it to collect data to show the relevance of the Success Profile in identifying and developing Intrapreneurs.

Only later did we realize that our research tool itself was a product that would be useful for large organizations that wanted to develop their own intrapreneurs. We called it the Corporate Entrepreneur Profile™ because at the time the word Intrapreneur was not widely used. Organizations referred to their internal entrepreneurs as Corporate Entrepreneurs.

Some of the early adopters found it fascinating to see how different and divergent Intrapreneurs were to traditional employees. It was clear to them and to us that we had unlocked the mystery of who Corporate Entrepreneurs/Intrapreneurs are, how they are different and why it is important.

We had made our way through the list of characteristics, traits, and attributes in the chart above. From the start, we knew it was impossible for any one person to exhibit all those characteristics and even more difficult to measure all of them. Finding the ones that were relevant was our challenge and our end goal.

Over the last ten years, we have worked with many organizations to help them identify and develop their internal entrepreneurs. Our data shows that the same competencies that were relevant than are even more relevant today. We continue to see that Intrapreneurs exhibit a unique combination of competencies that set them apart from their peers. They do things that are often totally opposite to things done in the core business. We have also seen that the same top competencies are exhibited time and time again in those individuals that are best suited for the role of Intrapreneur.

The key takeaway is that Intrapreneurs that have been successful in this role are the only ones that can help us understand the Entrepreneurial Orientation at the Individual Level. They have demonstrated their capabilities through their actions and the results they achieved. By looking at individuals that were already successful in the role helped define what it takes to be an intrapreneur. We identified seventeen competencies that enable Intrapreneurs to be more successful inside organizations.

The success profile also helped us understand the EO of the individual – their level of risk-taking, innovativeness and pro-activity. Embedded within each competency are behaviors that directly link to risk-taking, innovativeness, and proactivity. Plus, the individual results achieved by these intrapreneurs speak for themselves and directly link to firm performance and entrepreneurial success. The very thing that has been missing from prior work.

Present Perspective

We recognize that the academic world and business world still do not agree on what it takes to be an Intrapreneur. A key factor is the lack of understanding in the differences between personality assessments (measuring broad personality dimensions) and competency-based assessments (behaviors grouped into competencies for specific job functions.) The academic research has provided some useful information, but it has been incomplete.

It is only in working with the Corporate Entrepreneur Profile™ that we have come to understand the unique perspective that Success Profiles bring to understanding the competencies and underlying behaviors that motivate, inspire and engage individuals in entrepreneurial pursuits inside of established organizations. It is a comprehensive assessment of the full range of competencies of successful intrapreneurs. Many of the items identified in academic research are included in our set of competencies. We acknowledge the contribution that their research has made to this effort.

This article was designed to help you understand insights that have been useful in advancing our understanding of intrapreneurs and why the existing research has not been able to give us a complete picture of the Entrepreneurial Orientation at the Individual level.

We believe that our research has helped move the discussion forward in positive ways that contribute to a better understanding of the nuances that distinguish intrapreneurs from their peers and to understanding the Entrepreneurial Orientation of Intrapreneurs.

About the Author

Susan Foley, Managing Partner
Corporate Entrepreneurs LLC.

As an experienced corporate entrepreneur (Intrapreneur), Susan understands the challenges of building corporate entrepreneurship (Intrapreneurship) as a core competency inside of an established organization.

Susan has spent the last twenty-five years helping organizations develop new growth businesses that have generated millions. She helps organizations identify and develop their internal entrepreneurs and entrepreneurial leaders.

Susan is a national and international speaker, the author of numerous articles and two books *Entrepreneurs Inside: Accelerating Business Growth with Corporate Entrepreneurs and Acceleration: Changing the Speed of Growth.*

She has been an Executive in Residence at Babson College, has taught Corporate Entrepreneurship at Babson Executive Education and Social Change at Suffolk University and has been a fellow at the Center for Innovation and Change Leadership at Suffolk.

Susan works with Fortune 1000 and medium size businesses that are under pressure to deliver new business growth. She helps these organizations build the entrepreneurial competencies needed for success. Susan's mission is to help business executives, innovation teams and individuals understand the value of corporate entrepreneurship (Intrapreneurship) in accelerating business growth and to help individuals develop their capabilities as internal entrepreneurs. In doing so, she is awakening the entrepreneur in all of us.

Prior to this Susan was the Executive Director of the applied research centers at Babson Executive Education where she managed the Business Innovation, Process Management and Knowledge Management centers. Before that Susan was Vice President of Research Services at Standard &

Poor's where she built and managed a venture funded initiative to create the Industry Services business. She also held senior positions at 3M, Hewlett-Packard, Digital Equipment, DMR Group (now Fujitsu) and Arthur D. Little.

Susan has a BS in Business Administration and an MBA in Marketing Management from Rochester Institute of Technology, a post graduate degree in Health Administration from Simmons Graduate School and Executive Management Training at INSEAD, France.

Affiliations include the National Speakers Association, The Boston Club Distinguished Leaders Series, Treasurer and Board Member of NSA New England and she is a Certified Hospice Volunteer.

www.corporate-entrrepreneurs.com

Made in the USA
Monee, IL
04 November 2026

67383011R10174